THE
CAN-DO
MINDSET

THE
CAN-DO
MINDSET

How to Cultivate Resilience,

Follow Your Heart, and

Fight for Your Passions

Candace Parker

GET LIFTED BOOKS

A **zando** IMPRINT

NEW YORK

GET LIFTED
BOOKS

Get Lifted Books is an imprint of Zando.
zandoprojects.com

First Edition: June 2025

Design by Neuwirth & Associates, Inc.
Cover design by Christopher Brian King
Cover photograph by Ramona Rosales

Ladybug on page v by Sri Utami from Noun Project

The publisher does not have control over and is not responsible for author or other third-party websites (or their content).

Library of Congress Control Number: 2025933459

978-1-63893-218-5 (Hardcover)
978-1-63893-219-2 (ebook)

10 9 8 7 6 5 4 3 2 1
Manufactured in the United States of America

To the people and passions
that fuel my purpose.

CONTENTS

Introduction:
Allow Me to Reintroduce Myself   *ix*

PART ONE
Community

One   **The Apple and the Tree**   *3*

Two   **Built Different**   *15*

Three   **"Left Foot, Right Foot, Breathe, Repeat"** *27*

Four   **Forks in the Road**   *49*

Five   **Something New**   *66*

PART TWO
Authenticity

Six   **This Is Anya, My Wife**   *79*

Seven   **The Real Candace Parker**   *93*

Eight   **Fumbling Together**   *102*

CONTENTS

PART THREE
Negativity

Nine **Different Isn't Always Bad** *119*

Ten **Better the Hard Way** *140*

Eleven **When to Hold Them, When to Fold Them** *160*

Twelve **Bouncing Back** *176*

Thirteen **Don't Let Up** *204*

Fourteen **Who Will We Choose to Be?** *226*

PART FOUR
The Dash

Fifteen **My Life, My Choices** *257*

Sixteen **Love Is a Verb** *270*

Seventeen **Rule of Threes** *289*

PART FIVE
Opportunity

Eighteen **I Did It My Way** *303*

Nineteen **What More Can I Say?** *319*

Acknowledgments *331*

About the Author *333*

Allow Me to Reintroduce Myself

It was a sweltering-hot Saturday in late eighties Illinois, when my dad piled my brothers and me into the car for a trip to the park. This was our tradition—as a family, we often spent our Saturdays playing tennis. Being the youngest of three, by eight and eleven years respectively, I wasn't able to join in the matches just yet, so I'd spend my time jumping in between the playground and the tennis courts where my brothers competed. I wanted so badly to be grown-up like my big brothers, going head to head on the court, but I still enjoyed the slides and the swings. Throughout the afternoon, I ran wildly with my shirt clinging to my skin and my braided pigtails trailing behind me in the wind of my own creation. I was the only girl, but I loved to insist that I could still hang with the boys. When my brothers finished their match, they would join me in the playground, bounding from slide to swings and back again. With the wind on our backs and sweat streaming down our faces, we ran and ran and ran until the summer sun finally demanded we pause for water and rest.

As we guzzled water, my brothers pulled their sweaty T-shirts over their heads and let the breeze cool off their slick skin. My brothers were my heroes. A combination of idolization and the need to emulate pushed me to compete with them at every moment. It was my way of proving that I was better than them or could at least keep up. I immediately moved to do as they did, yanking at my sweat soaked shirt, when my father scolded me. "You're a girl, Can. You can't do that," he said. I watched my brothers, scowling. My shirt was clinging to me, too. What did being a girl have to do with me needing to cool off, I thought to myself.

The moment my dad turned his head, and before I could think about getting in trouble, I quickly pulled off my shirt and ran away with my tiny chest sticking out. My pigtails still followed me, anchored by my barrettes and bows, but I was no longer weighed down by my sweaty T-shirt. My brothers looked to my dad half anticipating their baby sister to be reprimanded and scolded. Dad watched me, chuckling and sighing in the same breath. There goes Can-Do.

When I was a baby, everyone naturally shortened my full name to Can. I was the youngest of my siblings with a pretty wide age gap, which made me the doted-on little girl of the house. The stereotype of youngest siblings is that we expect everything to be handed to us, but I was the complete opposite. By eight months old, I'd already started walking, and I rode a bike at three with no training wheels. A daredevil by nature, you could routinely find me jumping off stairs, climbing high into the thin branches of the trees, and playing outside from the morning until night, covered in a mixture of dirt and sweat. My stubborn independent streak would flare anytime someone told me no, and my blood would boil if they dared tell me I couldn't do something. By the time I was two years old, my mom extended my nickname from Can to Can-Do.

My nickname made me feel invincible. It was my secret superpower. Can-Do got me through everything: learning to tie my shoes, countless tests, being the tallest kid in class, big games, and devastating setbacks. Every time I heard someone saying, "Girls can't do that!" I heard my mom saying Can-Do: yes, you can. Whenever I faced challenges or doubted myself, my mom would exclaim,

"Can-Do!" When I felt overwhelmed by the shadow cast over me by my brothers and how amazing they were at everything they did, my mom would whisper, "Can-Do." And when I did revert to my role as the little sister with Dad wrapped around my finger, my brothers, Marcus and Anthony, used to joke that Can-Do was short for "can do anything and get away with it."

Can-Do has never been about success or failure, but about believing in my abilities and having the confidence and courage to "do." It's always been a mantra and reminder to take that first step, defy limitations, believe in myself, trust who I am, and dare to be different. The mentality that if I'm going to do something, I'm going to do it well whether that be the most mundane task or the most high-stakes opportunity. My dad was one of the first people to instill that value in me. I remember coming home from school and telling him that I'd gotten the highest grade in class on a test that day. I was beaming with pride, exam held outstretched in front of me, when my dad asked, "Is this your best?" I couldn't believe it. He must not have heard what I'd said or seen the grade. It was an A, and no one else in the class had done better. But my dad didn't care about everybody else and how they did. He didn't want me to be sidetracked by that, either.

"The moment you start measuring your finish line against others, you've already lost," my dad told me. There might be days where I'm not the top of the class and other days where I'm running circles around my peers. The only thing that mattered on both days was whether I'd done my personal best, properly prepared, and put in the maximum effort I could have. No matter where I landed, that should be enough for me. But if I was in an environment where doing better than others didn't demand the best I had to give, I owed it to myself to give consistent effort. Rain or shine. Win or lose. Crowd or empty bleachers. I needed to constantly be seeking areas for improvement and ways to continue getting better, no matter the result. The mindset it takes to succeed the first time might take an adjustment or more to keep you there. You have to have the drive to keep working, without comparison being the only motivation. I couldn't do it for the applause because I wouldn't always have it. Most days all I'd have was my inner voice, and that had to be enough. I had to matter enough to myself to hold myself accountable.

From that day on, I've always held myself to that standard. I was a strategic and hardworking kid. I always have a plan. I sacrifice daily conveniences for bigger-picture goals and aspirations. Early in life, I mastered the mindset needed to achieve what may seem impossible to others. I learned regret is a hard pill to swallow. I've gone after what I've wanted relentlessly, and any opportunity that didn't come my way wasn't because I lacked work ethic or commitment. My family nickname had evolved from positive self-talk into a way to actualize the lifestyle I desired. A nickname that motivated me turned into an acronym that would do the same, with even greater specificity on the how. Can-Do came to stand for:

Community

Authenticity

Negativity

Dash

Opportunity

Community is where I come from, the people I surround myself with, and who I choose to be for them—it's everything to me. My community teaches me my worth, and they fuel my growth, confidence, and motivation. Particularly as you find more success, the need for those who can lovingly hold you accountable grows. I'm grateful for my foundation, who deftly balanced the need to instill confidence in me, ignite my ambition, and remind me of the importance of humility. I realize that everyone isn't so fortunate to grow up in a community like I had, but adulthood offers a blank slate and opportunity to develop community in new ways.

Authenticity is the only way I can face myself in the mirror. I try to never confuse the what and the who—what I've done versus who I am. Authenticity is about staying honest and true to yourself, even when it's difficult. It's about loving who you love and demonstrating that strength for your children. It's about not being afraid to be different, or the same, not to prove a point but to draw closer to the most honest parts of yourself. It's about your actions and daily habits, aligning with your morals, values, and intentions. No matter what room you walk in, table you sit at, desk you work from, or person you talk to you are *you*. It's about staying humble and human, being honest about your missteps and true to your word. It's about realizing that just because no one has done something before doesn't mean it can't be done, especially if you feel in your bones that it's possible for you. And it's about, at the end of the day, hanging your hat on the work you've done and not the credit you receive or people's opinions. (After all, you have to live with you.)

Negativity is a part of life, and I think people are scared of it. But the truth is adversity builds and reveals character, and it's necessary. The greats are defined by what they choose to do after adversity, and embracing the lessons negativity holds for me has been game-changing. After all, the greatest leaps forward come from choosing to learn from the missteps and losses in the game of life. The deciding factor in handling the inevitable negativity is your reaction. Navigating and sifting between hate that needs to be ignored and lessons that lie within each obstacle that stands between where you are and where you have the potential to be. If you let it propel you to greater heights, it can and will.

The **dash** is the journey—there's a start date and an end date, but life is what happens between those things. Legacy lies in what you repeatedly do. You can't always control the end results in life, so by relinquishing the desire to control the outcome, you can fully focus on the process. In my every day, the dash means presence over presents—showing up with my full heart to every relationship and every commitment I can. Be where your feet are, there's power in the present in a world that has a constant pull to plan for the future and dwell on the past. Understanding that time is important and how you spend it both demonstrates and dictates your desires. Choose accordingly.

And lastly, **opportunity**. This is what allows us all to rise. I've been in a lot of situations where taking opportunities meant being the only one who looks like me at the table, and I had to realize that being underrepresented didn't make me less valuable or make the job any less mine. On the contrary, it meant I had a responsibility to take up even more space and bring others along with me. The only job beyond that is to recognize the people who made those opportunities possible and make sure you leave the door open wider for the people who follow you. Accomplishing what was once deemed impossible is what being a visionary is all about. Just because something hasn't been done doesn't mean it can't or shouldn't be.

Can-Do has served me through so many life phases, anchoring me through choppy waters. Though the world attempts to limit me to certain lanes, I pride myself on being versatile and taking up space in a number of industries, which requires being secure in who I am and what I bring to the table. I am led by curiosity and I am unafraid to ask questions. As a result, I've always had my hands in multiple jars at one time. I love to read and watch documentaries, especially about politics and history. I listen to John Mayer and Jay-Z, and in the shower (I think) I sing like Adele. I am obsessed with *Jurassic Park* and equally soak up true crime documentaries. I love to read nonfiction, and one of my favorite authors is Malcolm Gladwell, but my favorite book of all time is a novel, *The Alchemist*. Traveling and learning about different cultures is one of my passions, and I am obsessed with trying different cuisines. A true foodie through and through, I enjoy pairing my entrée with a fine bottle of a bold cab or a nice burgundy.

I often go down rabbit holes about space, aliens, mindfulness, equity, organic food, and a million other things on any given day. My day jobs these days include president of Adidas Women's Basketball, NBA TV analyst, and adviser to Avenue Capital Sports Fund. I serve on several boards, and I've got my hands in private equity and venture capital. Some of my proudest professional moments were interviewing President Barack Obama and giving a TED Talk. But if you ask me, all those things pale in comparison to spending time with my family and being there to witness my daughter execute a perfectly timed slide and flawless spike at a volleyball match! My cup is the fullest on a lazy Saturday when my wife, daughter, two sons, and three dogs all pile and cuddle up in our enormous bed. As our laughs and giggles echo throughout our house, they fill up my soul. I wear many hats, have millions of flight miles, meet many different people, and get to have so many experiences. But I realize all that I am and all that I have become is a result of intentionally leaning into the Can-Do, relying on my community, remaining authentic, handling negativity, understanding the importance of the dash, and seizing and creating opportunity.

Oh yeah, and I was pretty good at basketball, too . . .

THE
CAN-DO
MINDSET

PART ONE

Community

ONE

The Apple and the Tree

"Pretty good" might be downplaying my basketball career just a smidge. Let me back up and say that I'm immensely proud of what I've been able to do on the court. I'm proud to say that I have won a championship at every level the sport can be played, and I have won a championship on every US team I have ever been a part of. I'm proud to have won two gold medals representing my country in the Olympics and to have been recognized as the most valuable player at the 2012 Olympic Games. I'm proud of being a three-time WNBA champion, two-time MVP, Defensive Player of the Year (reminding people I can play a little defense too), and the 2008 Rookie of the Year, the first and only WNBA Rookie of the Year and MVP in the same season thus far. I'm extremely proud of my career at the University of Tennessee—bringing back-to-back championships to Knoxville and being able to come back from injuries again and again. I'm also proud of the career I've been able to establish off the court, as a television analyst for the NBA and the NCAA tournament, president of Adidas Women's Basketball, and adviser to Avenue Capital Sports Fund. All of this was possible because I picked up an orange ball and fell in love.

It still amazes me that this orange ball has afforded me all these opportunities, experiences, and relationships. Before any awards, championships, endorsements, or titles, there was just Lil' Can bouncing her basketball up and down the court. Basketball upheld its end of the bargain, and I would like to say I kept my side as well. It has taken so much more work than most people imagine to get to the places I've been, and to win. None of those wins would have been possible without leaning on, learning from, and creating intentional community. The Candace Parker that people know and celebrate today is a by-product of those microinvestments that my family made in me. Before I can reveal any of my "keys to success," I have to honor the source. Community is my who, what, when, where, why, and how.

I grew up in a basketball family in every sense of the phrase. My dad played basketball at the University of Iowa from 1972–1976. My mom, an athlete in her own right, grew up in Des Moines but because of the lack of opportunities for women in sports in the 1970s, had to settle with just playing recreationally. My parents met at the University of Iowa and were married with a baby on the way by junior year of college. Born from their union was my brother Anthony and three years later Marcus followed. I was a bit of a surprise and came eight years after Marcus. Athleticism was in our blood and from a young age my parents threw my two older brothers into sports. Baseball, football, soccer, and yes, of course basketball.

With Anthony and Marcus both being so much older than me and playing basketball, the choice seemed made for me long before birth. My first crib had a plush basketball in it. I attended my first in-person game when I was only two weeks old. Though I was born in St. Louis, Missouri, around the age of three we relocated to Naperville, IL. My family was always at Spring-Field Park hooping on the weekends, so naturally I tagged along. As they ran up and down the court and back again, I impatiently sat on the sideline until it was my time to shoot in between games. I had hesitantly agreed to start playing on a YMCA team at around six years old, which my young mind rationalized as me enjoying one of my many hobbies. I was always tall and athletic for my age, so I stood out immediately among my peers.

Being so surrounded by basketball, one might think it was a given that I'd become the player I am today. You might be surprised to know that I was very resistant to falling in line. Just because I can do anything doesn't mean I wanted to follow a path outlined for me, even if my family were the ones doing the steering. Marcus was brilliant, and Anthony was already nice at basketball. Though I couldn't always articulate it, I was always afraid of being pigeonholed into someone else's shadow. I was born competitive and, I dare say, I feared not being as good as my two big brothers. Instead, early on, I invested my energy into soccer and volleyball—two sports I could claim as my own independent interests. Basketball would always be a bonding activity for our family, I thought, so I could play around when I wanted without it becoming my thing.

Around age five, I set out to play my first competitive sport. I'd always been off the charts in every physical way for my age group. Each doctor's visit when they'd take my weight and height, I was always in the ninety-ninth percentile and my brothers would joke that I'd hit the genetic lottery! I had no control over my growth and yet I loved that I was winning yet another unsaid competition without even trying. Naperville had a kids' soccer team (YBA), and I immediately asked my parents to sign me up. I'll never forget beaming with pride as my entire family lined the sideline to watch *me* play. As a family, we always showed up and supported one another. As the little sister, I was the one always tagging along and taking naps at my brothers' practices and games. I was always finding things to do at their many tournaments, but now it was my turn. It was finally my time to be front and center. We made it a priority to be one another's biggest fans. There's a confidence you have when you know you have people there watching and rooting you on from the sideline.

Dad never lied to us—ever—about how we performed; he always told us what we needed to hear without beating us down. During workouts, I watched Dad yell at my brothers, question their commitment, and challenge them to improve weaknesses and master strengths. When Dad was in charge, the workout never really ended, either. On the way home from the park, especially on days when my brothers weren't putting in enough effort, Dad drove in the car with me in the back seat and my brothers running up and down the street next to the car to keep up. With time, they learned to only agree to stop by the closest parks to the house when Dad asked if they wanted to work out. Games were another thing. My dad wasn't like the other parents, cheering on his kids and shouting encouragement no matter what we did. My dad was locked in on every element. No emotion was honestly better because if we weren't giving full effort or weren't being aggressive, then he stopped watching altogether. He'd sink back into the bleachers with his back leaned almost flat. His gaze would be directed straight up into the air. My mother was the yin to my dad's yang. She cheered, loved on us, gave us the benefit of the doubt, and was our biggest fan at any and everything we did.

We didn't talk about games for twenty-four hours after they were completed because my Mom established a rule to keep the peace and sanity in the household; time gave us a better perspective and less emotion. Other parents thought it was too much, and by today's standards, my dad would probably be banned from all sporting events, but Dad coached hard on purpose. We knew he cared about us, he loved us, and he pushed us hard. He never asked us to do anything we weren't capable of doing. When people asked him to go easier on us or Mom told him not to be so critical, he would ask us if we wanted him to go easier, and we would always say no. He'd exclaim, "Tell me if you want to be good or great. Good, I'll leave you alone. Great, and I'll take you to the brink of what you think is impossible."

I was on the sideline a lot when I was too young to play and had a front-row seat as my dad yelled, screamed, pulled, and pushed every ounce of effort and energy out of my brothers. My dad was never results-driven in a stereotypical way. You could have dropped thirty and still not have played well in his eyes. He was always most proud of a well-rounded, versatile game in which we were aggressive and confident. After what he considered bad games, Dad would seethe and scream, demanding what he knew my brothers had capacity to do but weren't giving on that particular day. I can hear him say, "I will never ask you to do something you can't do." No matter how well you thought you played, he was never satisfied. He would always point to the little plays or small possessions within a game that we could rarely remember. So much so that at times it ended in arguments and tears. Watching Dad coach Marcus and Anthony spurred a bit of jealousy in me. I wanted "it." I wanted to be pushed, yelled at, and coached. At the end of a long workout with Dad, my brothers were both drenched in sweat and tired beyond belief, but there's a satisfaction one has after you know you got better.

Don't get me wrong, there were times, few and far between, where my dad would look us in the eyes and tell us good job. When he said it, we knew he meant it. Sports and workouts were physical activities, but my parents always strived to push us mentally as well. In school, we were held to extremely high standards. Our brains were exercised with deep, far ranging questions around the dinner table about a wide array of topics that were meant to make us think. We were encouraged to ask questions and be curious about everything, instead of trusting that others had all the answers. Whenever we asked how to spell something or what something meant it was met with "look it up." At that time, before cell phones, it was a task to find an encyclopedia and look up answers to our questions. But even while rolling our eyes and kicking and screaming, we did it, and as a result, we were well-versed in a wide range of topics. We were challenged at home to be great, not in just one area, but all-around.

Greatness began at home, and my parents knew how to pull it out of us in their own ways. While my dad pushed us on the court, Mom was really intentional about family being at the center and strengthening our self-worth. We always ate dinner together, and Sunday mornings were spent around the breakfast table in front of fresh, hot homemade waffles and amazing conversation. And boy, we loved to joke around! We all kept one another extremely humble at all times. Don't misstep, misspeak, wear a questionable outfit, or do anything that is worthy of being made fun of. Nobody was off-limits! Dad dished it out, but the love was always there. One Saturday morning, Anthony had a friend over when my dad suddenly stood up from the breakfast table and began looking through the cabinets. We all knew not to ask, but Anthony's friend was newer to the Parker household. "Mr. Parker, what are you looking for?" My dad exclaimed, "Anthony's jump shot, hahahaha!" That was our childhood; we joked around, humbled one another, laughed, debated, and celebrated together. You could never take yourself too seriously in our house.

By the time I was seven, Anthony was off to Bradley University on a full athletic scholarship and playing basketball on a bigger stage. We tried to attend most home games and would make the drive two and a half hours south to Peoria, Illinois, to cheer my big brother on. Many Saturdays my parents would take me to my basketball games at 8:00 a.m., then rush over to Marcus's JV games, and finally scramble to make the drive to catch Anthony's game at Bradley. Those were the good ol' days. Quickly, Anthony emerged as a star and we all had front row seats. Not only to the spotlight and applause, but to the results of all his efforts. Only our family knew how much work he had put in to excel on a stage he worked so hard to be on. One spring during his junior year, Bradley made the NCAA tournament, and we traveled sixteen hours up to Rhode Island to watch his team face Stanford. The game was tough, and Stanford came out with the win, but Anthony put the nation on notice as to who this smooth shooting guard was with an impressive double-double performance of thirty-four points and ten rebounds. Anthony made a real name for himself that day and ended his junior year being ranked as the number one shooting guard in the country.

When we weren't taking the two-hour road trip, it was often only Marcus and me at home—even though he was just a few years away from leaving for college. Marcus has always been incredibly smart; from a young age, he aspired to go to a top medical school. With his eyes set on Johns Hopkins, he decided to focus more on school and exams than basketball. As he focused on a career path he'd dreamt of since he was five years old, basketball was relegated to a hobby. His hard work finally paid off when he was accepted to Washington University and, later, the prestigious Johns Hopkins medical school.

Both of my brothers were shedding their childhoods and making their dreams come true while I was just getting started. My mom tells a story about me coming to her one day crying inconsolably. "What's wrong?" she asked me, to which I replied, "What am I going to do?" After my mom prodded some more, I revealed, "Marcus has school, and Anthony has basketball. What do I have?" I didn't want to be left behind, but Mom helped me see that I was running my own race in my own lane. I'm grateful for my Mom always knowing how to comfort her baby girl, when I felt like I wasn't enough. My time would come, and in the meantime, I had the best teachers and role models right in front of me, my brothers.

Anthony's draft night for the NBA, and the months leading up to it, also had a hand in that. With his dream so close to being a reality, our family became consumed by an electric energy. We'd drive through rich neighborhoods imagining which house Anthony would purchase. We walked into dealerships so Anthony could test-drive expensive cars and picture himself in the future. We saw the work he put in, he deserved everything that was to come. After years of playing basketball for fun, Anthony was our incredible reminder that this sport could take us as far as we dared to imagine. For the first time, I saw basketball's potential to unlock and open up new doors and horizons. That our skill sets and natural talents made us great, but the time and dedication we put in made us special. Watching

Anthony take the leap from college to the big leagues made me grow up a little. The dreams I had for myself required hustle and sacrifice.

I learned so much from both my brothers about resilience and discipline. I was young and was shielded from a lot, but I noticed that they were both frequently underestimated. My father's coworkers asked about Marcus's educational pursuits. When these colleagues heard how much my brother was thriving, they wondered aloud and in front of my parents about whether Marcus was admitted through a program for minorities. They didn't believe he could be accepted on his own merit. Raising us in Naperville was a strategic move for my parents. As children of the civil rights era, my parents heralded education as the great equalizer. For many Black middle-class families like mine, moving to a suburban neighborhood with great schools was the only American dream worth pursuing. Anything else was deemed an intergenerational setback. But these neighborhoods were more often than not predominantly white and subjected the children of ambitious Black adults to spaces absent of diversity, where we were mascots for the Black community. Everything we did was stacked up against the stereotypes the white people around us believed. "You're so well-spoken." Read: Black people can be eloquent . . . but not all of them. "You got into Johns Hopkins?" Read: Black people can do things other than sports . . . but only through affirmative action.

It also reminded me of stories my grandparents had shared with me. I was lucky enough to have all four of my grandparents in my life well into adulthood. Throughout my childhood, I spent hours on end with each of them, and even a couple great-grandparents, listening to their stories and understanding how they saw the world. I've always been fascinated with history and enjoyed hearing about specific time periods because it indeed shaped me into who I am. Through my loved ones' eyes, I understood their fears and motivations and how external factors shaped them. My paternal great-grandfather, Clarence Duke, was a landowner and one of the first Black Americans to ever graduate from college in Oklahoma. He endured so much to migrate west and offer his children the opportunity to bloom beyond white supremacy's reach. Each of his three daughters graduated from college, and my great-grandfather ended up leaving Oklahoma to teach in Illinois.

One of his daughters—my dad's mother, Joan—was the epitome of her ancestors' dreams. A tall, slender woman, my grandmother played basketball in high school and, in her adulthood, worked for the government throughout the fifties, sixties, and seventies. We don't think of Black women in the mid-twentieth century as having independence, but my grandmother did. In addition to her high-powered civil service job, Grandma traveled often across Europe while still raising her boys to be conscious of race and racism in America. None of this was easy; Black ambition has always been hard-fought, especially in my family, so it's only right that my brothers and I see ourselves as part of that legacy. I come from people who have mastered this tightrope act of doing what hadn't been done, and I would master it, too, in time.

Witnessing moments and hearing stories about racism and resilience helped me walk into my own future, eyes wide-open. I understood that people are primed to see the world, and all the people in it, through labels and boxes. They take one look at you and make a split-second decision about what they think you're capable of. My job is to never let other people determine my worth or potential. As the kid already hell-bent on defying expectations, my teenage years only strengthened that resolve. I wanted it all. I wanted to take the foundation my parents laid for my brothers and myself and succeed.

I have to also credit my parents for instilling in me a strong sense of self. I'd been playing tug-of-war with basketball, but I finally gave in around twelve when my dad began coaching me in middle school. It took a bit of convincing from my mom to get my dad to agree to coach me. She wanted him to teach me the game, just as he had coached Anthony and Marcus. I'm grateful that my parents cared enough to give their time and energy to their little girl, just as they had to the boys. My sports weren't treated any differently than my brothers'. My parents made the decision to lean into my hopes and dreams. We started our own team, The Illinois Jaguars. And so our journey began. My dad and I entered the era that I had always hoped and dreamed for. My poor mother knew that with this new adventure beginning, she would have to play peacemaker once again. But all three of us were excited and I was elated that it was finally my turn!

Like he had with my brothers, my dad coached me rigorously. He's always known how to motivate me and what makes me come alive. My competitive streak was second to none. I'd race you at tying my shoes or to the car after dinner if you goaded me on enough. When practicing basketball, Dad always "questioned" whether I could do something, knowing I'd do anything and everything to prove I could not only do it but could do it better than anyone else. Even when I knew what he was doing, I couldn't help myself; his playful banter still motivated me. He knew the buttons to press and how to pull the strings to get me to where I wanted to go. My dad's philosophy was very simple: I'm going to teach you basketball IQ and push you past your comfort zone every chance I get. "When you're gliding, that means that you're not doing what you're supposed to do," he'd chide me. Champions don't settle for easy.

As I mentioned, my father played basketball at the University of Iowa from 1972–1976. His career ended after blowing out his knee, but his love for the game continued. There was always a basketball game on in the house. Growing up in the western suburbs of Chicago in the '90s, of course we watched the Bulls dominate the NBA. And when we all sat on the couch to watch the game, Dad didn't just watch, he dissected them. He would always point out specific sets the Chicago Bulls would run. Instead of pointing at the high-flying, flashy, unbelievable moves Michael Jordan would do, my dad would point to the little things. Michael's stance on the defensive end, his pump fake and how he made the defense believe he was really about to shoot it. As a result of those daily basketball lessons,

I had been recognizing defenses and coverages since I was five years old. He refused to let me coast through basketball off physical ability, I had to master the mental aspect as well. In the end, it served me as I learned to dribble, shoot, dunk, pass, communicate, and study the game to enhance my basketball IQ. My versatility stems from him and his refusal to allow me settle for mediocrity. I was tall and he refused to fall into the trap of standing me under the basket. We were playing the long game and eventually others were going to be just as tall, long, and athletic as I was. So I needed to develop my skills now to be successful then. I learned that we don't stop because others are clapping. Stay focused on what you need to do. Seek out weaknesses and don't hide from them, improve them. Once my father ignited my passion, nothing could keep me from basketball. Even when he was no longer coaching me, I couldn't get enough. I was skipping school dances for tournaments and Friday night kickbacks for workouts. I only agreed to attend prom if we could leave the first thing the next morning to make it to an out of state tournament.

The same summer that Anthony was drafted into the 1997 NBA draft, the inaugural season of the WNBA began. "We got next" was their slogan and I went from dreaming of playing for the Bulls to imagining that I was a starting forward for the Houston Comets. Finally it was our turn. Little girls everywhere had a league to aspire to play in now. We had role models who looked like us and were tired of being on the sideline. Our hopes and dreams of playing basketball professionally were possible. My future in basketball wouldn't be cut short because of a lack of opportunity. I could be drafted just like my brother. All that stood in between my lofty dreams and myself was work.

I literally had two road maps and blueprints on how to succeed in whatever I wanted to do. Anthony and Marcus both taught me that, by refusing to be out-worked there's nothing you can't achieve. Marcus brought his hunger to the classroom and it turned into a career in medicine as a radiologist. Anthony was just as ferocious on and off the court, eventually transitioning from playing basketball at the highest levels to working his way up and serving as a General Manager in the NBA. In both of their cases, the key to their success wasn't found at the finish line but at the starting point and in the choices they made throughout their journey. It began with a willingness to be challenged, evolve, rinse, and repeat. Those two, guided by Dad's stern hand, gave me a front row seat to resilience.

As I got older and had the opportunity to form relationships and build my own community, I became extremely intentional with who I surrounded myself with. My goals were important, but who I was and became in the process were just as crucial. I needed people around me who challenged me, were curious, loved to learn, valued hard work, believed in support, held one another accountable and most of all *loved* hard. There's this illusion in life that there is no overlap in the people you surround yourself with and what you aim to accomplish. Show me someone's circle and that will tell a lot about who they are and what their goals are. It is difficult to accomplish anything alone. Over and over I have heard and seen firsthand that you win in life with people. On those tough days, you need someone to lean on, pick you up, tell you what you need to hear. Too many times we want to skip steps, skip growth, stay in comfort, but we all need that someone or someones who will ride with us through the fire, who supports us through the ups and downs in life, and who reminds us who we are when we lose hope and belief. We all have benefited from that "plus one" who instilled confidence in our dreams and motivation to our doubts. I was told to chase people and passion in life and you will never fail. I've been fortunate to have amazing people around me who have inspired me, shaped me, and grown with me. Perhaps the only better feeling I get than receiving support is being in a position to provide it and be for someone what so many have been for me.

TWO

Built Different

You'll be dedicated and that's what you should
want to be in anything in life—whether it's sports
or academics or your relationship. It all stems from
finding that fun, that thrill, that excitement.

—BRANDI CHASTAIN

I n middle school, my eighth grade basketball coach pulled me aside to talk about my long-term plans and goals. In gym class a few days before, I'd dunked a tennis ball with ease at just thirteen years old. When I turned around, all the teachers looked transfixed as they whispered among themselves. "You have the potential to be the top player in the state," Coach said, beaming with pride in our one-on-one meeting. As Coach continued talking about what I needed to do to get there, all I could think was "state?!" I'm shooting way higher than that. I smirked as I reminded myself "we don't have Molly goals and we for sure don't have Molly expectations."

Molly is a girl I played soccer with when we were in elementary school. Or I should say I played soccer and Molly mostly did . . . her own thing. We were young and this wasn't professional sports so the focus was on learning skills, roles, and how to play together. Not everyone had the most competitive spirit, but most of the team had found a lane that worked for them on offense, defense, or as the goalie. Except Molly. The whole season, Molly picked flowers during practice, rarely focused or tried hard during drills and training, and games—well, she barely touched the ball when she was in, let alone scored a goal. Our coach was extremely passionate about everyone scoring a goal and by the end of the season, everyone on the team had scored with the exception of Molly.

In one of our last games of the season, we were up against a team that we were going to easily beat. Our coach pulled another forward on the team and myself aside and encouraged us to pass to Molly to help her score. During halftime orange slices and Hi-C juice boxes—why our parents gave us that sugary drink during sports, I'll never know—our coaches made the change to keep Molly at forward. She was instructed to not play defense to increase her chances of breakaways and scoring opportunities. There were several close calls during the game where Molly almost scored; the entire parent section, coaches, and players on the sideline all jumped up in anticipation and every time it was met with an "awwww." It took nearly all game but finally Molly was headed right for the net when one of my teammates kicked her the ball. We all watched as Molly stopped the ball with her shin guards, ran to catch up to the ball, and kicked it. Everyone held their breath, the soccer ball rolled to a stop, just passing over the line. Goooooaaaaaaalllllllll! Molly threw her hands in the air triumphantly at what was likely the first goal she'd scored in her life. We all ran over to celebrate with her, slapping high fives and showering her in love. When the game ended, Molly's father scooped her up and onto his shoulders. "Let's go get ice cream to celebrate," he yelled in excitement as little Molly giggled in the air.

As I watched the scene play out before me, I couldn't help but be confused. I'd scored six goals in the previous week's game alone. My teammates and I had actually put in the effort to contribute to our team's success, yet Molly was riding off in the sunset as if she'd just scored the game winner. Where was my celebration?! After the game, my dad quickly pushed my comparisons to the side saying, "We don't have Molly goals and we damn sure don't have Molly expectations."

We don't measure our success against others, Dad reminded me. Someone's greatest achievement and wildest dreams could be your baseline. He wanted me to know that getting too excited by others' limited expectations of me would only cap my potential. "Let Molly be excited by her first and only goal of the season, but that's not your path."

Since that day, I've always dreamed bigger and shot higher for myself than what others wanted for me. Their track wasn't mine and not because they underestimated me necessarily but because they were comparing me to their perception of "excellence." I couldn't blame them for not seeing what I saw. I only needed to stay focused on my vision. So fast-forward from that soccer field to half a decade later and I again proved to my middle school coach that I was headed somewhere no one in Naperville saw coming.

By my freshman year of high school, I was 6'3" and just ranked the top female basketball player in the *country* of the class of 2004. So how does the top-ranked player in the nation stay hungry enough to chase something bigger than those early accolades? What does it take to not become so consumed by the cheers that I forget to do the work? Humility. I naturally always wanted "more," but my most important people around me never let me settle. I saw my weaknesses and knew I had a lot more to grow in my game. That just because I was "at the top" at the moment didn't mean I had even scratched the surface of what I was capable of. Set big expectations and standards for yourself and then work to achieve them, then when you do, work some more. This was my first experience realizing that my crazy dad might be onto something.

The only time I let myself get a big head was when I realized that my brothers were only 5'5" and 5'7" when they entered high school. My growth spurt hit earlier than theirs and if we didn't have such a wide age gap between us, I would have relished towering over them. Outside of that, I kept my head down and remained addicted to the grind of practicing. Doing what others wouldn't do had taken me places they couldn't go and I didn't want to settle for peaking now. I had natural talent for sure. Again, I was 6'3" when I was fourteen years old! But I also had a mindset and a work ethic that set me apart even more. There was so much more to dream of than high school. I was thinking about college and all that came after that.

During my middle school years, all eyes were on Pat Summitt and the University of Tennessee. My parents recognized early on that Tennessee plus Summitt equaled success. The Lady Vols won the championship in 1996, 1997, and 1998. Three straight wins led by the Three Miques (Chamique Holdsclaw, Tamika Catchings, and Semeka Randall). Helming a dynasty like Tennessee is exactly what I'd dreamed of and my dad knew it. One day while on a business trip, he saw a UT hat in an airport store. He immediately purchased it and wrote on the brim in black Sharpie, "I don't coach effort." My Dad knew how to motivate me. I hung that hat on the coatrack outside my room as my reminder of what I was working toward. I didn't want to just attend Tennessee, I wanted to be recruited by them and win championships for that team. As I did my nightly routine of brushing my teeth, washing my face, and doing push-ups to get stronger, I'd look up and see that orange hat.

Recruiting didn't begin until sophomore year but I still received hundreds of questionnaires from colleges expressing early interest. I didn't look at or open most of them because, in my eyes, I hadn't arrived yet or accomplished what I knew I could. The time for celebrating would come but this was too early. I broke my rule only once. One day in early 2002, I went out to the mailbox and was so excited to see the Tennessee Lady Vol Power T in the corner of the envelope. I ran inside the house waving the letter around in my dad and mom's faces. After years of my dad playfully taunting me about not being great until Tennessee wanted me, finally the day had come that *the* Pat Summitt and the best of the best at Tennessee were interested in recruiting me. My dad smiled and my mom waited as I opened the mail to see what was inside. I opened it up and my smile faded quickly. The questionnaire wasn't from Pat Summitt or the basketball team at all. It was from the volleyball team who wanted me to consider playing for them.

We laughed long and hard with my dad using this for even more fuel. "See, you're not there yet!" Yet was the keyword. I loved volleyball, but not as much as basketball. I didn't want to be a Lady Vol without being a hooper. It was great to be recruited for two sports I cared about but my eyes and heart were locked in on becoming the best on every basketball court I stepped on. I used moments like these to keep me focused on becoming stronger, faster, and more agile. Thankfully I wasn't shooting in any gyms alone. I always had the support and love of my mom, who chauffeured me to and from workouts, treatment, school, and practice. My dad was always there with his encouraging tone and commitment to doing challenging things, regardless of what people expected. It was him who first challenged me to dunk, knowing I had the ability to do it.

We began by dunking tennis balls and volleyballs throughout the end of middle school and the beginning of high school. When doing that became easy for me, we advanced to attempting dunking with actual basketballs. I am fortunate to have always had huge hands, thanks to my mom's side of the family. (My maternal grandfather wore a size 16 ring!) Great genetics on both sides allowed me the physical ability to not only be long and athletic, but palm an NBA-sized ball with ease. The first time I ever dunked it was at the Edward-Elmhurst Health and Fitness Center in Naperville when I was in the ninth grade. Our workout concluded and my dad casually bounce passed me the ball and I gathered the dribble, palmed the ball, gathered my steps, and dunked the basketball. When my feet landed on the ground, my dad was already cheering and hoisting me into the air unable to contain his pride. We raced home where we told my mom who joined us in the excited freak-out we were having. I wasn't thinking about what this meant for my career or for women's basketball. I simply couldn't wait to call my brothers and let them know I'd gotten one down at fourteen years old when they hadn't dunked until they were sixteen. Like I said, we could be a bit competitive in the Parker household!

When I dunked for the first time in a game at the Dundee-Crown Christmas tournament, the gymnasium erupted with cheers and surprise. I jogged back across the wood floor pumping my fist and looking to the stands. My brother, Marcus, and his wife, Glenda, jumped up celebrating with excitement, my father pumped his fist but maintained his stoic seat on the bleachers, and my mom, the real MVP, insisted on recording my Christmas tournament from up in the stands. She'd caught the dunk on camera and, in doing so, captured the real beginnings of me being thrust into the spotlight. Reporters and sports journalists appeared on our front lawn the next morning. All were buzzing about the teenage girl in Illinois dunking, rebounding, and doing everything else under the sun. Could I live up to everyone's expectations? No, I would far surpass those because my expectations far exceeded what anyone thought I could become. I didn't play for those lights or the applause that came with it. I genuinely LOVED the game of basketball. I found joy in the work, playing the game in a packed gym or alone on a Sunday afternoon workout, and in defying what's possible in a world that loves putting limitations on females in general. Looking back, at times I wish I would have relished and lived a bit more in the moment. I was always raising my own bar, which is a gift and a curse. But, now that I had everyone's attention, I was going to show them what was possible.

I also began to look to people and players who had what I wanted. Not material things, but grit and determination and unapologetic passion. Some of those archetypes came through the media, like the iconic Brandi Chastain World Cup moment. I was a teenager when I joined tens of millions of Americans in watching Chastain score the game-winning penalty against China, securing the World Cup for the US Women's National Team. When Chastain pulled her sweaty jersey over her head and swung it around victoriously, I understood that. Most people spend their whole lives chasing a feeling as euphoric as that one and when you finally reach that moment, you want to relish it. The next day when all anyone could talk about was Chastain's sports bra and not how incredibly she'd played, I remembered all the times I'd been told something wasn't ladylike. Whether it was passion in the midst of a game or what I wore or how strong I'd become, I was used to people being both impressed and confounded by me. But Chastain didn't let that stop her and even on a stage as large as the World Cup, she allowed herself to be free of those judgments. I wanted to be as courageous and bold, and leave my own footprint on women's athletics and what it meant for girls and women to be seen as competitors and not sweaty sex symbols.

Another example of an athlete who was unapologetically themself is one of my favorite basketball players of all time, and the reason I switched the number on my jersey to #3 after high school: Allen Iverson. There was so much to marvel at when it came to Allen Iverson. The fact that in high school he was so versatile that he led his basketball *and* football teams to state championships. His ability to stare down adversity and still come out on top, as he did after being unfairly incarcerated as a teenager. Every step of the way—from the neglected hoods of Virginia to the hallowed halls of Georgetown University to the NBA—Iverson entered each space with a commitment to being himself. After making your dreams come true, many in Iverson's position would play it safe but that would be a betrayal to all that made him him. Though the NBA held a more corporate aesthetic at the time and accepted Black masculinity in a very specific and "respectable" look, Iverson insisted on donning braids and wearing streetwear. Culture wasn't a costume you put on or took off, he seemed to be saying. Celebrating our differences doesn't mean flattening them and we should be proud of who we are at all times, not just when winning on the court but also outside of a game or media junket. Allen Iverson's defiance allowed players like Russell Westbrook and James Harden to turn the NBA tunnel walks into a runway, and the NBA as a whole to become a driving force in culture and fashion.

Even though I didn't dress or play exactly like him, I could appreciate how much Iverson transformed the game forever. He refused limitations put on him and championed more imagination for the league overall. At 6'0", Iverson was fairly short as far as an NBA guard is concerned. Most point and shooting guards had several inches of height as an advantage and, still, Iverson outscored most of them. When you watched him play, you could see the passion and heart shine bright through the cornrows and tattoos. Iverson allowed Black people more permission to take up space in professional athletics and bring Black culture and our origins with us. Did he make mistakes? Sure. But the game was, and is, better because of Iverson. His confidence was contagious and I can recall waiting in line for hours to cop a pair of his Reebok Questions and Answers, sneakers I played in for years after.

Tina Thompson was another inspiration for me, having been the first college draft pick ever for the WNBA and leading her team—the Houston Comets—to four consecutive championships! As if that wasn't enough, Thompson was also a gold medal Olympian and led the league in scoring for years even after retiring. Back then, Thompson and the Comets had girls across the country "raising the roof!" I loved Tina because she was a post player who had a pure jumper and a smooth turnaround. She played the game her way. In fact, she wore bright red lipstick on the court every game. I loved players who brought their own swag and personality to the game. She was an example of someone who was feminine in nature and looks, but brought a ferocity to the game that was anything but "ladylike." She did it her way. She carved and forged her own path. I always dreamed of doing that. No matter what uniform I put on, I wanted to be *me*.

Idolizing athletes on my television screen had taken me far, but I've never been someone to believe that you can only be inspired by people you don't know. My brothers had always been my first motivations, teaching me that no goal was unreachable and no challenge was insurmountable. They always say "don't meet your heroes," but I was raised with mine. I grew up wanting to be even a fraction as cool, smart, and talented as they were. Anthony and Marcus had set the bar incredibly high as to what the Parker children could and would accomplish through grit and perseverance. I had to live up to their example and I fell in love with the process of proving to myself that I was made of the same stuff as my brothers. We were simply built different than other kids our age. Physically gifted, yes, but mentally as well.

When my brothers left home and I saw them less, I craved mentorship and guidance from someone other than my family and coaches. Enter: Jenni Dant. Jenni Dant is a brilliant coach and hooper who I first met when we were teens. Jenni was four years older than me and headed to play basketball at DePaul. Though I was ascending on the basketball scene, Jenni seemed to me to have already made it.

Luckily for me, Jenni was as kind as she was skilled and we spent a lot of time together in the year before she graduated from high school. We talked about the recruitment journey, what to look for in coaches, and she even taught me how to drive! She gently encouraged me from the passenger seat as we wound through empty parking lots and it was as formative for me as any basketball advice she'd offered. Simply because she'd taken the time out of her day to pour into me. It meant the world as an underclassman to have someone as successful as Jenni spending so much time and energy with me. I soaked up every piece of advice she gave me and channeled it into the explosive high school career I knew I was capable of. She may not even know her influence and what she meant to my basketball journey. We don't still communicate and I haven't spoken to her in years, but her presence, character, influence, and love for me was influential at a time when I needed it. I realized through Jenni Dant that sometimes you have no idea the impact you can have on someone's life. I learned through different relationships to pour and lean into people, but also, by just doing and being me I could very well serve as inspiration and a role model for so many who desperately need it.

In my second half of high school, I never lost a game I played in and became the basketball player to watch. When they said I only dunked on "girls," I played and won co-ed dunk competitions. When they switched it up and said all I knew how to do was dunk, I racked up points, rebounds, and assists. (I probably hold the record for "almost triple doubles.") Even when I was wide open, I sometimes intentionally went for layups and held out on dunking until I decided to. I would never be anyone's one-trick pony or gimmick. There was a lot of pressure to put on a show and bring more visibility to women's basketball but I didn't want to dilute my craft. It would be a disservice to everything my parents taught me about doing it for me and not for the praise.

But the praise came anyway, and the country began to pay attention to girl's and women's basketball in a whole new way. After years of watching others make names for themselves, it was my turn. Since the late '70s, the McDonald's All-American game has been the high school–level's premier All-Star exhibition. The best high school hoopers across gender all assemble for individual competitions around dunking and three-pointers, and a game between the East and the West.

During my senior year of high school, in March 2004, I joined the top basketball players my age including Dwight Howard, Sylvia Fowles, Tasha Humphrey, Shaun Livingston, Charde Houston, Sebatian TelFair, JR Smith, Sa'de Wiley-Gatewood, Josh Smith, and Alexis Hornbuckle. By this point, I was already a Gatorade, Naismith, and *USA Today* Player of the Year. My game was undeniable but the McDonald's All-American game was the chance to showcase and measure your game up against the best of the best across the country. The opportunity came about to enter the dunk contest after practice one day. I was hesitant at first, as I was nine months post–ACL surgery and still donning a huge knee brace. But, "Can-Do, right?" So I entered the men's dunk contest as the only female participant.

The games were being held at what is now known as the Paycom Center in Oklahoma but the dunk contest was hosted a few miles away at Carl Albert High School in Midwest City, a sprawling campus with the stands and bleachers buzzing at the future of the game of basketball. The men's roster alone had 5–7 guys who would be lottery picks in the coming months in the NBA Draft. When I entered the gymnasium, I looked up and around at the packed stands. Every inch of the bleachers was filled with sports journalists, ESPN camera crews, fans, and family. A black backdrop blocked off one end of the gym and dozens of people who couldn't find a seat stood against the walls opposite it.

I was up against some incredible competitors and, perhaps on another day, maybe they would have put me to shame. But I knew most of the people in that room were waiting to see what I could do. Girls rarely competed in the dunk contest at that time and I knew this would be many people's first time seeing a woman dunk live. The anticipation should have made me nervous, but I'd been preparing for this moment since I was thirteen dunking tennis balls with my dad.

Rudy Gay went first and dunked but missed both of his next attempts. Darius Washington Jr. was up next and threw down two nice ones, including one behind the back and over the dome jam. When my turn arrived, I made my first dunk with one hand and circled my torso before hitting my second dunk on the second attempt. JR Smith made an impressive dunk when he touched the left side of the backboard with the ball before dunking it on the right. We left the first round of the slam dunk contest with JR Smith and Joe Crawford tied at first, Washington at third, and me at fourth place.

I teed up the next round just happy to be there. I had zero expectations and was actually just having fun. No one expected me to win and I am an extreme realist, I didn't expect to win. I entered to get a couple dunks down and take a seat. But accuracy was my strategy. I made all three of my attempts, covering my eyes for the last one. The gym erupted with the crowd jumping to their feet. Shocked that a "little high school girl" was able to actually slam dunk. I sat back down and waited for the other competitors to bring down the house! Darius Washington's first attempt of the second round was beautiful but he didn't make either of his next two attempts. JR Smith only made the last of his second round attempts and Crawford missed two himself. While most of the competition missed nearly as many as they made, I'd made all but one of my dunks across both rounds. When Crawford didn't make his last attempt of the round, the corners of my mouth turned upward immediately and the other girls near me began congratulating me. I'd just become the first girl to win the McDonald's All-American Slam Dunk contest.

In the media frenzy that followed, some celebrated the feat, others questioned it, but what it came down to was I made my attempts and others missed them—MJ shrug! And that's where it began. My name became synonymous with dunking. But through the dunk contest, more people tuned in to watch our game the next day and actually see women's basketball. The skill set, the pace, the versatility, the physicality, and the style. Our game was growing and I was thrilled to be a part of it. So many fans to this day come up to me in all walks of life and proudly state that the first time they fell in love with my game was watching the 2004 McDonald's All-American dunk contest. I'm grateful for the stage that was fought for and provided by so many other girls who didn't have the chance to play in the game until 2002, I'm proud that I was bold enough to take the chance and enter the dunk contest, and I love the fact that even to this day, when the 2004 boys and girls roster gets together, I can talk shit to JR Smith because he went on to win the NBA dunk contest, but he never beat me!

THREE

"Left Foot, Right Foot, Breathe, Repeat"

Individual success is a myth.
No one succeeds all by themselves.

—PAT SUMMITT

I was on the road with the Los Angeles Sparks at the time, traveling to an away game when my phone rang. Any time the area code 865 would pop up on my phone I knew it was Knoxville, Tennessee. Ever since my college coach, Pat Summitt, was diagnosed with early-onset Alzheimer's five years prior, there was an uneasiness whenever I saw the familiar area code on my phone screen. I picked up before the third ring, anxiety wracking my thoughts. As the person on the other end of the call began to speak, my eyes filled with tears, and my stomach dropped. I looked down at the tattoo on my forearm. "Left foot, right foot, breathe, repeat." The year before, I elected to make one of my favorite quotes—one I learned from Coach—permanent for moments such as this. Pat wasn't doing well, and they suggested that I come and see her, and soon. I took a deep breath, knowing what this meant. I rearranged my travel and headed to Knoxville as soon as our game against the Minnesota Lynx was finished that night.

The entire way to Knoxville, I obsessed over what I would say to Pat to convey just how much she meant to me. How she brought the best out of me in a way no one else could. How winning with her was sweet, but boy, the lessons I learned in the face of the losses were invaluable. Even that was a half story, though, because our relationship was so much bigger than basketball. It washed over me that this could be the last time I spoke to Pat. I didn't think of the 1,098 wins she amassed by the time she retired, the most by any coach ever, or the eight NCAA championships she led the University of Tennessee Lady Vols to. I thought of how grateful I was to have her as a role model for all these years. Everything Pat did was a master class on work ethic, passion, and people. She was so much more than an incredible coach; she was a leader, educator, mother, motivator, competitor, and my muse. Pat's hustle knew no bounds, and we bonded over our stubbornness and insistence on doing it all. The woman nearly gave birth forty thousand feet in the air, proving it to anyone and everyone who dared look into that icy stare and doubt her. Coach was traveling the country nine months pregnant to recruit new players to the Lady Vols when she began contracting mid-conversation. Home was nearly two hours away by air, and a medical professional probably would have told Pat to go to the nearest hospital, but Coach refused to give birth anywhere but Tennessee. When the pilot announced that he was going to make an emergency landing in Virginia, Pat apparently gave the staff the same look she'd given to many a referee before. "She knew what she wanted and she was going to do what she had to do to get that," her ob-gyn said of that day.

Pat beat out nature, gravity, and an entire crew of pilots and flight attendants—because that's what she did. She made a plan, and she executed. It's what we all admired about her.

Pat didn't feel like she could let up—on herself or others—and I understand why. Women's basketball was still in its infancy as Pat built and cemented a dynasty. She loved the sport and the women it empowered, and refused to shortchange the opportunity to scale it to where she knew it could be. At just 22 years old in 1974, Pat Summitt accepted the head coaching position at the University of Tennessee. During those years, women's basketball was just beginning and needed someone like Pat, regardless of how young she was. Just one year older than some of her collegiate players, she coached them hard, tough, and intensely to set the tone for what it was to be a Lady Vol. But, ever since those early days where she balanced being a graduate student, was paid just $250 a month, drove the bus, taped ankles, did laundry, and coached, she insisted on all of her players calling her "Pat." All of her players from that time on continued calling her by her first name—she demanded it. I was uneasy at first, as I was brought up with Mrs. or Coach or Ma'am, but after a couple practices where she refused to answer, I relented and called her Pat.

She came from a small town in Tennessee called Henrietta and she grew up competing against her brothers and being challenged and disciplined by her father (sounds familiar). Pat learned hard work from an early age and as a result, she replicated it and demanded it from everyone who put on a Tennessee Lady Vol uniform. I don't know if Pat ever set out to change the course of women's basketball as a whole, but she saw opportunities that weren't there and fought to create them, she used her voice in a way that most women hadn't, and she didn't ask for respect, she demanded it because she was willing to roll up her sleeves and outwork you.

In my quiet moments of anticipatory grief, I realized that my love for Pat superseded what we accomplished, which is saying something because we accomplished *a lot*. Pat was and remains my favorite person to win with, but some of my favorite memories with her involve a lot of losing and adversity. It's who she became, and who she called me to be, in the midst of those moments that made me love, respect, and listen to her so closely.

More Than a Coach

The moment I first set foot on Tennessee's campus, I could sense that Pat would become more than a coach to me. I couldn't wait to play as a Lady Vol, so I was devastated when I had to sit out my freshman year with a knee injury. I worried about the lost time and was gutted to realize I couldn't do the one thing Pat had brought me to Tennessee to do: play basketball. While I was anxious about being deemed a bad investment, Pat didn't stress at all. Quite the opposite actually, Coach was determined to spend extra time with me. Though I was feeling unproductive and unworthy until I was back on the court, Coach saw the opportunity I didn't. She continued pouring into me and took advantage of the chance to get inside my head and learn my language.

During my freshman year, Pat asked me to have lunch with her every Wednesday and to bring my homework with me. There, in her office sitting atop the gymnasium, we talked about everything: basketball, family, adjusting to college, getting along with my teammates, hopes, fears, physical therapy, my parents' divorce, and so much more. During that time, Pat took everything in. She learned about my brothers and how much basketball was an extension of family. She learned my favorite foods, least favorite workouts, and long-term dreams.

I didn't always know how much Coach lived by this until my parents would visit and I realized Coach had remembered their birthdays. *When did I tell her that?* I wondered to myself. But it wasn't worth trying to figure out. Coach knew everything that mattered, recognizing that the little things make the big difference. She knew everyone's name—not just the staff at Tennessee but also from colleges across the SEC. When we traveled to away games, Pat remembered nearly everyone and made it a point to call them by name and be intentional about giving them the time and respect they deserved. The more I reflect on Pat's leadership style, the more I'm baffled at how she managed to do it all. Somehow she made it seem effortless and yet I know how much it takes to maintain even one relationship at the depth that Pat knew all of her players, assistant coaches, and supporting staff.

Coach carried herself with expectations of greatness across the board, not just in winning games, but in how she was able to see and relate to people. Because Pat invested so much in the people around her and expected so much from each of us, it made me value her advice that much more. Pat's opinion carried serious weight with me and I always wanted her blessing on anything new in my life. Perhaps that's why I waited so long to tell her about the forward at Duke who I'd started seeing. I was almost as nervous introducing him to Pat as I was for him to meet my parents—and he was probably just as nervous as well.

We'd just concluded a televised game against Stanford when I received a Facebook message from a 6'7" forward from Duke University named Shelden Williams. I replied and things seemed to really flow after that message. It just so happened that a month or so after those first DMs were traded, the Lady Vols played at Duke. Shelden's and my first official meeting in person was in the lobby of a Durham hotel the night before our game against the Blue Devils. A couple of our teammates were present, as we all laughed and chatted until curfew when it was time for me to go upstairs and prepare for the game the next day. From that moment, we agreed that once the season was over we both wanted to spend more time with each other.

Shelden was a projected lottery draft pick, playing at the mecca of college basketball and still so down to earth, kind, and humble. Our relationship grew over the phone and Skype where we realized we were quite similar. Both of us were *extremely* focused and didn't like going out or partying much, opting for small intimate gatherings instead. It was amazing going through the ups and downs of college and basketball with someone who knew firsthand what it felt like to navigate the challenges of playing a sport on a big stage.

We also had our differences. He was always ten minutes early and I was always racing to get there ten minutes late. I was also more outgoing than Shel, but there was a way that I brought out his personality and he allowed me to be sensitive and soft. I would sit on the telephone just listening and he would do the same for me, allowing me to vent and express my frustration of not playing well, etc. Time flew and things became serious. Oftentimes, he would make the trip to Knoxville to only have a couple hours with me. We'd work out in the arena and I remember this one specific day we bumped into the coaching staff. I was so nervous to make it official. I fumbled around making small talk before finally introducing Shelden to Coach Dean, Holly, and Nikki, who couldn't stop smiling. Then came the movement as all eyes turned to Coach Summitt, who was standing not far behind. Coach walked toward us methodically and though it likely took her only a few seconds to reach us, it felt like hours. When she stood before us, I remember hearing Shel swallow hard. I looked over and could visibly see his nerves as I noticed my own heart beating fast. Shel stood up straight, stiffened up, and was nervous like I had never seen before. My voice shook a bit as I made the official introduction. "Nice to meet you," Pat exclaimed in her deep Southern drawl. I looked over again at Shelden, who nodded and locked eyes with her in the most respectful way before replying, "Yes, ma'am."

I laughed the second we got out of earshot of the coaches at how scared Shelden seemed. He chuckled, too, and admitted Coach Summitt was intimidating. I couldn't really blame him. Her crystal blue eyes had the ability to look through you. Anyone who ever got caught in her stare can attest to how it had the ability to pull fear and accountability out of you in an instant.

Shelden and I quickly grew as a couple and every moment that was possible, we made an effort to see each other. I can remember a number of times he would surprise me by driving or flying up to see me after practice. One time, when I was playing USA basketball in the fall of 2006, Shel popped up at Duke for our exhibition game against Australia. The Cameron Crazies (as the student section was called) started chanting Shelden's nickname "The Landlord." I smiled at him with the biggest grin, grateful that he had come to support me on my senior national team debut. My love language has always been quality time so it meant the world that he'd made the effort to match what always had truly mattered to me.

Pretty soon Shel was a regular around the team and the University. Pat welcomed him in because she knew that he was important to me. Pat and Shelden developed their own relationship even as Pat warned me about taking my time and being deliberate. Pat was disciplined and driven, but always reasonable. She was very open and honest and communicated her expectations and rules up front. In the end, Coach also knew there were some things I needed to experience on my own. Anything we chose to do (or not do) had a cause and effect. A reward or a consequence. Instead of grilling me, Pat would ask about how things were going and whether Shelden was respectful. After that, she always reaffirmed her trust in me to make the best decisions on how to balance my personal life, basketball, and school. Instead of accusing me of anything, I felt Pat's trust and confidence, which made me accept even more responsibility to maintain that trust.

Looking back, there's a lot I wish I'd done differently throughout my time with Pat, but I took note of how loved she always made me feel even in the midst of messiness. I wanted to do that with the people I loved going forward. Affirming someone gets you way further than questioning them.

Lead by Example

Long before I played at Tennessee, Coach Pat drafted up her twelve keys to success, which she dubbed her Definite Dozen. Every principle was described at length in her book *Reach for the Summitt*, but each mantra also had an accompanying poem, so to speak, of what that principle looked like in practice. All twelve principles were printed and hung on the walls of the locker room for players to internalize. Every year, Coach started the school year by assigning each player a principle to embody. We didn't all receive the same principle, either. Coach took the time to consider each of us individually, our growth opportunities over the coming year, and what we needed to internalize in order to rise to the station Coach knew we were capable of. I spent four years in Tennessee, and every single year Pat called me into her office and assigned me the same principle: "Handle success like you handle failure."

> You can't always control what happens, but you can control how you handle it.
>
> Sometimes you learn more from losing than winning.
> Losing forces you to reexamine.
>
> It's harder to stay on top than it is to make the climb.
> Continue to seek new goals.

Coach really hit me over the head with that one. (She could be *very* demanding.) Pat knew when you weren't giving your all and she worked hard to break the habit of under committing or half-assing anything. She insisted that we each discipline ourselves so no one else had to. Coach had no problem holding us accountable, which we all learned firsthand. But she was all about empowering us to *want* to do what was needed. No one should need to yell at or chastise you if you care enough to be intentional about your inputs. Beyond her Definite Dozen, there were other mandates like always sitting in one of the first three rows of class. In the moment, some of Summitt's rules seemed unnecessary or over-the-top but they've served me far beyond any basketball court or classroom. I was recently at an Adidas conference in Germany, and the whole first row was empty. I immediately took my seat in one of those chairs and cracked a smile thinking of how proud Coach would be. Let your body language speak for you, she'd tell us. By sitting in the front row, you're asserting your willingness to lead and be seen as a leader. Those little things add up. That mentality has carried me further than I ever initially dreamed, but it took time for me to submit to the Summitt Way as a passionate, young hooper.

I'll never forget one of my worst games as a Lady Vol. Or rather, I'll never forget how disappointed and furious Pat was. Not that we'd lost but that we didn't seem to care enough to bring our best. Throughout the game, we'd been sloppy across the board, and Coach wasn't having it. She chewed us out in the locker room that day and specifically got on me about being a leader. Pat knew what she was doing; I didn't like to be told I couldn't do or hadn't done what needed to be done. The next practice wasn't up to her standard at all, either. Tempers were brewing, and sometimes my stubbornness worked against me. The more Pat dug in, so did I. I could tell Coach was extremely frustrated because when she's really mad she doesn't yell or scream, she ignores you. Before practice ended, Pat asked me to leave and go back to the locker room because she was tired of my energy. Essentially, I was kicked out of practice.

The next day, I was ready to prove Pat wrong and show that no one was more committed to the team than me. I woke up extra early to arrive at the gym long before practice was set to start. I loved it in the morning; the building was so quiet, and most of the hallways were dark and still, awaiting the buzz of players, trainers, and coaches who weren't set to arrive for another two hours.

As I drove past the front of Thompson-Boling Arena where the coaches' offices were, to go and park my car underneath the arena, I noticed a light on in one of the offices. After parking my car, I rushed up the stairs and into the coaches' offices to see who was there. Sure enough, Coach was already in her office flipping through papers, watching film, and drawing up strategies. I shook my head as I tiptoed out and back down the stairs to get dressed in the locker room.

There I was, thinking I was going to show *her*. Meanwhile, without saying a word, I learned a lesson I will carry with me forever. To be one of the greatest of all time, you can't forget the little things that got you to the top. You don't have to shout from the rooftops about what you are doing or the amount of energy and effort you are putting in—just do it, quietly and deliberately, over and over again. All the extra time, showing up early and staying late, is necessary in the process and battle to stay great. There was no outworking Pat Summitt, and she remains one of the greatest basketball coaches of all time for that reason.

Coach would always say, "I will not start your engine." That phrase perfectly encapsulates her leadership style. She first demands your commitment to yourself and your ability to want to be great. Pat was not into begging someone to try, but boy if you committed to starting your engine, she sure would rev it! She never asked you to do anything she wasn't already doing; Pat expected everyone to meet her at her level so they could see their full potential. Leaders get to where the team needs to be and pull you there. Bosses push you from behind, sometimes to places they have never been or would never go. Pat was a leader. She built teams and showed through her everyday actions just how committed she was to the team. All you could hope was to match her consistency and work ethic. Anything and everything was possible on the other side of that.

We Over Me

During my entire time at Tennessee, I never wore the name "Parker" on my jersey. None of us did. As Coach reminded us over and over again, we didn't have our names on the back of our jersey because it was about playing for the Lady Vols and not playing for ourselves. "You play for the name on the front." Teamwork was another one of her Definite Dozen principles in action: "Put the team before yourself."

Teamwork doesn't come naturally. It must be taught.

Teamwork allows common people to obtain uncommon results.

Not everyone is born to lead. Role players are critical to group success.

In group success there is individual success.

During my last year at Tennessee, we were chasing back-to-back championships and when you're the reigning champ, you are the hunted and not the hunter. Just before the Christmas holiday, we lost to Stanford in overtime—our first loss of the season. We had a little over a week before our next game against DePaul in Chicago and practice was intense! Pat hated losing, especially when she felt we weren't at our best. Because the away game was on January 2nd, we traveled into Chicago early as a team to practice and settle in. Had we been in Tennessee preparing for this game, we would have had the New Years' Eve holiday to ourselves, but staying in a hotel as a team meant a team-wide curfew. After the designated time, no one could leave or enter. Any other year, I wouldn't have minded much because I've never been one to chase big parties or crowds. But

Shelden and I had recently gotten engaged and I wanted to bring in the New Year by his side. He'd traveled all the way to Chicago for me and I couldn't imagine being so close to him without spending the evening together. If we were playing a home game, Shelden and I'd be doing the same thing in my Knoxville apartment, so why should this be any different?

After weighing the potential outcomes and consequences, knowing that we didn't have a game the next day on January 1st, I did what I knew I shouldn't have: I strolled right out of my hotel room and headed to Shel's room on a different floor. I didn't even bother to be inconspicuous because I knew I wasn't technically leaving the hotel. Shelden and I were simply going to lounge in his hotel room since he had to catch an early flight out the next morning to get back for practice. However, a few hours into hanging out, Shelden's hotel room phone rang. Weird. When he picked up the phone and began repeating the words "yes, ma'am" over and over, I knew we'd been caught. He didn't even try to deny it or give me cover. Shelden immediately admitted I was next to him and promised to get me back to my hotel room as soon as possible.

This was a moment when I saw Pat's deep sense of responsibility to people beyond herself or her "star player." The team needed to know that no one came before the team and that anyone could and would be held accountable for putting themselves before the collective. I was angry at the situation that I had caused. I gave Coach no choice but to discipline me. What kind of example would she be setting if she let me get away with this? I had to respect her insistence, even after she announced she'd be benching me for the first half of our coming game against DePaul. Of course I was devastated, as this was my one and only game that I got to play at home in front of my family and friends. I could also tell it hurt her as much as it hurt me to see me on the sideline as all of Naperville watched from the stands in confusion. Still Pat didn't budge and, over time, I came to admire her consistency. Once the stubbornness and emotions passed,

I respected Coach and her decision even more. If we didn't win that would be on all of us, but it wouldn't keep her from leading this team the way she intended. Accountability for your actions.

Coach held herself and others to a high standard because she knew our collective commitment could yield unimaginable results. Why take it easy when we could simply rise to the occasion, together? She never took credit for herself and always championed the chorus of people who made the Lady Vols go round. So long as we each played our role and played it well, nothing could get in our way.

One of the ways Pat insisted on challenging us to be the team she knew we could be was by signing us up for one of the toughest NCAA schedules in the country. She didn't believe in padding our record with easy wins or soft seasons. She didn't care if that meant we weren't the number one seed or what commentators thought about it. Her philosophy was to face every possible situation during the regular season so that we could adjust and learn before the NCAA tournament. During games, Coach cared far less about the results on the scoreboard than on what she saw and felt about our commitment. We could be up by thirty, but if we had given up offensive rebounds or missed an assignment on the defensive end, we'd hear about it in the huddle.

In 2007, we were playing the UNC Tar Heels in the Final Four. We were down by twelve with a little over eight minutes left. We had twenty-one turnovers, and after I got into early foul trouble, it was a less-than-smooth night. I walked into the huddle and took the lead. My teammate Nicky Anosike and I challenged our team to rise to the occasion and dig deep. To fight the feelings of exhaustion and the desire to give up. We had worked far too hard to give in. We asked if we all could commit to the tangible goal of getting five straight defensive stops. Every member of our team was locked in and nodded their head. Pat Summitt heard the last bit of the huddle at the end of our challenge to our teammates. Pat, picking up where we left off, wouldn't let us give in. As we wrapped up the huddle and headed out to the court to resume play, I could see Pat nod to one of the assistants. She was proud of Nicky and me for taking ownership. We were prepared. We were prepared because of all of the tough practices, the games on the road in a hostile environment, the drills that prepared us for THIS moment. I'm grateful for things not being easy because we found out what we were capable of in the uncomfortable and challenging times. We knew we could win because in those tough practices and games, we figured it out together. In the postgame interview after we stormed back to win and head to the NCAA championship, Holly Rowe asked me what I'd learned about myself that night. "I'll tell you what I learned about my team," I said earnestly. "I learned that we could play through adversity." Pat had prepared us in more ways than one for that moment. I was proud that we won, sure, but I was most proud that in our toughest moments, I had been the leader the team needed me to be.

Communication Is Everything

While I take pride in knowing that my relationship with Pat was special, I also revel in the reality that she made everyone feel like the only person in the room when she was talking to you. Coach bent over backward to show people she cared about them. She didn't treat us each exactly the same because, like a true parent, Coach knew that we are all unique individuals, and the same tactics won't work universally. What Pat mastered was the ability to treat us all with the same level of respect and pull time out of thin air to get to know us each intimately. If you were standing in front of her, you were the only person that mattered at that point. She listened to everything you said, and to what you didn't say. This was one of Pat's core Definite Dozen principles.

Communication eliminates mistakes.

Listening is crucial to good communication.

We communicate all the time, even when we don't realize it. Be aware of body language.

Make good eye contact.

Silence is a form of communication, too. Sometimes less is more.

Pat strongly believed that you have to teach people and teams how to communicate with one another. It takes work on both ends for a message to be conveyed and implemented. Receiving a message in a productive and open way is just as important as delivering the message in a way it can be understood. It all boils down to our intention. Coach communicated her intentions and her love for the game and striving toward greatness, but also winning. The way she loved the game showed itself in how she prepared and focused, as well as in her energy. Actions are a way of communicating even more so than words and every time Coach was on the court, she oozed with respect for the craft. That respect manifested as a willingness to give it everything she had, every time she entered the athletic center.

Communication is easy with people who are alike, but as we all know, not everyone comes from the same place or thinks the same. Learning to communicate through differences and with different-minded individuals is crucial in a team setting. As a result, Coach implemented ways to hold us accountable for the way in which we communicated with one another. In Pat's eyes, there were five areas of communication to be vigilant of: eye contact, body language, listening, "rebounding" or applying what you heard, and submitting to shared expectations.

Eye contact was a must and went hand-in-hand with body language because, as Pat reiterated, energy shows up long before someone opens their mouth. Anytime someone addressed us, the expectation was that we gave that person our attention and communicated our concentration with deliberate eye contact. This wasn't something you only saved for important people like coaches; our teammates, referees, fans, reporters, and anyone else who stepped foot in the gymnasium deserved our attention and care. Especially when representing the Lady Vols, Pat needed our body language to speak that the team was greater than our individual circumstances. Bad body language usually means you are feeding into yourself and not pouring into the team and what it needs.

Listening is a crucial element of communication and Pat listened a great deal. Whether we were in huddles, meetings, or watching film, Coach encouraged us to lean into not just hearing, but listening from a place of trying to understand. Everyone on the team came from different environments, cultures, and backgrounds, so the only way that we could truly get the best out of one another is if we each felt heard. If any of us had a problem or an issue, we were expected to communicate and talk about it openly, not to go tit-for-tat, but to better comprehend how to be better for one another. I had an issue with the twelve hour study hall rule for all freshmen. I hated going to Thornton Center where all the athletes went for tutoring and study hours. An environment that was designed for efficiency only left me feeling distracted. I felt I was responsible enough to get my work done on my own and I told Coach so. Pat listened intently before responding. She decided not to bend the rules for first semester, but if I received a 3.0 GPA or higher then she would allow me to forgo twelve hours and only do six. Her willingness to compromise with me made me feel seen, heard, and motivated to secure that 3.0 but also to understand what I could get out of the study hall hours while I was there.

An essential aspect of listening is ensuring you properly digest what has been said, *and* that you will implement the feedback in the future. Feedback, especially from a coach or teammate, is a major gift and allows us the chance to be better with and for one another. Shrugging off criticism not only keeps you stagnant individually but also keeps the team from reaching the next level. So, Pat developed a system of ensuring we always acknowledge and consider feedback in real time. Rebounding in basketball is a way to start a possession over or begin again. You have the opportunity after a missed shot to recover and improve. Anytime a correction was delivered, we were to respond with one word: "rebound." That signaled we'd acknowledged the miss and were committed to catching it and doing something about it.

"Candace, you need to get back on defense faster."

Rebound.

"You missed blocking out."

Rebound.

By keeping it short and sweet, Pat also wanted us to remember not to hang on to negativity. Next-play mentality demands we keep the game going without being burdened by the message. See the mistake. Acknowledge the room for growth. Apply it. Receiving a message and having the ability to move on is paramount in a fast-paced and high-stakes game. We used a similar strategy when complimenting one another. The point was to congratulate good behavior without becoming full of ourselves or distracted. Good behavior was met with a simple: "two-points." If your energy and effort were exceptional or if you drove the lane and found a teammate for a good assist and were complimented for such, your response would be: "two points." Consistent communication was Coach's preferred way of working with others. Rules were given at the start of each season that left no room for ambiguity: class and school were not optional but priorities. Missing class was met with a suspension of games and lots of running at 6 a.m. Pat cared enough about us to know that we couldn't be basketball players for life. We had to develop as people and excel in the classroom.

These five pieces would protect us against misalignment, confusion, or harmful assumptions. Emotion can exacerbate miscommunications, and Pat wasn't having that no matter how good you were on the court. Ego and wins didn't drive Coach, effort and intention did. Pat understood that you bring the best out of people by caring for and listening to them. Taking the time to figure out how we were each wired allowed her to then coach to those unique perspectives. Sure, she still yelled at and challenged us, but she invested just as much time in listening to and trusting us. I've borrowed that style of individualized leadership not only in the workplace, but also in how I parent.

Pat taught me that the people you love are always worth the extra effort. Coach often went out of her way to show us individually and collectively that we were seen, heard, and valued. If we expressed a desire or fear, she wanted us to know she was listening and finding ways to make our lives better. Whether that meant advocating for us behind the scenes with athletic departments or exposing us to beautiful experiences like Broadway plays and nice restaurants, Pat's actions always matched her words. She was impeccable with both, and that has since formed the foundation of how I communicate with and prioritize the people in my life.

Legends Never Die

Pat Summitt was the vanguard of women's basketball. She transformed the ferocity and athleticism that people associated with our game. Unfortunately being first often means being a martyr, and Pat frequently sacrificed herself and her personal life to be her best as a coach. And she was the best, every single day. But that wasn't without loss. I believe it's why Pat insisted on pouring into each of us players and ensuring we were supported holistically as students, community members, and women. She gave up so much to give us the world; she didn't want it to be so difficult for the next generation of women in sports to have more balance.

Coach invested everything she had into leading the Lady Vols. And when you thought she had nothing left, she reached down deeper and mustered up more time, more energy, more mentorship, more commitment. She never complained or vented. She simply did what needed to be done before someone had the chance to wonder who could do it. Pat would. Like a true pioneer, being so excellent often meant suffering in silence.

Decades later, Pat began to notice differences in how she communicated and reacted. Considering she'd always been incredibly deliberate, Coach sought help understanding what was changing and was ultimately diagnosed with early-onset Alzheimer's disease. I'll never forget her sharing the news and then checking in on *me*. "There's not going to be any pity party," she said to anyone and everyone. "If you try and throw me a pity party, you'll be the only one there." I remember thinking, *Pat, I'm supposed to be taking care of you now*, but she couldn't stop being that same coach, mentor, and friend she'd been since I'd first met her as a teenager. She couldn't turn off the fight, the positivity, the challenge. Through good and bad, ups and downs, Pat remained true to her values. She practiced what she preached, whether she was winning or battling a terrible disease. That was what I respected the most about her. She never changed due to circumstance or difficulties.

When she was first diagnosed she spoke of how this awful disease had never met an opponent quite like her. That she was going to fight as hard as she could, but also bring awareness to help find a cure. She constantly was thinking of others. Even when she was at her lowest, Pat spent her energy picking everyone else up off the floor. It was how she lived, and she wasn't about to stop. "How do you do it?" I asked her. "How will we beat this?"

"Left foot, right foot, breathe, repeat," she told me.

Pat never made herself the center of attention, but both her presence and absence are always felt. She shifted energy and grounded me in what mattered. Not being able to pick up the phone and call her for advice still makes me sad to this day. There are so many heartbreaks and disappointments I've endured and thought, *If Pat was here, she'd make it all better.* When I look out and see friends and colleagues still being mentored and coached long after leaving their universities, I see a dynamic that I'll never have again. But I often find myself feeling grateful for the lessons I didn't truly grasp in my younger years, but that I appreciate and understand now.

All the clichés about grief and loss are true. They say, in the end, you won't remember what someone did but how they made you feel. Stats and accolades faded to the back as I remembered Pat's jalapeño corn, the best hands down! Her homemade ice cream and the look on her face of pure joy as we often overindulged in all the deliciousness! Food and barbecues were her love language so attending them now, it's hard not to have her on my mind. I often imagine what it would have been like to have her over to my house and cook for her. I think my upbringing of family meals coupled with dinners at Tennessee primed me to view a night out surrounded by good people and fine cuisine as my idea of heaven. I wish we had many more years of grubbing, but I know she's guiding me even now.

I always speak Pat's name and honor her as my North Star. Pat has always guided me home to my best and most authentic self. I feel her presence and energy so heavily in those moments. When I've pushed myself, when I've put someone else in a position to succeed, or when I'm parenting my kids, I feel her. The words *for Pat* are stitched into the tongue of all my sneakers to ensure that her name and legacy are never too far away and can serve as a reminder of what I can do when I put one foot in front of the other and commit. "Left foot, right foot, breathe, repeat." Whenever I'm gearing up for a big business meeting, I wear her Angel perfume as a reminder to represent all she taught me.

I even find myself trying to emulate Pat's commitment as a working mom. I used to watch in awe as she would land from a speaking engagement in Washington, DC, and jump right back into coaching and taking us through our preseason workouts. Pat would be yelling at us as we worked our way through drills. But when the time came, her demeanor changed as she rushed out. Before we could finish catching our breath, Pat was headed out to catch Tyler's summer-league game. Wherever she was she gave her all, and I carry that with me in everything I do.

After I had graduated, I brought my daughter, Lailaa, as a toddler to a game to visit everyone. Watching Pat love her and prioritize my child, hugging her, talking to her, carrying her during practice is forever etched in my mind. My heart was so full because she loved Lailaa so much; watching her allow Lailaa to get away with things made me giggle. I have no doubt in my mind she would have done the same with my sons. I can't give them her physical presence, but I can carry on and pass on what she stood for, how she lived, and how she made people feel. I hope in due time, Hartt understands what his middle name symbolizes. He will never have to ask who Pat Summitt was because we plan to keep her name and legacy very much alive in our household. I realized long ago, as I was standing in Pat's hospital room holding her hand, you honor someone not in the words that you speak, but in the actions that you carry forward.

Lupita Nyong'o once wrote that grief is the price of love, and I feel that deep in my bones. I carry my love for Pat with me into every room I enter and ask myself, how would Pat have transformed this space? Who would she have brought along with her? In what ways can I do her legacy justice by implementing her teachings and principles here? I try to sprinkle a little Pat into everything I do. Our son, Hartt Summitt Petrakov Parker, was named after the woman who made me not only the player and leader I am today, but the *person*. When I called Pat's son Tyler up and asked for his blessing, he smiled and nodded immediately. "Mom would love that."

A summit is a peak; the highest point of a hill or mountain. The summit isn't manufactured by others but built over time through both pain and patience. The mountains we now stare up at were once flat pieces of Earth biding their time. When the tectonic plates beneath the dirt shifted and collided with one another, the earth buckled and rose with the movement. When the dust settled, a full mountain range was left in its place. And where the earth rose higher than any point, that's where we find the summit. This is who Pat Summitt has always been, and the legacy she leaves behind. No matter how difficult life was, she grounded herself and prepared for the elevation that could only come with consistency. Her commitment to the journey more than the achievement, and to lifting the people beside her up, is what took her to heights no one else has seen. Even as new peaks are formed, Pat Summitt stands alone as one of one. A generational talent and gift that I'll cherish for many lifetimes to come.

FOUR

Forks in the Road

Clear is kind. Unclear is unkind.

— BRENÉ BROWN

S helden and I were the definition of young love. Facebook messages exchanged when I was nineteen, dating by twenty, engaged by twenty-one, married at twenty-two, and a baby shortly after my twenty-third birthday. I always envisioned settling down early, so when our baby girl, Lailaa, arrived it felt cosmic. I wanted to be a wife and a mother so badly I used to play house growing up and write down potential names for the "four children" I was planning on having. My image of marriage fell between the representation of love I saw growing up in my parents' union and the movie *Love & Basketball*. To imagine falling in love with someone who not only loved basketball, but also infused that love into their career, was the cherry on top. In my mind, when you love someone you are on an island, separating yourself from the bullshit that has the potential to fester and destroy everything you have built.

Since Shelden and I started dating during his last semester at Duke, I watched the NBA draft from my couch as the commissioner took the stage and announced that "with the fifth pick of the 2006 NBA draft, the Atlanta Hawks select Shelden Williams from Duke University." At that point I was only a small part of his journey, but I was excited for him and his family. His work and dedication helped him achieve every hooper's childhood dream. Shel and I wouldn't be far apart, either, as Atlanta was only a three-hour drive south from Knoxville.

Throughout the summer and into the fall, I tagged along for some of his monumental life moments, buying a house, purchasing cars, and becoming an adult with bills and advisors, agents. Shel was so gracious and kind in wanting me to be a part of all of it. I saw from very early that he valued my opinion and was excited to have me as part of this exciting time in his life. He oftentimes would emphasize this being "our journey" and not just his. Just within the past year, my parents were going through a far from pretty divorce, I had limited my time going back home, partly because so much had changed and I didn't want to go back to a place that felt so different from what it was before I left for college. At a time in my life when I was very much searching for a "home" I was excited and needed to build one with him, together, the way we wanted to. Picking out couches, bedroom sets, guest rooms, washers and dryers seemed a bit like playing house. Quickly our relationship grew and expanded. That winter, just months after dating, we spent Christmas with each other and were able to shape and determine how we wanted to live and what our household would represent.

Shelden's rookie year was tough, the transition to the NBA on the court was far from perfect. We were up for the challenge. I was entering into my junior year and focused on winning the national championship our program and city so desired. I spent most of my time in the gym, in class, doing homework, or talking/being with Shel. Young love will do that to you. My off days were spent making the drive to Atlanta and as soon as either one of us got our schedules, we mapped out how we could see the other. Shel would fly in from time to time on off days and catch some of our games.

That first full year together set the stage for not only the joys and excitement of new love and learning about each other, but the realization that people had a lot to say about our relationship. How we would deal with our various careers and balance that with our relationship served as a challenge. Regardless of how much I acted like I didn't care or didn't read what people said, I heard the whispers, the opinions, the "hate," and it stung. I struggled in a world that expected women to never shine brighter than their husbands or where husbands were demoralized for supporting their wives. Public opinion was like the high school groupthink as to who should, and shouldn't, be together. Some days it seemed like no one wanted or expected me to be with Shelden. The echoes were loud and came as insults, jokes, comments, and questions. We struggled with communicating throughout that first year. I don't think we named our frustrations about our public relationship. We brushed off most things as unimportant and moved on, but lingering thoughts seeped into who we were to each other. When there are too many people who have a say, everything can sway. Especially when we didn't really talk about what was going on. In a public relationship, it was even harder to keep things between just him and me. I didn't know if he read or saw something, or was he just mad over his game? It was a challenge at times to support someone who was adjusting and adapting while also balancing my own career.

We made it work because we wanted to. Even after I was drafted into the WNBA and we knew we'd be living and working in different cities, we found a way. Shelden sat courtside at my games holding Lailaa like the movie relationship I idolized between Monica and Quincy in *Love & Basketball*. He was indeed a dedicated father who loved Lailaa and wasn't a knucklehead. Shelden was extremely dependable and trustworthy and early on, I loved how he would always talk to his mom every day on the phone. His focus inspired me and his diligence in getting tasks done served as the example I needed.

I felt safe with Shelden. His goals and dreams of family at the foundation were the same as mine. We had all the things I thought I desired. Marriage, kids, house. But somewhere in all of that, I got lost in what I imagined versus the reality. I like watching *Love & Basketball* and forgetting it's just a movie. The life stuff that happens and the perfect ending is all of an hour and a half. This was work. When Shelden and I said "I do" in a little chapel in Lake Tahoe on November 13, 2008, with just the two of us, a baby girl in my belly who was due in just a few months, we were in love and looking toward the future. None of the other "stuff" mattered. We both were in the early stages of our careers and basketball dictated our lives. Wherever the ball bounced that's where we went and in between those bounces we did the best we could to spend as much time as we possibly could together. We established our goals, the way we would go about accomplishing them we could work out later. But as time went on, I understood the wisdom and patience others tried to bestow on our young love. Before you can grow in a relationship you have to be able to evolve and grow *you*.

IN 2005, at the SEC tournament during my freshman year of college, both my parents traveled down to South Carolina to support the Lady Vols. Even though my injuries kept me from playing, they'd made the long trek and I needed it more than they knew. It had been a long and arduous few months and I really missed them both. In the weeks leading up to the South Carolina trip, they both were hard to reach and I could only ever seem to contact one of them at a time even though they lived together.

"Can you hand Dad the phone?" I'd ask my mom after we'd spent some time catching up. "Call his cell phone," she'd reply, which seemed like a lot more work for someone in the same house. Seeing them in person confirmed what their weird phone calls hinted: my parents were hiding something from me. Their dynamic was off, they barely looked me in the eye, and they behaved awkwardly as if they hardly knew each other despite being married for nearly 30 years. I got approval from the team to eat with my parents that evening. We went to dinner and their interactions and energy only reconfirmed my suspicions. Something was off.

The next day my brother and sister-in law appeared, which would have been normal in any other season except this one. I was injured and unable to play. Why had they bothered to come all this way if I couldn't suit up? I had questions but my love and genuine excitement to see them outweighed any need for answers. Later that same day, my sister-in-law and I went for a walk and I asked her outright, "Are Mom and Dad okay?" She looked at me and told me to ask them, in a voice that said it wasn't her story to tell. The next few hours were incredibly uneasy as our family hung out with a tense and weird energy hanging between us. As everyone tried to pretend everything was fine, I looked around at the family that I grew up wanting to emulate. This was the family I sat at thousands of meals with talking, laughing, dreaming and we couldn't even put our words together to share our feelings. My parents talked me through my greatest heartbreaks and helped me achieve my greatest feats, but where were my role models and their lessons on leaning into vulnerability now?

As the evening went on, I grew angrier and angrier. In the moment I felt as though my parents weren't doing and being who they'd taught us to be. At one point, I couldn't hold back my feelings and confusion. I abruptly asked what was going on and the silence that followed was thick. After what felt like an eternity, they answered. Divorce. As they began to talk about how they didn't make the decision lightly, my mind went blank and I began to daze out. It was like swimming underwater and watching a conversation play out before you. I only heard general sounds as my father spoke. Eventually my mom stood up and walked out of the room mid-conversation.

My subconscious was piecing everything together, connecting the dots, and making assumptions. After a bit, I looked around the room and realized I was the only one overwhelmed and taken by surprise by everything happening. Everybody else knew. Initially, that only made me angrier and less receptive to what was happening. I was the baby of the family but that didn't make me an actual child. Or so I thought. I was eighteen years old, and yet my family was giving me the white-glove treatment. I was the last to know and, seemingly, the only thing standing in the way. Almost no time passed between me being out of the house and them separating. Were our family days a way to placate Lil' Can? My world felt flipped upside down and in so many ways I felt betrayed. I was alone with my thoughts, fears, regrets, and hopes. I continued the pattern I always had growing up when things got tough—I shut down and stopped communicating. A blank stare took over my face and as someone whose face has always had subtitles, it was hard to hide my true feelings.

Toward the end of the conversation, I became self-conscious about the fact that everyone was watching for my response. How long had this part of my family been kept from me? How long had my brothers known and just allowed me to live in the Neverland illusion that I envisioned? Everyone else around the room had gotten the courtesy of a private reaction. My personal life felt completely out of my control as though I were too fragile to handle more notice or involvement. What about me in particular signaled, "we should hold off on telling her"? I was the youngest by eight years, but it stung to realize the distance between myself and my family was greater than I realized. I was eighteen and angry that everyone knew and they sat me down to tell me as a group. I cried for the separation and how it would impact me, but I also cried because I felt distant from my family. How could they keep this from me? Hadn't I always been forthcoming and vulnerable with them? But then I started thinking about the intimate details about my life and whether I was really sharing with them. Did I tell them about my mistakes, or about the dumb decisions I had made thus far in college? No. This moment was a revelatory fork in the road showing where what I thought was true diverged from what actually was. That was scarier than anything. Real power and intimacy and love is leaning into your vulnerability (shout out to Brené Brown).

Only a few months into being away from home, "home" as I knew it changed forever. A lot of my emotion stemmed from the fact that

I was still hanging on to the Parkers I'd grown up as. The Parkers had always been a close-knit clan. We cheered on our favorite teams together, ran up and down the court together, laughed, cried, and fought together. It's all I'd known. My two-parent household was the only normal I'd seen up close so I believed my parents would be together forever. We spent my entire childhood around the table, every single one of us. The Parkers always ate dinner together so we didn't just look like a model family, we felt like one. We were big on showing up for one another when and where it mattered so I always envisioned having that forever and being that family even after us kids grew up. Suddenly, though, I had to face the idea of fragmented holidays and going home for Christmas or Thanksgiving to what exactly? Would we decorate the tree together like we always did and bake cookies while opening presents? Would we even be in the same room?

Even the word *divorce* felt taboo to me as a child; it was never something I imagined being a product of—or participant in. Whenever they would fight or have periods of the silent treatment that was deafening within our household, I would break down in tears thinking the worst. They would assure me that everything would be fine. But here I was, sitting in the reality. I couldn't help but envision my world grinding to a halt and crumbling right at my feet. I became very guarded and grew less trusting of people. It didn't help that I was also battling a nasty knee injury and didn't have my love and favorite outlet to turn to. As I continued to turn inward and close myself off from others, the isolation both comforted and scared me. I'd never felt so alone and I hated that there was seemingly no warning for it all.

I became self-centered, as most of us do when we are trying to navigate tough times, especially as children. We are conditioned to look at each situation from our own vantage point. How does this impact *me*, why didn't they tell *me*, what does this mean for *me*? Ignoring how huge of a change this has to be for *them*! My parents had been married for thirty years. They'd shared three decades worth of laughter, loss, new beginnings, ambition, monotony, and evolution. For the first time in a long time, they weren't putting the needs of their children first and, in hindsight, they deserved the space to figure that out. Oftentimes, we as children forget how hard it is on our parents to navigate divorce themselves. How it likely took them a long time to dig through the mud and be okay with their decisions. How many nights they probably lay awake worrying about the impact it would have on us. How this isn't easy on anyone and there is no playbook or blueprint in working through life's tough decisions. With hindsight I understand that I was incredibly young despite the places college and basketball had taken me. My parents' relationship existed first and beyond their children, but they were also walking a thin tightrope in shielding and protecting me as the youngest and most immediately affected.

As kids, we always think that our parents have everything figured out. When I truly internalized that my parents weren't doing this to me, but that they were in the midst of an emotional separation and life shift, I had so much more grace for how long it took them to open up to me. They were in pain, and hurt people hurt people because they can't hold their own feelings and cushion everyone else's as well. If you're not whole and on your own two feet squarely, you won't be good for anyone.

My parents' story is theirs to tell or reckon with, and it certainly shaped me as a child who grew up thinking of her mother and father as invincible, emotionless beings who orbit around their children. Divorce forced me to see them as human beings with their own desires, dreams, fears, triggers, expectations, insecurities, habits, pet peeves, and hopes. Time helped me understand that they both were dealing with the separation in their own way. But from the outside looking in, I was looking to my parents to lead with a bit more truth and honesty in the problems they were going through. I wouldn't have been able to change the experience or outcome necessarily, but it would have put less of the burden on the people receiving the news. Closeness with someone doesn't mean that everything they experience is instantly your business and, at the same time, you should feel comfortable communicating with people close to you. Honesty in close relationships is saying "here's what's on my heart, and I'm not comfortable sharing the other piece right now" while having that being respected. You can still let someone know the how without the what.

Even when my knee healed up, the void of the nuclear family I'd known all my life remained. The holidays had always been my favorite time of the year, enjoying delicious food with my favorite people. Suddenly, I had more angst than excitement trying to figure out which parent was hosting what and where I wanted to be. As time went on, their strained relationship bubbled over and touched each of us in different ways. Big and small inconveniences became the norm. Throughout my collegiate basketball career, tickets became a hassle. My parents couldn't sit next to each other and I would have to double- and sometimes triple-check to make sure they were nowhere near each other, but their tickets were similar because I didn't value one over the other. It became exhausting trying to see them both without letting them see each other. It especially became difficult when they would bring significant others to my games. Postgame became something I dreaded, who do I hug first, at times I just wanted to go to dinner. I didn't want to make decisions about who I went with. I hated the way it made me feel. Every moment I was asked what I wanted to do, I felt like I was picking my favorite parent. Dividing time and energy between the two left me with the feeling that no matter where I was, someone was missing. As young kids, you do as you are told while your parents work out the specifics. As an adult, you have agency.

Divorce got ugly, and as a result, I chose to run from it. I stayed at school the entire summer and took classes as opposed to going home. I visited Shelden during short breaks, instead of taking trips back to Naperville to bounce back and forth between my mom and dad. He became my "home." I was angry, confused, and began to deconstruct and analyze my whole childhood. Was everything a lie? During this time, I wanted more than ever to create my own community and home. One that could have the hard conversations, that leaned into constant improvement and evolution and somewhere that was at its core the way things appeared on the surface. Their divorce didn't cause me to give up on love. It actually did the opposite. I became more intentional, almost obsessed with wanting to build the type of love I envisioned and desired, right then!

The first Christmas Shelden and I spent together was in 2006 in the home I'd helped him pick out. Shelden and I decorated together, ordered the tree we wanted, designed the menu, and for the first time did the holidays our way. There was a sense of excitement in transforming this house into "our" home as we made these festive decisions and choices together. We were intentional in laying the foundation of what we hoped would be many more holidays together. It was both of our first times creating what we wanted for the holidays. Just a year before, I was experiencing my first Christmas with my parents being separated. I spent the morning with my mom in the house I grew up in and the evening I went to visit my dad in his apartment. It was surreal and difficult. Christmas was always our favorite holiday as a family and we were rooted in traditions. From decorating the tree as a family to the way in which we opened presents on Christmas morning. On Christmas Eve, we always watched *National Lampoon's Christmas Vacation*, all piled together on the couch. Now, all of us were attempting to reestablish what our future traditions would look like. With Shelden by my side I was excited for the first time in a long time to go into the future with someone. To have a say in our traditions, the home we would build, and the future that was possible to create.

"ARE YOU HAPPY?" Lailaa asked me one day.

Lailaa had just turned five and we were cuddling on the couch. Around us was an Encino mansion overlooking mountains. Our dream house. It was a slow morning with just the two of us in the home. Shelden was gone for his first stint in China. We had all the things we had dreamed of: house, cars, a beautiful daughter, even two amazing dogs. And yet, I couldn't shake this emptiness. I tried my best to shield my emotions from my daughter, but my feelings over the last couple days and weeks engulfed my mood and sucked my energy. One moment, her eyes glued to the TV and the next, she turned to me and asked, "are you happy?" Lailaa has always had a high emotional IQ; she feels emotions and at times almost too much, even from a very young age. I was stunned, her brown eyes that still contained that twinkle of child innocence stared at me, waiting for an answer.

"Yes," was on the tip of my tongue but I stopped myself. I couldn't lie to my daughter. I shook my head, looked her in the eyes, and said, "I am working to be." She gave me a hug and a hilarious scene in her cartoon interrupted the moment. She chuckled and her attention went back to watching the screen. I was left to my own thoughts. What would bring me back to happiness? When exactly did I become unhappy?

Everyone has a plan and then life happens. Looking back on my journey, Shelden's and my relationship always felt rushed. Basketball dictated our schedule and life moved from game to game, season to season, and team to team at a breakneck pace. Initially, he was playing for the Atlanta Hawks while I finished out college at Knoxville. Then, during my rookie year in the WNBA, Shelden traveled with me as much as he could. From domestic games all the way to Beijing for the 2008 Olympics, we finally had some quality time. But things were different. It became really hard to support Shel through the lows in his career because everything was going right for me professionally. It was hard to really understand what he was going through. The moment I knew I was pregnant, life changed. Shelden and I were not just looking at the schedule to plan when we could see each other, but instead to coordinate childcare. I was a young mom and adapting, adjusting, and learning on the go. Early on Lailaa had to be with me—as I breastfed her for fifteen months. I was set to take just a few weeks off, before heading overseas to play for Yekaterinburg, Russia. One day, I was sitting with Shelden venting about everything on my plate and decided to go against my norm. Playing abroad brought significantly more income into our household and had the potential to change our lifestyle. But Lailaa was only a couple of months old and I still needed shoulder surgery. "I don't know," I began hesitantly. "Maybe I shouldn't play abroad this year and instead I should recover at home." I didn't know it then but I was asking for permission in a way. I've been an overachiever and people pleaser my whole life but, just this once, I didn't want to have it all together. I wanted my husband and friend to lift some weight off my shoulders and validate my feelings. But I didn't say that. I posed the hypothetical and prayed for an out. Shelden replied quickly saying I shouldn't turn down such a lucrative opportunity. "You can do it," he told me. I knew he was right but it wasn't the response I was looking for.

Since Shelden's schedule and my own didn't line up, my mom stepped into a caregiver role as I traveled abroad to play—and from time to time during my WNBA season when Shel also had to play. My mom traveled with us and put me at ease knowing Lailaa would be taken care of while I was at practice or during games. "Honey" as Lailaa would call my mom, loved her granddaughter and seeing their relationship blossom was special. I'm grateful that my mom dedicated the time and energy that she did; I can't imagine what we would have done without her.

Most of the year, Lailaa, my mom, and I were a trio who scrounged time with Shelden as much as our schedules would allow. Even when I was no longer breastfeeding, I became used to having Lailaa everywhere with me. It became comfortable and normal for Sheldon and I to be apart. We had thrust ourselves into our professional basketball careers, playing in different cities from the beginning. Our arrangement worked well for parenting Lailaa but it weighed on our marriage. I didn't realize how distant our marriage was nearly from the onset; half the year at the least we spent months and months apart. I also didn't realize how much I grew silent in my struggle and how distance was driving more than just physical separation, but emotional as well. At times, I was going through life, ignoring and silencing the voice in my head, asking myself, "Is this what you really want?"

Then my fourth year overseas came and life began to spiral. My grandmother suffered a stroke and my mom was needed to help care for her. The stroke was obviously unexpected and with mom unavailable to join us, we had too little notice to arrange visas and travel for someone else to take her place. For the first time, Lailaa and I traveled overseas with just the two of us. No Honey. Lailaa was three years old and at an age where I could bring her to practice, games, and road trips. When I was on the court, Lailaa sat close by with someone from the club—mainly my translator—watching her. It wasn't ideal and no one would look after Lailaa like my mother, her father, or I. But we had to make do. That year, I also found a school across the street from the gym where we practiced so that I could drop her off right before practice and pick her up immediately after.

Suddenly, I was a de facto single mother. Every minute of my day was spent working out, practicing, playing, or parenting. As soon as I was off the clock and court, I was racing to my baby. There were no days off for me. No matter how much you love your child, everyone needs a break. At times part of my immaturity was staying silent in my pain and discomfort and unhappiness. No one can understand your feelings if you don't express them let alone if you are thousands of miles away. I was strained and in desperate need of support, which seeded resentment. That resentment swelled and ballooned with the realization that as I struggled to keep Lailaa and me together, Shelden had the freedom to design his parenting schedule around his work and not the other way around like I had to. I couldn't go anywhere without my daughter. I wanted her there—and that was indeed my plan—but I also needed the support of her other half. The flexibility he had was such a stark contrast to my limited capacity, and it exasperated me.

Everything about balancing my career with motherhood felt like a fight; fighting with my body to do what I knew it could, fighting with my schedule to create time I knew I didn't have, and fighting with the expectations placed on mothers by society to do it all. Shelden always supported me before, but at this stage of our lives, our careers were going in opposite directions. Shelden was struggling to find a home in the NBA and bounced around between seven teams in six NBA seasons. Then, he'd signed his first stint overseas to play in Chalon, France. It was far from easy for him, I'm sure. But then again, we didn't talk much about it. The adjustment from playing domestically to overseas is something I knew all too well how hard it could be. I should have been there for him more but at the time my tank was empty. I struggled and felt alone and a lot of my feelings, insecurities, and fears were not met with a sounding board on his end either. So I did what I had always done, put my head down, gritted my teeth, worked myself through it, and shut down. I purposely ignored his needs in subconscious retaliation for all the problems we had just ignored in the past.

Meanwhile, I was finally healthy. I had worked my ass off post-pregnancy and to recover from a string of unfortunate injuries. All the work I had put in was on full display. I was back to being one of the top players in the WNBA. The cracks in our relationship were coming to light. People's opinions and snide comments about us were taking up real estate in our ability to grow. Shelden, rightfully so, struggled with jokes and comments comparing the two of us. There were the random interactions in the airport of fans coming up to the two of us and asking, "Shel, can you beat your wife one-on-one?" This happened numerous times, even to my brothers. Anthony would laugh it off and make some type of joke back, but

Shel didn't take it so lightly. But what wasn't fair is how I found myself dimming my light to make room for his. I didn't know how to be proud of myself without taking away from him. Basketball, which steered our relationship at its inception and was the foundation of its existence, turned out to be our demise.

Shel and I had become misaligned. I'd been used to pushing myself mentally and physically so I approached this time in my life the same way. I had always been all gas and no brakes, being optimistic I could fit everything into one day. Asking for help, in my eyes, was seen as weakness and I struggled trying to shoulder everything. I was hanging on by a hair in terms of balancing motherhood, basketball, and self-care. But, I was also pushing people away who wanted to help, acting like everything was fine, and drowning in my loneliness.

You can't grow from what you don't talk about and there I was becoming what I despised. A person one foot in her marriage and one foot out. Not open or vulnerable; not candid or honest. Merely going through the motions and avoiding the communication and work needed to keep a family together. Marriage is about the union being at the forefront. Children are beautiful and integral parts of a family, but to have a great home the two adults at the center have to want to be there and put in the consistent effort to maintain it. Or have the courage to speak the hard part aloud and give people the honesty I've always asked for. Being dishonest with others is a form of cowardice and I didn't want to be a liar anymore. The root of the problem is that I was dishonest with myself. If you can lie to yourself and pretend to be living in your morals and values and explain yourself away from the truth, you have no problem doing the same to others. Because regardless of what made me feel good in the moment, I had to admit to myself that I was a shitty wife to Shelden. I hurt a lot of people and became someone who was defensive, hotheaded, unhappy, dishonest, and resentful. That behavior had nothing to do with anyone but me. I am not proud of the lies, the cheating, the immaturity, and most of all the avoidance. When you deliver truth in a deliberate, honest way, you actually are respecting the person enough to be open, which is a lot harder than lying.

This season of my life taught me even more grace for my parents and also forced me to look at myself in the mirror and demand accountability. I rewound back to the pain and anger I had as a child watching my parents' divorce. Yes, I was sad about them separating, but I was most upset that I lost trust in them because they hid the truth from me for so long. As an adult, I realized the fear my parents had. It turns your stomach, keeps you up at night, and wedges doubt into your decision-making. For the first time, I realized that you can paint the picture of the journey, prepare, say what steps you would have taken, but until you experience the tests and the obstacles, you never know how you will react. I had an opportunity going forward to choose to do what's right. Normally, we know deep down inside what is right and what is wrong. Right is usually hard. Choose hard. I have vowed to try and steer clear of sharing other peoples' stories in this book. I want to respect my family and friends and their journeys. So I will leave out the details of how we told Lailaa about our divorce, but I will say that I vowed during that time to be honest. I made a number of mistakes, I don't know if they would have changed the result or not, but what I do know is I'm not running from them.

There is no perfect time or place to share with your children about your marriage. Everyone dreads the conversation. So have conversations, plural. I vowed that my life would not be one-off tough talks. Instead, I decided to learn from my experience. Lailaa deserved it. Sometimes my heart beats fast, fear takes over, and all of that is normal. Do it afraid. Talking through the difficult, uncomfortable, and messy moments is essential to any strong relationship whether familial, romantic, or professional. There will be pain no matter what, but how you handle it—with grace, love, and intention—can make all the difference. Everyone needs to be seen and heard to show up as their best selves and shutting down instead of communicating keeps that from happening. I had to learn to be transparent about my feelings and not to be vindictive when I'm unfulfilled.

Oftentimes I think about the "what ifs." Not in the sense of if I hadn't gone overseas, but what if I began to actively work on myself then? Communicate my needs clearly and upfront? Not shy away from conflict? Stuck to the promises I made even when the circumstances that I made them in changed? What if I had stopped using unhappiness as a crutch to justify straying in a marriage that I entered into willingly? What could have been unlocked earlier if I was upfront about the way I felt so as to not drag a relationship out and string along hope?

In order for me to be the type of mother, wife, daughter, sister, and friend I aspire to be, I needed to embrace radical vulnerability, especially when I wanted to hide my flaws or uncertainty. Growing *you* and evolving you is key to being unshakeable so that when life gets tough, you can still lean on the morals and values that you have cemented. The end of Shel's and my marriage was tough. I did not walk that journey perfectly. I made many missteps and had my faults. But walking that journey taught me a lot about myself and who I was in the process. Most importantly, I learned who I wanted to work to be. I have my daughter's name tattooed on my wrist and, underneath it, "my reason." I realized all these years later that personal growth and self-discovery precedes a successful relationship and/or marriage. I wanted to be great for her! I wanted to demonstrate, and be a positive representation of, love and all that comes with it. So, I went to work on me!

FIVE

Something New

One is loved because one is loved.
No reason is needed for loving.
—*THE ALCHEMIST*, PAULO COELHO

Growing up, I always was a sucker for those trashy teen girl magazines with the quizzes on what type of lover you needed. I took every single one and giggled at the series of surface-level questions like "What's your favorite genre of movie" or "What subject in school do you enjoy?" Love seemed so simple and easy. I imagined the partner I desired appearing, wrapped in the package I expected them to be: Prince Charming.

As a young adult, I read *The Alchemist* for the first time and realized that our paths and destinies are frequently not what we think we want, though always, in the end, what we truly need. The novel follows a young man named Santiago as he pursues a treasure he dreamt about. En route to that hidden treasure, Santiago meets a girl named Fatima and falls in love with her. After professing his love and asking for her hand in marriage, Santiago is dismayed when Fatima tells him she will only marry him after he completes his journey. True love comes exactly when you need it and are ready for it. Not a second sooner.

Anya and I officially met for the first time at the London Olympics in 2012. I was representing Team USA and she Russia. It was a quick encounter in the athlete village one afternoon with a fellow hooper, and before we parted ways, Anya told me that she'd signed to play for the same Russian women's basketball club, UMMC Ekaterinburg for the following season. When I arrived in Russia that fall to begin the season, I remember I told a joke at practice, and she was the only foreign player who laughed. Having attended college in the states at the University of Louisiana Lafayette, Anya's English was nearly perfect, and as a result, I learned, so was her sense of humor. From her banter, you could tell An, as I call her, had spent a lot of time in the South and around Black people, which always surprised people who expected something very different from her. An was always full of surprises! She had an affinity for hip-hop and R&B, loved Ginuwine, and could recite every word to any Craig David song. Pretty quickly we spent more and more time together. Her eyes and smile were electrifying, but her brain is what stopped me in my tracks. Her energy jumped out to me immediately. Calm and patient, but deliberate and intentional. There was never any small talk; we immediately jumped into deep and meaningful conversations. When flying to and from games, the two of us would sit huddled on the team plane whispering, laughing, and talking about everything under the sun. Though the plane was loud and full of people, even then, I couldn't help but hang on to every word she said. *Who is this beautiful, smart, and direct woman?* I thought.

As a newbie to all things Russia, I was pretty overwhelmed by the amount of cultural differences to learn and history to better understand. Anya was both a friend and tour guide as she gave me a crash course in traditional Russian dishes and culture. I followed her around like a puppy, hanging on every word. We were in her home city of Moscow for a game, and she was proud to show me around. We walked through the Red Square (Moscow's de facto city center near the Kremlin, where many historical events took place, from military parades to czar speeches). We drank coffee overlooking the Kremlin and I tried *borscht* for the first time at a restaurant next to the gigantic statue of Peter the Great. I followed her lead and completely let my guard down, immersing myself in the culture. I would even break out the Russian I learned in tutoring, though I was always too shy to speak. An was always so proud hearing me order food or talk with someone in her native tongue because I was earnestly trying to adapt and adjust. Anya told me about her family members who'd served in various wars and pointed out memorials honoring their service. We'd wander around museums for hours looking at Russian literature and poetry, as well as their natural history museum, which stretched back in time. We bonded over Pushkin, the Russian poet, and his gorgeous way with words. When historians discovered and unveiled Pushkin's African American ancestry, we laughed at the irony, adding it to our growing list of inside jokes.

I soon realized Anya had experienced many of the events I had read about in history class. The day the Soviet Union collapsed, she casually described school letting out early and seeing tanks on the streets of Moscow. Only to get home and turn on the TV and see Boris Yeltsin riding through the same streets of Moscow on a tank, signaling the collapse of the Soviet Union and the rise of Russia once more. We visited the Great Patriotic War museum, which Americans know as World War II. (Even that distinction signaled a lot.) The museum's lack of English subtitles and translation thwarted my need for deeper learning. I asked Anya to translate every single word in the museum, and she happily obliged, understanding how interested and curious I was about the topic. Hours later, I felt like I had a different perspective on Russia and WWII, but this experience had deepened my understanding of Anya as well. Plaques, memorials, and the museum as a whole brought out conversations we probably wouldn't ordinarily have had. I was grateful to better understand where she came from and her feelings and thoughts. We realized pretty quickly—despite growing up in countries that couldn't be more opposite in their wildly different ideologies—that Anya and I brought out the best qualities in each other: listening to understand (not to agree, oppose, or be right) and finding joy in the other's excitement. We could have days full of serious, intellectual curiosity followed by days of silliness and pure fun.

I'll never forget the time we went dog sledding. The morning air was freezing cold, so we both bundled up in as many layers as possible with Anya leading the way, as usual. I loved seeing Russia through her eyes. When we arrived, I quickly realized our activity wasn't nearly as regulated as it would be in the States. I'd expected a trained guide would direct the sled with us as nothing more than passengers. Instead, Anya and I were shown the functions of the sled and handed the figurative keys. The rest was up to us and those huskies. I was terrified and unprepared, but Anya's confidence convinced me to see it through. Dressed in all black with gray UGGs, I felt like the shadow of the Pillsbury Doughboy as I climbed aboard the sled and took my seat behind the harnessed dogs. Anya perched herself behind me on the part of the sled designed for steering. My only job was to keep an eye on the dogs and help to avoid trees. Otherwise, Anya was our captain and, as someone who was comfortable with and used to leading, I surprisingly didn't mind relinquishing control and following for the first time in my life. As the large dogs glided through the snow, dragging us with them and only pausing to poop, I couldn't stop laughing in glee. *This is so cool*, I kept thinking.

At one point, Anya and I switched places. Wrong move number one. I was now in the standing position guiding the dogs as we sledded down the snowy pathways. We hit an area that hadn't been ridden over before, so the snow was piled up in mounds. As we raced through, the dogs moved with ease, but our sled rocked side to side struggling to find a flat snowy path to settle onto. I was flung from the sled after an intense bit of turbulence while Anya never lost her place in the front. "Push the brakes," Anya yelled as the dogs continued to carry her and the sled down the path. *How?* I wondered incredulously as I laughed and ran behind her on foot. I tried to catch up as Anya gracefully remained on the sled. After chasing the sled for a good few minutes, Anya managed to slow the dogs down enough for me to climb back on. I sported a gnarly bruise down my right side from the fall and we belly laughed for hours about our adventure. When we made it back to the welcome center, I didn't want "this" to end.

For a long time I never stopped to ask myself, *What was this?* I had never felt like this before, both about someone else, but also about myself. I liked who I allowed myself to be in her presence. Slowly but surely, I realized that person I allowed myself to be was actually *me*. Yet still I fought my feelings and tried to play like they didn't exist. I pretended that it was normal for your heart to beat fast and your stomach to turn into butterflies when your platonic friend walked into the room.

I never envisioned being attracted to a woman. My attraction to men is what prevented me from realizing that this was also possible. That one didn't negate the other. Being romantically interested in a woman went completely against the play I had drawn up for myself. I supported others loving who they desired. Why couldn't I be okay with my feelings? I fought the internal battle in my head, my mind competing with my heart. I felt the attraction, but unpacking the emotions and admitting how I felt went against everything I thought I was and always wanted. The internal struggle was exhausting: No matter how hard you try, you lie to yourself. Ultimately, I'm grateful for that confusing time because our connection grew even deeper since the foundation of our relationship was friendship.

We pretended for quite some time that our deep connection was instead surface-level flirting. The depth of our relationship was really established in the time we spent apart. I longed for our FaceTimes and texts. I remember vividly when my dog Fendi passed away, Anya lay awake on the phone with me for hours. I openly sobbed and was unafraid to show her my emotions. She too leaned on me, opened up, and allowed me to be there for her in difficult times. Her strong, upfront, and tough exterior would turn to mush! I finally built up enough courage to tell her that I loved her. She took her time to respond, as she always does, but I knew that when she said it back, she meant it.

By this point, I was obsessed with Anya, her mind, and how much fun we had when it was just the two of us. She opened my eyes to realizing I had so much to learn and life could still surprise me. Since I was a teenager, I've had millions of eyes on me, and it forced me to grow up fast. The amount of expectations I carried on my shoulders forced me to become guarded in so many ways. With Anya, I could shed the need to prove anything. I could just be, well, *me*. By her side, I could be imperfect and, something I resisted for so long, vulnerable. Nothing was off-limits with her, and it was refreshing in ways I didn't expect. Anya and I talked about our deepest fears, weird desires, icks and pet peeves, childhood memories, and everything in between. We often uttered these words to each other—and we still do: "If I say it to you, it doesn't exist, right?" We became each other's homes and vaults. When we were apart, I missed the way I felt when I was with her. She made the most mundane tasks thrilling, and she made me feel unashamed, cherished, and, for the first time, understood. Not just in the good, but in the uncomfortable, the unfamiliar, the difficult.

Love Hard and Communicate Harder

I love love and always have. I don't do anything lukewarm. Deep passion is what wakes me up in the morning and what I go to sleep burning with. I wanted a love that matched the level of fire I pursue professionally and in every other area of life. A best friend who is a partner, lover, adrenaline rush, but also one who calms my soul, all wrapped in one. The representations of love that I witnessed growing up were a lot more grounded and full of a quiet, sturdy love.

I admire my maternal grandparents so much, especially for their longevity. Having been married for fifty years, you could feel the love they had for each other in the way they communicated with more than just words. Little nicknames, winks, a quick connection in the kitchen while cooking. The way they would fuss over little stuff until B-paw diffused the situation by laughing and embracing Mimi until she giggled. In everything they did, they took the time to show love, even all those years later, in good times and in hard times. I never saw extreme displays of affection or loud, bold declarations, but their love was enduring. My grandmother took care of my grandfather for years after he got sick. Mimi would sit for hours in the hospital next to him, holding his hand and supporting him in any way she could. Her days revolved around caring for him and cooking, driving, giving him his medicine. Even after all that time, there was beauty in their actions, which still spoke louder than words. No matter the type of love you have—exciting, daring, loud, patient—how you show up for the other person is what matters most. In good times and in tough ones; convenient and otherwise. Saying "I love you" is different than *living* it.

Living love became my mission. My love for Anya was hard to contain, deny, and disclose. How could Anya and I live love when we were fearful of anyone finding out about us? Now what? Anya and I were in love, but that was the least of the hurdles we had to clear. Everything felt so natural and yet I was constantly overthinking. It was as though my mind and body were at war with each other. One day, I'd tell myself the anxiety was all in my head. "Just do it, Can," I'd coach myself. "If she makes you happy, that's all that matters!" Then the next day I'd be immobilized by negative scenarios, unable to be honest even with myself. I was battling with more than whether she was "the one." I was at war with myself over my self-identity.

There was a deep loneliness to my initial phase of self-acceptance. Why did this have to be so confusing? In my past relationships, I responded to conflict by retreating into myself. It's always how I've

dealt with anxiety and loneliness, but it often exacerbates the problem. Anya didn't let me retreat, and I in turn did the same for her.
We talked about feelings we were afraid to give a name to and we
sifted through the jumbled up emotions to find out what truly made
us happy and how to protect that.

There weren't many grandstand events to mark my evolving relationship with Anya, but there were subtle signs, like the way my
heartbeat quickened when she walked into a room and how much
I anticipated more time with her. How afternoon coffee breaks
after practice would last for hours and they still felt too short. How
quickly we developed inside jokes and an intimacy that felt years in
the making. How closely An pays attention to the little things that
make me smile. How she intently listens to what wakes me up in the
morning and keeps me up at night. How she holds me accountable
to my words and my actions and forgives my missteps. She taught
me how to listen when we disagreed. How she understood being a
mother came first for me and that she not only respected that but
cared to develop her own relationship with Lailaa, not only as an
extension of me but as a little human with her own passions, desires,
and tics. How soft we could be with each other while sharing the
weight that makes life challenging to begin with. Anya's "selfishness"
for her desires, wants, needs, dislikes, and dreams helped me realize
it wasn't selfish at all. Prioritizing yourself is power and necessary. We
seemed "right." But we both deserved more. I didn't always know that
until An showed me.

Together, we chose to stand in and on what we meant to each other.

Settling into Love

Some people mark the beginning of their relationship with first dates
and first kisses, but I'll never forget the first time I built up enough
courage to grab Anya's hand in public. The day itself wasn't very

special but I was more nervous than I'd ever been. We were walking through the mall and my mind was racing as I reached out my hand to grab hers. My palms were sweating profusely, not because of her, but because of what others would think. When we went on dinner dates, we always showed quick displays of affection so as not to get the glares and stares that accompanied two women. When we had to leave each other for long stretches, An would pout and we'd steal a quick kiss so as not to attract attention. At first, we cared deeply about what others thought, but soon I realized that we couldn't ignore our feelings. An was becoming a huge part of my life and we deserved to honor that unabashedly.

A big part of my love for Anya was how much I admired and was impressed with her. It wasn't lust; it was reverence and awe, which made it easier to love and let myself be loved by An. I'd only ever let myself pursue these feelings with men, but the closeness with Anya consumed me like a wave that keeps you underwater tumbling and suspended by an unfamiliar gravity. So much of the narrative around the LGBTQ+ community is centered around resilience and hardship, bypassing the undeniable love and energy that I know to be true. When people ask how my life has changed since opening myself up to her love, they expect to hear about hardship and how difficult it was to come out to my friends and loved ones, let alone the world. Being in the public eye has never been a walk in the park, and being a Black woman means I'm no stranger to proving or defending myself. But loving Anya wasn't this difficult, challenging decision to make. On the contrary, allowing myself to feel what I feel for her has been freeing in every way possible. Making the decision to open up our love to others' opinions, thoughts, comments, and judgment was the difficult part.

Anya made every monotonous task seem like a thrill: A trip to the grocery store would leave us laughing as we raced up and down the aisles with Anya making me put sugary items back in exchange for healthier options. On long car rides, we often played old songs and reminisced about the stupid boys we'd mistakenly thought we were in love with and couldn't live without. Even activities I hate—like shopping!—were things I loved to do with her. They say you should marry your best friend and I had found mine. I eventually said in my wedding vows that sometimes when I was mad at her I would want to call her and talk about her.

Food was often a source of comfort and company when Anya and I were together. We had a few favorite restaurants in Russia that we went to all the time together, eating all the fresh seafood we could stomach. At one restaurant in Yekaterinburg, I fell in love with the salted dorado fish. Anya turned to me and said, "I can cook that." The fish was so decadent, I didn't believe her, but she did. There in her kitchen, I watched her gut the fish, cure it in salt, and serve a dish even more delicious than the one in the restaurant. There's nothing she can't do, and she never accepts defeat.

An and I have always enjoyed similar flavors and trying new things, but the meal itself was never as special as the company. It was really the experience of being with her. Whether indulging in the finest black caviar or a simple burger and fries, date night meals symbolized quality time with my favorite person. The new things I learned from her, the way her eyes watered and how her laugh would fade and get weaker the funnier our conversation got. No matter how long we'd been together, our connection grew and swelled. As more time passed, I realized I wanted to always carve out time and be intentional about those moments. We began keeping the wine corks from memorable dinners and experiences, which for us meant that our collection soon was too overwhelming to continue. We wrote little messages on the corks, explaining the experience we'd had and one word to describe the memory. The good food began as the vehicle and turned into nostalgic recollections of our time together. Recalling a dish would bring up a flood of feelings, joy, and love.

Anya and I did the little things naturally, which headed off big problems and the strain of what the world can put on love. We didn't always share the same passions, but I quickly realized Anya encouraged me to be more open to trying new things and experiences, which opened up my eyes to things I could never have imagined. I now *love* caviar, for example, but no matter how many times I try, I will always pass on oysters. I normally read nonfiction, but I actually enjoyed *1984* by George Orwell. These are all moments Anya goaded me into exploring. In a way she drove me, even more so, back to my core of being intentional with my time and unafraid of the unknown. The person I was before the world got a hold of me.

As our relationship blossomed, I pushed for us to read *The Alchemist* together. Slowly but surely, I realized this tall, blue-eyed, gorgeous inside and out woman was in fact my Fatima, guiding me to who and what was meant for me. There is a difference between infatuation and being in love, but boy, I felt *both*. And I respected her enough to want to work on myself. We had the depth, but we also had levity that completely disarmed me and allowed me to not take myself too seriously. Anya saw me and cared for me in ways that I never had before and introduced me to a tender, smart, and knowing love that transformed the way I saw myself and others. When we least expected it, Anya became my person. And I hers.

PART TWO

Authenticity

SIX

This Is Anya, My Wife

*Nothing I accept about myself can be
used against me to diminish me.*

—AUDRE LORDE

I absolutely *despise* the concept of coming out. Loving Anya came easily and naturally. Why did I need to explain or justify that? Though I've been a people pleaser at various stages of my life, I've never subscribed to the idea that people were entitled to intimate details of my life, and coming out felt so antithetical to that. The drama of having a series of sit-downs didn't sit right with me; like I was succumbing to society's unfair expectations. Nothing had changed about who I was as a person and yet who I chose to share my life and go to bed with threatened existing dynamics and exposed how vulnerable I was.

It took Anya and me quite some time to adjust to the idea of us pursuing a future with each other. So much so we would lie awake at night and dream of a time when everyone would know and we would be free to be ourselves outside our home. Kind of crazy, right? Free to feel at ease with someone and something that brought us so much happiness. In a world that feels so advanced and accepting, it was hard to not feel like I was letting people down. Harnessing the love I felt was difficult, but in a way, we reasoned it was necessary to protect it.

The angst and anticipation is what stressed me out the most. I realize now there are so many people who are connected to the stress of "coming out." The parents who are unsure of how to support their children, the teacher who sees their students struggling with something but can't talk about it. The individuals themselves who don't see an out. Without knowing it, our support systems sometimes place conditions on their love. It's not always malicious; oftentimes a rational understanding of the world makes people fearful of how the world perceives and treats the LGBTQ+ community. The looks, the glares, the eye rolling, the comments of "poor children, poor family." The Bible being thrown in our face. People want to protect those they love from unnecessary pain but end up compounding that hurt instead. Even those who mean well and attempt to be "supportive" do more harm than good by singling LGBTQ+ people out and making us feel alone in the process. No matter how well-intentioned, after the seventh "love is love" and "you're so brave," you want to crawl into the deepest, darkest hole you can find. As strange as it sounds, we just wanted our love to be normal.

I pretended I didn't care what strangers thought, when in actuality I did. Not in the sense of their actual love—because anyone allowing my life to occupy their thoughts is lame—but their comments and looks still stung, a constant reminder that our love may never be "normal." But my family and friends were everything to me. What would it mean to start a new chapter without their blessing? I hoped I wouldn't need to find out.

My big brother Anthony is one of my favorite people in the world. We talk nearly every day and are fully involved in the other's life. He is open-minded and supportive; he always knows the right words to speak in any given situation. Calm, calculated, and slow to react and quick to support. We didn't really become close until he returned from playing overseas and I was in my twenties. Since then, he has in a way become my moral compass. Almost *What Would Anthony Do?* The guilt of withholding such a huge part of my life and happiness from him was weighing heavy on my mind. I would send his phone calls to voicemail when I was with Anya; I didn't want to have to explain or lie. I was exhausted from keeping up the "she's just a friend" front.

I had a road trip while playing for the LA Sparks and for the first time in a while, it was going to just be him and me. Before the trip, I convinced myself this was the perfect opportunity to tell Anthony that I was in love with Anya. Sitting across from him, though, it was clear I'd underestimated how nervous I'd be. Dinner came and went and I couldn't find the words. Every time I opened my mouth, a lump swelled in my throat and my heart began to beat out of my chest. Then the tears would form and I changed the subject. Worst-case scenarios swirled through my head and immobilized me. My nieces and nephews were my absolute babies. I couldn't help but imagine, what if my siblings wouldn't allow my nieces or nephews to come visit or look at me as a role model.

After dinner, Anthony and I returned to the hotel and were just sitting around but he felt my stress and discomfort. I tried my best to express the jumble of emotions I was going through inside. In my angst, I was using gender-neutral pronouns to refer to this "special person" in my life, and Anthony cut right to the chase. He disarmed my biggest fear and said, "You know, if this special person is a she, we will still love you and support you." A weight was lifted from my chest, and a flood of emotions followed. I gave in and told Anthony how much Anya meant to me . . . as more than a friend. He wasn't fazed, and I felt relieved and grateful that I'd always be his little sister. I was grateful because he just listened. He listened to me go on and on and brag, rant, rave, celebrate a feeling of love that I had kept bottled up for so long. I cried myself to sleep that night. I knew not every conversation would go as smooth and accepting as Anthony's, but my hope grew: that one day, Anya and I might live in a world where we didn't have to hide our love.

Not everyone responded the way he did, but Anthony's vote of confidence helped me to realize that while I *wanted* my loved ones by my side, others not understanding wouldn't or couldn't keep me from Anya. I wasn't asking people to agree with my love, but I was demanding respect. When my more skeptical family and friends saw that clear resolve in my eyes, they also saw how serious we were about each other and—in time—matched our energy. And some didn't. And that's okay. Fear would not deter me from living my life. At times we both were strong, some days Anya had to carry forward hope and I would lean on her heavily with all of my thoughts, fears, and hesitations. Other times, I would become the beacon of hope and have to inject hope and belief and reminders into Anya's doubts.

I'm so grateful for the community I had around me and how they encouraged me to be my full self. People who were open and honest about who they loved helped me to fully internalize that Anya and I deserved to be happy. Robin Roberts was a huge source of strength for me during this season, as were Chelsea Gray and Tipesa Moorer, and Ann Wauters and Lot Wielfaert. These are people who'd been in my position—or were traversing similar roads—and could be a listening ear when I needed one most. I also received support from friends like Dwyane Wade and Gabrielle Union, Vanessa Bryant, and my former trainer Jenny Moshak, who were instrumental in normalizing our love. We could double-date or hang out as families without feeling "othered."

I can't say every conversation was easy. And some were more difficult to have. Not because I didn't think they would love or support me but because, even if just for a second, I could see the flash of disappointment across their face. They'd try to disguise it, but I'd see it and know. Anya's parents didn't speak to her for six months, which was hard on us both, and required new levels of patience. Even beyond family, it was incredibly difficult to have conversations with people who had made homophobic comments in the past. No matter how big or small, those moments pulled back the curtain and showed me what they really thought. Now, I had to pretend that I didn't remember, or worse, confront those toxic beliefs head-on. I once had a coach confront me about things he had heard. He told me that I wasn't like that and to not let other players convince me to join that "lifestyle." Ultimately, though, I refused to let others' potential disappointment keep me from being gracious with myself and others. I remember telling Anya that it took her, and me, a long while to be okay with our lives not fitting into the plan that we had had for ourselves. Let's allow our family members time and grace to process. Our one nonnegotiable was we refused to stand for any negativity around Lailaa. She is and always has been my world, and I wouldn't allow anyone to insinuate that Anya and I weren't prioritizing her interests. That somehow we weren't being solid role models or good representations of love.

There was also the fact that Anya was a woman and a white Russian woman at that. It's hard enough to introduce the one to your family. But I was also dealing with the insecurities that accompany introducing someone you are unsure they will approve of, not because of who they are but what they look like. From the outside looking in, Anya and I check every box as to why we shouldn't be together: American and Russian. Black and white. Both women, with me being a single mom. Yet somehow, despite all that, we believed we were made for each other. Anya was the person who my parents told me I should be in search of, but she just happened to not come in the package that we all had imagined.

I knew all of this leading into my conversations, and it wasn't fair. Again, communication was my saving grace. Though I'm aggressive and a leader on the court, in my personal life I can be more avoidant when it comes to challenging moments. But I had to address people's expectations and that it wasn't going to change how I lived my life head-on. Anya and I talked often and candidly about everything going through our heads and how to honor our commitments to ourselves while being sensitive to the nuance of the moment. As long as the two of us were in lockstep, everything else would fall into place when it needed to.

I can only imagine all the people out there going through something similar. The feelings of fear, anxiety. I empathize with those who depend on the very people that they are seeking approval from. I can't imagine the fear that they must feel and how powerless it must be. That instead of lying awake worrying about acceptance, you lie awake not knowing if you will have a place to stay or a way to take care of yourself, a job, etc. Going through this situation not only grew my ability to be okay with disapproval, but it increased my knowledge of the need for more people like Anya and myself to live authentically and serve as a beacon of hope for those who are struggling. Who knows who's watching. The mother who wants to support her child, but doesn't know how. The sister who doesn't have the words to comfort a sibling who is struggling with who they have fallen in love with. A father who is struggling with a culture of hypermasculinity. I want to serve as an example for those who need it. No matter who you are or what you have, being fearful to express who you are and who you love is lonely and scary. Until you have been in that position, you can't understand the emotions and feelings that accompany the journey. That understanding made me change my view on "coming out" and lean into the opportunity to celebrate *us* and live in the open.

Choosing Each Other

With the love of our family and friends secured, I proposed to Anya and asked her to spend the rest of her life with me. Actually, Lailaa and I presented An with a cake that said "will you marry us"—a nod to the fact that Lai had always been a huge part of our relationship, especially when we were living abroad. I was nervous, not because I wasn't sure she'd say yes, but because this time I knew what I was getting into. It's easy to agree to something you don't fully understand.

I was eyes wide-open. I'd never been so sure of someone in my life, and that thought low-key terrified me. We'd worked through challenges, taken steps to better communicate, and matured. We had danced in the sun, rain, and snow—literally. I knew, no matter what, at least we were in this life thing together.

An and I existed within a bubble, and there was a blissful peace to the relationship we'd built. It took years for us to be okay with ourselves and fully accept that we deserved each other and this love. We'd both been in relationships with men before, but this was a new experience. We were finding our way with no road map or compass. Listening to what our hearts yearned for and not overthinking it too much. Once I knew Anya and Lailaa were happy and comfortable with each other, most of my angst dissipated, and we settled into a norm that was calm and easy.

There was nothing to "normalize" or insist upon. We simply were. Our life didn't feel particularly different outside of being in love. I soon realized that the blissful simplicity we shared was somewhat of an illusion, not unlike the stillness found in the eye of a hurricane. Whether I wanted to acknowledge it or not, choosing each other also meant assuming a new, politicized identity. After identifying as straight my whole life, I was coming to terms with what it meant to be gay in America.

Being openly LGBTQ+ in most parts of this country, and the world, is an inherently politicized identity. In choosing to love and marry Anya, I was thrust into a community and hadn't paused long enough to realize that I was navigating more internalized shame than I thought. When you can't see something, you don't know what possibilities lie in wait. Gay marriage had only been legal in America for two or three years when Anya and I began dating. The society I'd grown up in hadn't given me much space to see loving someone of the same gender as the beautiful act of love that I had come to know it as. We were building the road as we journeyed, together.

Some days it was exhausting and looking out at all the obstacles and hills we haven't climbed seemed overwhelming. How would we ever make it? We were jealous at times of other relationships that just were. No fighting, no clawing to just be. Love could be so beautiful, but also so challenging. My mind would go to the rooms I wasn't in, but my name was. I could tell by the uncomfortable smiles or whispers behind my back, the comments and questions that ensued. I would always introduce Anya as Anya and never would give her a title. I would lie awake, my heart jumping out of my chest and my stomach aching in anticipation of being "outed." I'm so grateful that my family, friends, and members of the media allowed us our time and our process to come out on our own terms.

Considering it took so much time and intentional work to get to a place of self-acceptance for Anya and me, imagine what we were stepping into by telling our loved ones. I didn't think I had the energy to invite so many people into our world. Though each conversation was unique and my people had lots of questions, I welcomed the chance to be a realer and more honest version of myself with the people I care about most. In some instances, I regret how conversations happened, while also honoring the validity of my fears. As a mother, I know how important it is to be a safe space for your children and that people withhold self truths because the consequences of radical authenticity are terrifying. Isolation. Ostracization. Severed relationships. My anxiety and fear led me to rush through conversations that could only happen slowly and openly. It wasn't that I didn't respect them enough to carve out more time, but I often felt frozen by how much was at risk if certain conversations didn't go well.

At times, it was terrifying to feel so exposed and unprepared. I couldn't quite train or watch film to best strategize for this next chapter, but I had to try my best anyway. I refused to let my own internalized thoughts keep me from the greatest love I'd known. I needed a marriage that felt as good as it looked, which meant not getting in my own way.

Thankfully we had some help. In a league full of queer women, my teammates and fellow players wrapped us in love and became part of our bubble. We could double-date or ask advice from people who understood the tightrope I was walking. Having our community be invested in our success as a couple meant the world. It's still an ongoing process in some ways to normalize what Anya and I have and not feel an incessant need to overexplain it. At the same time, explanation and advocacy is needed at times to ensure anyone and everyone can be their full self.

In most cases, my fears proved to be unfounded. Yes, there was tension initially, and tears were shed, but my family and I always found our way back to one another. After the initial shock, my people enveloped us as I knew they would. In other cases, people would ask questions like, "Why didn't you tell me before?" and I had to fight to hide my frustration that they couldn't understand all I was up against in a society that considered my identities as three strikes against me. What I really was thinking was shouldn't you be asking yourself why I didn't feel comfortable telling you? Why does this weight always fall on my shoulders? Time allowed for deeper conversations where the only important truths were made known: Anya and I were in love, Lailaa was safe, and the two of us being together was only adding to our collective happiness as a family, not detracting from it.

In 2019, before sixty of our closest friends and family, Anya and I said I do. We wanted to create a weekend-retreat experience for our loved ones. In addition to celebrating and crystallizing the love An and I have for each other, we also wanted our favorite people to meet and enjoy one another. We opened the long weekend with a massive dinner spread to welcome all our guests. The next day, we brought everyone together again for a boat day. There in the crystal-blue waters of Mexico, surrounded by friends, An and I got to be our full selves: in love and unapologetic about it. Getting to hold hands with and kiss my soon-to-be wife without worrying about who would see. Everyone knew and cared for us, not just as individuals but as a unit.

There were of course people we didn't have with us. Family members who had yet to accept our union. Friends and colleagues we hadn't come out to yet. Some of my co-workers at the time didn't even know I was taking off for my own wedding. In preserving the sacredness and privacy, there was still a bittersweet undertone, but we'd worked too hard to get to this point. I didn't need others' validation or presence because I'd marry An if it were just her and me in a courthouse.

The day of our ceremony was perfect in every way. We stood there—hand in hand—vowing to protect, love, and cherish each other. During her vows, Anya reminded me and our guests that we'd always joked about if we would made it to the altar. "I have news for you," she said to me. "We made it!" The perfect final touch was a quote from our favorite book, *The Alchemist*. Lailaa read it aloud: "And, when you want something, the entire universe conspires in helping you achieve it." There wasn't a dry eye in the venue. I had found what I had been searching for. The person who doesn't complete me, but enables me to do the work to complete myself. Anya and I jumped the broom, a Black tradition that was important to us both to keep alive within our family.

At the beachfront reception, we danced, drank, and sang our hearts out. Our parents, siblings, teammates, and other loved ones were there cheering us on. There were no NDAs, phone bans, or top-secret security. We expressed to our loved ones that this was intended to be a sacred weekend for only our invited guests, and they understood that. Everyone kept their memories close to their hearts, and not a single media outlet was any the wiser. I remember thinking it was the best night of my life. Until I woke up the next morning and realized nothing could be better than waking up and falling asleep next to Anya Parker every day thereafter. And so the next chapter began. I got to do life with my best friend.

Allow Us to Reintroduce Ourselves

The marital bliss from our wedding weekend was euphoric yet short-lived. In an ideal world, we would have transitioned straight from our festivities to a long and beautiful honeymoon. But, instead, I flew back to the United States the day after our wedding for studio, with our honeymoon delayed until the Christmas holidays. I didn't let anyone know that I had just experienced the best week of my life. When asked how my weekend went, I shrugged and said it was a normal one. It was a pragmatic solution, and an anticlimactic one. Anya and I both felt it. We had all this love and excitement yet could only share it with those sixty people we'd invited. It's like being a kid with no one to show your art project or cartwheel. All our emotions had to be bottled up and strategically meted out. There was no sharing wedding photos on social media, no recounting our favorite memories at work, no honeymoon phase. None of the authentic sharing that comes with having just married the love of your life.

As more people were introduced into our bubble, I realized just how shaky our foundation would remain so long as our relationship remained a secret. For a long time, I rejected the idea that our relationship was a secret at all. Anya has always been around and by my side. Anyone reading deeply between the lines would see us on red carpets and sharing inside jokes on Instagram. What we meant to each other was no secret, but I recognize that there are levels to secrets. Even though I had never entirely concealed our closeness, I omitted some information and allowed people to assume we were simply really great friends. But withholding the full truth and evading being seen still counts. I wanted our relationship to not remain hidden in the darkness, but to come to the light.

Unfortunately, there are a lot of people who feel entitled to approve of my personal and professional decisions. A *lot*. Fans, media, coaching staff, family, and even well-intentioned friends. For my entire adult life, people have picked me apart and offered up their unsolicited opinions on what I need to do to be great or to preserve my legacy. A loved one casually suggested that I wait until after I renegotiated my television deal to go public with my relationship. Sitting there in stunned silence, I tried to shield my deep hurt and hold space for the (albeit, misdirected) love guiding my family's apprehension. For a people pleaser like me, it became extremely exhausting to be accountable to what so many thought was best for me.

In the media and professional settings, I was making split-second decisions to prove myself and protect our love without diluting how much Anya meant to me. I still found myself introducing Anya by name with no context around who she meant to me. "Have you met Anya?" "This is Anya!" Innocent enough yet ultimately noncommittal. I wasn't insisting we be seen as a couple or that Anya in particular be publicly recognized as more than my friend.

But other people's expectations were waiting for me around every corner. On numerous occasions, fans came up to me and offered this backhanded compliment: "We are so glad you aren't like the other girls." I hated these comments for two reasons: There are no girls in the WNBA. We are women who are often infantilized into these caricatures of little girls cosplaying at a grown man's game. But the other aspect of those fan comments that bothered me was the way I was held on a faulty pedestal away from women I cared about and based on things out of anyone's control, like whom and how we love. There was a time when I thought nothing of statements like that. In fact, I even sometimes wore it as a badge of honor because I liked being different. I always supported loving who you want but was happy to stand out and defy the norm. Now, these comments stung because they weren't true. I was in a full-fledged relationship with my *wife*, and people would assume and praise me for being someone I wasn't. As the fans quickly snapped their pictures and walked away thinking nothing of the interaction beyond what they got from it, I was stuck. Those comments ate away at me.

It surprised me each time I avoided correcting people or clarifying our relationship because I knew I wasn't ashamed of Anya or of who we were to each other. I was more afraid and anxious about how people would respond. Was this the time and place to be so vulnerable? How would I defend us if expected to? Were we prepared for the onslaught of questions that would surely come, and were we in agreement on what to share? Frankly, it was pretty exhausting when the alternative was a private life.

Then almost equally as cringey are the people who think of themselves as helpful yet go out of their way to make sure I know they "*love* gay people" and "love is love" and all the other quips that drive me up a wall. Being in a lesbian relationship means being constantly met with people making sure you know they're an ally. The winks, wide smiles, and uncomfortably happy looks all feel like that awkward moment when a non-Black person tells you they have Black friends in their attempt to relate. I know most of these people are well-intentioned, but they unknowingly single me—and other LGBTQ+ people—out even more and make my sexuality the dominant narrative, rather than one small but important part of my life.

If I'm being completely honest, there's sometimes been an element of fake love that peeks through people's facades. I could always tell when someone wanted me to believe they were happy for me, but they secretly held a lot of criticism couched as personal opinion or care for me when I wasn't in the room. They would shout and profess happiness to my face, but talk about me and my decisions behind my back. "I just want to make sure she's thinking things through." "I mean, how are they actually going to make this work?" "I only want what's best for Lailaa." I had a heightened Spidey sense for bullshit and didn't appreciate those who pretended to know and care about my family more than me. Then there were others who claimed to have known all along, "from the time you were younger, I knew you were gay." I was stunned, unable to respond. How could you know something about me that *I* didn't even know? It was and remains frustrating to experience; I didn't realize how much my sexuality shaped the way people interacted with me, and vice versa, but it really did.

Some words of advice to people who have the best intentions in supporting loved ones who are "coming out": Do less talking and more listening. Make it about them and follow their lead! Validate their happiness, love, insecurities, fears—don't make it about yourself. And, under no circumstances should you say, "I knew all along" or "Why didn't you tell me?" It's okay to not have the words, need time to process, or have mixed feelings, but remember that you can't take words back once they've been said. It's always better to express that you've been caught off guard, but that you love and respect them, no matter what.

I wanted things to be as easy as "Anya and I love each other." I wanted to protect and preserve what we had. When Anya and I were alone or with Lailaa, an ease fell over us like a weighted blanket. We were secure in our love for each other. The introduction of others—their expectations, projections, and microaggressions—is what I thought would taint the peace we'd carved out for ourselves. In creating and cementing a bubble for our union, I thought I was safeguarding the people I loved. In actuality, I was only delaying the inevitable. Anya wasn't going anywhere, and neither was my public platform.

I remember bringing Anya to a huge family gathering and introducing her to my grandma. "Whom do you belong to?" my grandmother asked in typical matriarch fashion. I replied, hoping I didn't seem as nervous as I was. "This is Anya, my wife." Without missing a beat, Grandma said, "That's great," and continued buzzing around the house. Ten minutes later she approached me again, inquiring about the "random" Russian woman in her home. Dementia had already made Grandma forget their introduction, and so I repeated myself again through fits of laughter. "This is Anya. My wife." I didn't mind repeating those sentences as many times as Grandma—or anyone else, for that matter—needed. I liked the way it sounded.

SEVEN

The Real Candace Parker

Don't matter to me if it's a him or her.

—JAY-Z, IN THE SONG "SMILE," IN RESPONSE
TO HIS MOTHER COMING OUT

I came into the world of basketball passionately and with no self-imposed limits on what I could or couldn't do. I grew up in a Black family full of strong and independent women, so race and gender were never handicaps for me. I learned that the world wasn't as progressive when my high school career went viral before virality was a thing. Every time I dunked or leaned into a physical and aggressive game, people debated whether there was a place for that in women's basketball. It reminded me again of the fictional character Monica in *Love & Basketball*, my favorite movie of all time. Everyone from Monica's mother to her coaches to her star boyfriend, Quincy, chastised Monica for being unladylike or a hothead on the court even though she wasn't doing anything her male counterparts weren't doing. Being a woman was hard. Society told us to be strong but not too muscular, be competitive but don't be emotional, be independent but still subservient, and dream but within the confines of what box society constantly puts you in.

In one scene, Quincy and Monica are arguing about whether Monica's attitude is getting in the way of being recruited. Quincy seemed to think so, but Monica had other things to say. "You jump in some guy's face, talk smack and you get a pat on your ass," she retorted. "But because I'm a female, I get told to calm down and act like a 'lady.'" She then clarified, "I'm a ballplayer." There should be no room for double standards, and yet we have to be twice as good with a fraction of the fierceness. It's hard enough navigating womanhood in professional basketball. A part of me was terrified of how coming out would add yet another layer to how I'm treated trying to excel at the game I love.

Anya and I were married for two years before we made our relationship public. The people closest to me knew and loved her, which was all that mattered to me for a long time. When you're in the line of work that I'm in, you learn to keep your personal life sacred lest it be turned into a public debate and the subject of countless think pieces. In a league where storytelling is as critical as playmaking, I understand why it's important to curate your image, but I have learned to be protective against efforts to pack me up into neat, marketable boxes. I knew that the news of my sexuality and relationship would consume even more space with people debating why I'd married a woman and a white Russian woman at that. I didn't want to surrender to that level of scrutiny because I knew the conversations weren't in good faith and that the most curious ones would never bother to get to know Anya and me beyond the labels they assigned us.

My entire career, people have projected so much onto me, particularly when it comes to beauty standards, love, and family. It's not lost on me that in a league made up predominantly of LGBTQ+ Black women, fans and media makers alike put a specific type of players on pedestals: often white (or light-skinned) and almost always heterosexual. Coming into the league, I was respected for my prowess but heralded because I fit a convenient mold about beautiful and strong Black women.

Marrying my ex-husband only cemented the way the public saw me. Our union meant a lot to others, particularly those in the Black community who rarely get to see a successful Black couple thriving professionally and personally. Ending that relationship and publicly declaring my love for someone new—someone who wasn't Black or a man—would be different, to say the least. I wasn't rushing to rip the blinders off of everyone's eyes, nor did I want to be beholden to those projections.

People blanketly assumed that all basketball players were gay, and I pushed back against the myth that there was any one mold or archetype to define what a hooper looks and acts like. What I wasn't fully acknowledging was that a lot of WNBA players both historically and in the present *are* members of the LGBTQ+ community, myself included. That is a beautiful thing but hasn't always been recognized as such! But, somehow, identifying as gay placed all of these other stereotypes onto players. When I thought I was straight, I hadn't let myself imagine how isolating it could be to know who you are and be forced to hide that fact based on how others would respond to it. Yet here I was unpacking my own sexuality and having conversations about how my relationship might threaten my income and social standing. It may sound superficial from a distance, but my family's livelihood was on the line—as was the greatest passion I've ever known or cultivated.

But what kept ringing in my ear was the reality that I refused to give up on Anya and me simply because it would hurt some fans' feelings or put endorsements at risk. If the public wasn't ready to know the full me, then that would have to be their problem. I was ready to be the real Candace Nicole Parker.

I Am Who I Say I Am

As I was ruminating on these—and other—reflections, Lailaa forced my inner turmoil out of my body. My daughter is part of an unapologetic generation who say what they mean and mean what they say.

Lailaa taught me to be who I say I am out loud. My not-so-little girl unknowingly sparked a journey of truly stepping into my identity. My relationship is a symbol and vehicle for larger conversations.

Publicly and privately, I wanted to be responsible about honoring my wife, protecting both our peace, and leveraging my power toward a safer, more joyful world for other LGBTQ+ people. I decided to run toward, as opposed to away from, this new politicized identity.

When the winter of 2021 began to creep its way in, I knew it was time to tackle both the media and the public. Our first child together was growing quickly by the day in Anya's belly, and something about that looming deadline pushed me to accept the urgency of sharing our love with the world.

I distinctly remember thinking: I don't want our son to look up at me one day and wonder why I didn't publicly claim his other mother. As a family, I needed every member of our little unit to feel safe, loved, and included. Though Anya had never rushed me, I knew the time had long since come to take our relationship to a place we couldn't turn back from. We were ready.

I was already scheduled to deliver my first TED Talk late that winter and wrestled with whether that red stage was the best place to debut our union. I wanted Anya to have as much agency over how we introduced ourselves to the world and ensure that she was just as centered, especially considering she was pregnant with Airr at the time. Her safety and comfort were paramount.

After a lot of mulling over, I decided to use the speech to plant seeds that were sincere and relevant to both my personal and professional life followed by a more casual Instagram post to really seal the deal and let people in on who Anya and I were to each other. I felt, as I was writing the speech, like I was coaching myself. Telling myself what I knew I needed to lean into. As I rehearsed, I listened to my own words over and over. I knew then, more than ever, that I had to truly be me. True to myself and what I wanted. To be unafraid of leaning into who I want and my desires. Being fearful of what would come of me being me, of the box the world would try to put me in, would be counter to what I had stood for my whole life.

I wanted the public to follow my lead in seeing that us being together really shouldn't be a huge deal to others. Don't get me wrong: Anya is the sun, and my world orbits around hers. But I didn't want either of us to be fielding questions forever. Coming out shouldn't be this huge moment for LGBTQ+ people while straight people get to date and marry with no one batting an eye. I hoped the TED Talk would allow me to be vulnerable, and social media would help me to remind people that authenticity finds us when we least expect it.

When I stepped onto the TED stage to talk about breaking barriers and never accepting the limits put before you, everything in me was shaking. There were no teleprompters, and I'd worked tirelessly to commit my speech to memory, which definitely added another layer of angst. My heart was beating faster than ever before, my palms and underarms were sweating, and I felt as though my nerves were tattooed across my forehead. I'd played before tens of thousands of fans and had my athleticism amplified to millions more, but I'd never felt so terrified than when the soles of my black boots touched that platform and carried me to center stage. Here I wouldn't be dribbling a basketball or allowing the game to be my distraction. All I had were my name and my words. I hoped they'd be enough.

Standing there, I looked out in the audience and locked eyes with An who, in her calm nature, told me to breathe. I faced my fear and delivered the speech! I spoke to the audience about the lessons I had learned about not fitting into the boxes the world puts you in. Meanwhile, I was busy trying to fit into a box the world had put me in. I needed to listen to myself and my own words as well as the fierceness of Gen Z, my daughter in particular, who were being themselves, loving who they loved, wearing what they wanted, and talking about uncomfortable things.

As I kept talking, I hoped people recognized the multitude of ways to defy barriers and be uniquely ourselves. I was talking to myself just as much as the audience. In the past, I thought I was bravest when I did something others said I couldn't. Now I realized it took the most courage to do the things that make you happy and fulfilled, regardless of what people think. "We have to unite, to come together, to figure out why barriers are there in the first place." When I concluded the speech, roaring applause consumed the space. I did it. I'd said my truth and knew that—soon enough—fans would be picking that speech apart in every way imaginable. I was ready for them.

Stand in Your Truth, No Matter Who's Watching

During the twelve minutes that I stood on that TED stage, I tried my best to lay the groundwork for what I knew was to come. A few weeks after delivering the TED Talk, Anya and I were set to celebrate our two-year wedding anniversary. The previous year, we had an intimate, COVID-19-safe celebration with our loved ones as the violinist from our wedding serenaded us. It was beautiful but still kept tucked away from the public. This year would be different, I told myself. These were our last few days and moments of privacy. We savored them.

I was reminded that we were indeed still a secret every time we were out on a date and I was reluctant to grab my wife's hand. Or how the Beverly Hills paparazzi nearly caught us holding hands. How we always had to check if people knew where we were going so we could act accordingly. It was a terrible way to live. And all for what? I got sick and tired of keeping up this front.

Anya was ready, it took me a bit longer. But we had always discussed how we would acknowledge our love to one another, publicly. If we went the more formal route of sit-down interviews and traditional press, we'd be feeding into the flurry. Instagram gave us the nonchalance and control we wanted over our message. Two people loving each other is as natural as breathing air. That was our takeaway, and we wanted to set that tone from the very beginning.

Once we posted, there was no going back. No undoing the public's nosiness or getting a do-over at introducing the Parkers to the world. With that in mind, one might think I'd be meticulous in my word choice, poring over each word in the caption and which images to choose. Nope. I refused to overthink it. I drafted the post the same way I pack a suitcase: last-minute. When preparing for a trip, I firmly believe that what you reach for first is what's most important: key outfits for various events, necessary toiletries, etc. Anything left behind probably wasn't important, anyway, and would only weigh down the bags. When typing up my declaration, I started with what mattered most: our love.

> Happy Anniversary Моя жена! 2 years ago, I got to marry my best friend in front of our close family and friends. My heart could have exploded. I cried like a baby.... To know me or you is to know our love. This journey hasn't been easy. I am proud of us and what we have built and who we have grown to become both individually and together. Thank you for always loving Lailaa as your own, being my calm, my support, my voice of reason, my laughs, my cuddles, my dance in the rain, my happy, my home ... Thanks for constantly challenging me and telling me when I'm wrong. I LOVE YOU! I appreciate you, I value you and what we have.
>
> We've always dreamed of growing our family.... it's surreal that we now have a baby on the way! Lailaa is pumped to be a big sister!
>
> You couldn't be more beautiful! Glowing, while understanding that I have to constantly love, kiss, and talk to your belly AND yes ... play Jay-Z for the baby (Goose knows

"Song Cry" already by heart!) I can't wait to embark on this next chapter in life with you!

"So, I love you because the entire universe conspired to help me find you." -Alchemist

I pressed Post, silenced my notifications, and continued on with my day. The media frenzy ensued—as anticipated—with every major publication speculating about our marriage. They could have that. The guessing, projecting, and interrogating. Anya and I were too busy reveling in the joy of our second anniversary, not to mention the anticipation of baby Airr, who was still cooking in An's belly. A few days after my post, Anya jumped onto Instagram with her own reflection:

I always prefer to be present with you than post on social media, so please forgive me for being late with this post.

I am SO lucky to call you my wife. The last two years have been a dream. Our love never wavered, although like you said, our path has not been easy. And I can't be more proud of the family we have grown into.

You talk about not fitting in a box . . . We laugh how we are NOT a typical couple. Different Nationality, race, upbringing, same gender . . . Yet some days I feel like we could not be or think more similar. I GET you. I SEE where you are coming from and can understand WHY you operate the way you do. You have an incredibly huge heart. You always put family first. No matter how busy you are or how many thousands of messages you have on your phone, you always make time for me and for us.

You break records, win Championships, shatter glass ceilings with such ease. And you never brag. Seems like every day there is a reason to celebrate your new accomplishments, yet you never make it about yourself. I'm in awe of your strength and your power, and glad to be by your side in those moments.

I can't wait to have our baby with you . . . You love him so much already. You do talk to him each day, with your daily affirmations to Jay-Z lyrics . . . he kicks every time he hears your voice. I'm going to melt when I see you hold him . . . and I can only imagine what a sweet big sister Lailaa will be.

You taught me to be vulnerable. You taught me how to trust and showed me real love. Unconditional, all-encompassing and caring.

I am still learning to open up to the World, so bear with me. I'm learning to be brave like you.

"Remember that wherever your heart is, there you will find your treasure" the Alchemist.

I've found mine.

Looking back, we always seem to remember things as being easier than they actually were. An and I reflect on the fear we had then and ask ourselves why. Why were we so anxious and hesitant at times when the end result has been nothing short of magical. Things now seem like they always were this way. The family holidays, dinners, hand holding, normalcy . . . it feels like it's been this way forever. It's been only a few years since that Instagram post, and I know there are others out there struggling with the same journey I am now on the other side of. What would I say to that version of myself? *It's okay.* It's okay to feel what you feel, to be unsure, to not know your next step, and to question whether you are making the right moves. Give yourself grace, but always work toward your happiness. Don't give up on what you truly want and need. I've found that—and more—in An, and I only wish I'd welcomed this love sooner.

EIGHT

Fumbling Together

*We don't know where our first impressions
come from or precisely what they mean,
so we don't always appreciate their fragility.*

—MALCOLM GLADWELL

hen Lailaa was nine years old, I was preparing to take a work trip. Since she was born, Lailaa has come on almost every trip I've taken, whether for work or personal enjoyment. We were a team. Always had been, always would be. But this time, Lailaa was exhausted from traveling and didn't want to come with me. "I want to stay with Anya at home." At the time, Anya and I weren't yet married, and her nieces were in town, so I needed to check with her and make sure she was okay with having another little one to watch. That only sealed the deal for Lailaa, who thinks of Anya's nieces like her cousins. Of course, Anya agreed, and it was settled. Their first time truly alone without me.

Ahead of my trip, I remember being borderline obsessed about doing Lailaa's hair before I left. My daughter has beautiful coily hair that is bouncy and independent. It easily stretches out when natural and loose, so I wanted to braid it up or otherwise style it. Lailaa pushed back, and a few days before my scheduled departure, Anya said, "I can do her hair." It was a record-scratch moment, and in my head all I could think was *No you can't.*

I didn't want to hurt Anya's feelings, but I realized at the moment that I was carrying a lot of Black-mom guilt about my child being "presentable" in public. Every Black parent knows what it's like to be accused of not caring for your child when they look "unkempt." Ashy knees, undone edges, frizzy hair, and wrinkled clothes can all be used against us to make us feel as though we are negligent. It happens subtly, but the feelings are there. With all that context, I didn't believe Anya knew enough about Black hair to meet that standard.

More than that, I began to notice that my own childhood experiences with my hair and journey to loving it were also shaping the way I approached Lailaa's tresses. Growing up, I always wanted my hair to lie down straight on my back and stretch as far down as my classmates' hair did. Why couldn't my hair be less kinky and longer? The texture of hair and style was criticized no matter what age you were. If your braids weren't fresh or your hair wasn't tamed and combed, it could be the subject of debate and comments. All these experiences from my childhood impacted how I saw my hair and the responsibility I had to make sure my daughter's hair was "well kept."

The world, at that point, still wasn't comfortable with Black people wearing their natural hair. As I got older and gained more attention for basketball, my hair became a point of contention even outside my comparisons to my white peers. If I played a game or made an appearance and my hair wasn't perfectly styled, I knew I'd never hear the end of it from those within my own community. More than anyone else, it was Black men and women who made nasty comments. I knew how much it could hurt, and I didn't want Lailaa to have that same baggage that I'd carried.

Anya initially insisted and then began digging into the root of the problem when she saw how reticent I was. "Lailaa doesn't even need her hair done, and she likes it natural, and it's beautiful however she wears it," Anya said. "Why are you being so specific and micromanaging her?" I didn't think Anya understood me or Black hair enough to have an opinion. As we continued going back and forth, Anya proved that she'd done her research and disagreed with me on my approach to parenting Lailaa. "You want to raise a confident Black girl who loves her hair the way it grows out of her scalp, and yet you disparage her natural hair and relentlessly try to manipulate it." Damn. She had me. I loved that she cared enough about me and Lailaa to not walk on eggshells around a topic that mattered to us both.

By this point, Anya had been in Lailaa's life for *years*. If the three of us were going to be a family, then Anya couldn't be on the bench or think of Blackness as out of her scope and, thus, not her concern. In my head I fought the need to retreat; all I could think was, *She has no idea how many layers there are to this.* We had a lot of differences to bridge, and in that moment I recognized just how committed my partner was to me and us. She listened as I was almost brought to tears, recalling comments, insecurities, and burdens I carried and never shared regarding the standard of hair. I struggled with not having "good hair" and my desire to risk breakage and my natural hair falling out to get it to lie the way that I wanted. I also came to terms with the fact that I had been the one standing in the way. Even though this was a Black issue, I had blinders on in some ways Anya helped me realize that I was actually perpetuating the problem. I had become the comments and insecurities that so impacted me growing up. Everyday I was teaching my daughter to love her hair less. Sometimes, we want the world to be open and accepting in ways that suit us without acknowledging how we've become part of the problem. Thankfully, Anya was patient enough with me to talk it out and to give Lailaa agency over her body, including her beautiful hair. *I* was the one who maybe needed to listen to some more India Arie and remember that we are not our hair.

Autonomy in Growing Our Family

Anya and I are very different people conditioned in very different societies. I was born in St. Louis and raised in the predominantly white suburb of Naperville around my Black brothers, parents, grandparents, and neighbors, who each treated me like a precious heirloom. As the baby of the family, my mother was a true helicopter mom, and I grew up feeling very responsible for the investments others have made in me. Anya was born in Russia and raised in a smaller Eastern European family. Anya's mother passed away when she was a young girl, and she was raised by her stepmother. Anya was encouraged to become independent early on. She taught herself American English when moving to the United States to play basketball. Those aren't where our differences end, either. Anya's a Sagittarius, and I'm an Aries. I'm a people pleaser, and she is serious about her boundaries.

But, despite our differences, An and I also have so much in common. We're both eighties babies who fell in love with basketball at young ages. Our determination and work ethic led both Anya and me to be Olympians representing our nations on the largest platform in the world. We read the same books and watch the same movies. From aliens and space travel to World War II, we can talk for hours without getting bored of each other. And most importantly, we wanted the same things out of life: happiness, health, love, and each other.

By leading with our love for each other and our commitment to each family member's safety and happiness, there was no conversation or decision too taboo to discuss. Hair was one of the first areas I really saw Anya invest her time and energy. She'd done her research and wanted my trust. My stubbornness and preconceived notions had gotten in the way of me seeing what Anya was capable of. When I finally gave in, I found out she was right. Was Lai's hair perfect? No, but she liked it! Anya was more than willing to learn about Black culture, and I'd fallen in love with learning about Russia years ago. We didn't need any metaphoric walls up in our house when life could be so much better by letting one another in.

Not every conversation or hurdle was as easy as learning new hairstyles, however. I was notorious for bringing old habits into our new relationship. In hindsight, it was a bit of self-sabotage, but I also showed up the only way I knew. When I felt unheard, I yelled. In some ways, I was following the example I'd seen growing up. The way disagreements were handled and settled wasn't always the healthiest. A lot of feelings were left unsaid and accountability was traded for "never mind." Discussions and disagreements with people who share love should also lead and lean on good intentions.

As we made major decisions about where to live and grow our family, getting real about race in America became urgent. I'm a Black woman, and all our kids are Black. No matter how much love and protection we provide in our home, the world they're walking into when they step out the front door is often an unkind one. There was a culture shock for Anya, who was truly internalizing just how much racism shapes our experiences. She didn't initially understand the historic context behind the fixation on light skin, dark skin, and various features. She didn't understand the systemic oppression undergirding modern-day systems. Most of all, she didn't understand why the current generations couldn't divorce themselves from that sordid past. But 2020 changed all of that.

When Breonna Taylor was killed in her home and George Floyd cried out, "I can't breathe," and called for his mother while crushed under an officer's knee, Anya and I were going through the IVF process to bring a baby into the world. While navigating the unprecedented COVID-19 lockdowns, we were spending a lot of time in the house imagining what our life would be like with a new baby. A Black baby. Perhaps a Black boy. What kind of world would we want him to grow up in? Certainly not one as violently racist as this one.

The families of Ahmaud Arbery, Breonna Taylor, Rayshard Brooks, and George Floyd appealed for justice while Black Lives Matter protests spread like wildfire, burning the myth of peace born of our silence. Volume was the name of the game, and in a league full of Black women, my fellow WNBA players rushed to leverage our collective platforms and resources toward this critical moment. I was both proud and frustrated. Companies and organizations rushed to do "something," and it was difficult sifting through what was only designed to save face versus legitimate steps to eliminate the difficulties of being a person of color in the United States. The basic human rights that caused city after city to rally for were the very principles our country was built on. When we were negotiating and discussing what we were willing to sacrifice, another player brought in an important perspective: Why did it always fall to women, and Black women in particular, to save the day? In the end, what we accomplished for the league and the country at large was historic, particularly in supporting Senator Raphael Warnock's candidacy. And more than that, I was humbled by our commitment to having intraleague conversations about racism, police brutality, and how we wanted to meet this moment. Hopefully, players would be met with more institutional support long term to be the change we wanted to see. Either way, we'd tackled some big conversations together and it fueled me to do the same in all parts of my life.

Being in the bubble with my wife and daughter made everything real for us as a family. Anya understood and supported me, of course, but her sadness and confusion were palpable. What did this mean for our children and the life they'd expect to have as Black kids in America? We'd talked about racism for years, but then and there, Anya truly came to terms with a society that was both foreign and shocking to her.

Looking back, it's as if Anya and I traded places. In the beginning, she was my tutor and guide, letting me in on the intricacies of Russian society—the good and the bad. I asked question after question, some silly, some serious, some that Anya couldn't quite answer, which led to hours-long debates. Now I was the professor schooling my wife on the nuance and legacy of white supremacy. Reading about history in a book removes the emotion and feelings, but learning and talking to each other about our own pasts and our countries' human rights legacies shifted the conversation from being black and white to very gray. We both came to the conclusion that listening and giving space to the other to feel the history was more important. The roles had reversed, and we were interrogating whether America could be a long-term and safe home for our children. I committed to being as patient and gracious of a teacher as she'd been with me. We had always been imperfect with each other and come out better on the other side. Now would be no different.

Our conversations weren't intellectual debates with one side playing devil's advocate. They were animated, and our emotions often flared because this mattered to us both. But we couldn't avoid the fact that we approached the topic of racism in America differently. I was born and raised learning to navigate both racism and sexism in this country, so I understood the stakes and pain intimately. Anya saw and understood that. Even though she would never fully understand the fear associated with being Black in America, she does know what it's like to love, birth, and care for people who are. Her insistence on fully understanding the moment we were in and all that had brought us here is part of what I love about her. We see each other, not in spite of our differences but with them front and center. I would never bear any burdens alone, and the fight to make this country a safe place for our family would always be a shared one.

Families Come in Different Ways

Lailaa was my first blessing and introduction to motherhood, but I always knew I wanted to have more children with time. Family is my fuel; having a house full of laughter and love is what I live for. Seeing how much having Lailaa opened up my heart made me want to experience that over and over, and to give Lailaa the sibling experience I had and cherished. When my relationship with Anya became more serious, my mind immediately went to how different motherhood would look in a same-gender relationship. From conceiving children to parenting and navigating homophobic social norms, I didn't have the home-court advantage I thought I'd have. We obviously couldn't lie down and create a child in the traditional sense, but we could with a little help from modern medicine. Everything was new terrain, but I wasn't in it alone. Anya and I talked often and openly about what we wanted for our family and the options available to us.

Not long ago, there weren't many options at all for couples like us—two women who love each other. The ability to create a family is something I took for granted when I was a young woman aspiring to motherhood. Suddenly, I was staying up late at night with the computer screen glowing back at me as I researched procedures like intrauterine insemination (IUI), in vitro fertilization (IVF), and gestational carriers or surrogates. With sperm donors, there are known- and unknown-donor paths, private and not, depending on how much you want to know about your donor and how much you want them to know about you. Many of these options didn't exist even a generation ago or were in extremely experimental stages. My independent research and conversations with friends encouraged me that science had advanced to a place that made motherhood more accessible than many would think for LGBTQ+ couples like us.

But the reality is that the existence of medical research is only one part of the conversation. Even when options and treatments grew safer, they were primarily marketed toward straight couples struggling with fertility with medical providers being hostile toward LGBTQ+ people or outright denying care. It wasn't until 1982 that a major sperm bank was opened and began supporting single women and LGBTQ+ families. It wasn't until 1999 that a gay couple both appeared on their child's birth certificate, and it didn't become illegal to discriminate against LGBTQ+ people seeking access to fertility treatments until 2008—only four years before Anya and I first met.

The history of LGBTQ+ family planning made the process seem daunting and isolating, with an endless amount of hoops we had to jump through to simply grow and love our family. But we also had a lot of gratitude for the answers and protections we do have that weren't available even a decade or two ago. We benefited from the advocacy and investment of those before us. Because of them, our journey wouldn't be quite as rocky, but it wasn't completely smooth, either.

The first thing we realized about LGBTQ+ family planning is how expensive everything is. And I mean everything. Securing sperm from a donor can cost thousands of dollars per vial, and you need a vial for each attempt at conception. Then there's the procedures themselves. IUI is one of the more affordable options, but it has less of a success rate because sperm is inserted into the uterus and has to fertilize the egg on its own. IVF—by nature of the egg being fertilized outside the body and then reinserted afterward—has a far greater chance of success but can cost upward of fifteen thousand dollars each try. We're lucky we didn't need someone else's uterus because don't even get me started on surrogacy. Whew! It's a lot and adds up quickly, with insurance often not subsidizing treatments until you are proved to be "infertile." (For some reason, many providers mandate heterosexual couples to show only three months of active and unsuccessful attempts while LGBTQ+ couples are required to demonstrate six months' worth. The double standards are real!)

Having more children was a mutual priority that we'd prepared for and we were privileged to have the resources to consider all of our options. This decision needed to be what was best for our family holistically, and only the two of us knew what that was. Luckily for us, we are blessed with many friends and loved ones who have explored these same options themselves and offered us their invaluable insights. Our network and village came through in a big way with reflections on what they wished they'd known earlier, options they should have asked more questions about, and referrals to medical providers we could trust.

An and I took it all in, debriefing with each other about what resonated. We didn't want to feel backed into any corners by what others thought we should or shouldn't do, so we didn't divulge much about the direction we were leaning until we felt confident about it. It's easy to be swayed when you're on the fence yourself. But with our feet firmly planted, we were the captains of the ship. This was especially import-ant to me because I didn't want our gender to change the way people respected us and decision-making as parents. I didn't consult anyone about conceiving Lailaa beyond general advice, and I didn't want to feel as though I needed a chaperone simply because we're two women.

What I learned during this process is how much agency matters. Sometimes a phrase is so popular that we forget its true meaning, but I never felt more pro-choice than when staring into the eyes of my wife knowing that the ball was truly in our court. There are no wrong answers generally, and people shouldn't be shamed or judged for what works best for them. What mattered to us was that we cre-ate a truly blended family where no one feels left out or unloved. We also wanted a donor who we felt was a good human being and carried traits we'd love to see in our kids.

In the end, An and I decided that she would carry our children and that we'd use a private sperm donor that we selected. For our first pregnancy together, we planned to use Anya's egg and then use my egg for our next with An being the gestational carrier for both, and the same sperm donor for both. With the weight of that decision off our shoulders, I realized another new vantage point to navigate: being the non-carrying mom. Motherhood and pregnancy had always gone hand in hand when I envisioned my future family. My bond with Lailaa began in the womb when I felt her kicks and made changes to my lifestyle based on the fact that I was literally responsible for grow-ing her inside me. I didn't question my ability to love children I didn't carry, but I did feel as though I was fighting for my place as a parent at times. Never with Anya, but with the outside world.

Our first doctor's appointments were my blunt awakening to how different motherhood would be for me this time around. With Lailaa, I assumed the position at the center of the room. The doctor asked me lots of questions, and I was the focus, responsible for my growing baby's care. When Anya and I walked in together, pregnant with our first child, the doctor directed everything toward her. Do you want to get this vaccine? How is the baby? Are you feeling movement yet? We want to see you next week and do XYZ in the meantime . . . It rationally made sense being that her body was the one nourishing and protecting our little one, but it was almost like an out-of-body experience. For the first time, I was the secondary parent as far as others were concerned.

Anya and I checked in about everything and made decisions together, but still I felt the need to assert myself. "Hey!" I wanted to shout. "I'm here and present, and I have opinions on my future child, too!" Especially early on, I took ignorance as disrespect. If people didn't assume I was a parent, as well, or speculated loudly (and wrongly) about our family dynamic, I felt a deep urge to correct and teach them. With time, I learned to separate those with good intentions from the nosy people who saw this beautiful moment in our lives as gossip to report on.

I also learned to rest on the fact that I had nothing to prove to anyone. Anya and I know how much we both put into having children together. From choosing our donor to being at every visit, my fingerprint was all over our future little one. Plus, I could support Anya in ways that others simply couldn't because I'd been in her shoes before. No two pregnancies are the same, but I knew the anxieties and changes she was experiencing. I could support, coach, uplift, and watch out for her in a different way because I intimately understood what she couldn't always put into words. It also allowed me to bring some levity and humor, goading An on. My brother would try to tell me that I couldn't crack pregnancy jokes since I wasn't the one carrying the baby, but I'd joke back that *he* couldn't say anything to his wife, but I'm literally built different and get the pass.

Watching my beautiful wife glow and grow through pregnancy was an incredible experience to witness. What I didn't love was that negativity had followed this pregnancy, as well. With Lailaa, the public debated whether having a baby at that stage was career ending. When we announced our pregnancy with Airr, or Goose as we lovingly call him, our comments sections were smeared with occasional nasty remarks about our child's missing father or how "unnatural" it was for two women to be having children together. It's mind-blowing to see how strangers could be so bothered by people they don't know loving, providing for, and raising their family. Particularly in a world where there are so many children who need and deserve safety and care that they aren't getting. It should be easier for people who want and have the capacity to be good parents to do exactly that.

In the face of so much unwarranted vitriol, An and I find affirmations elsewhere. Living in California meant that certain things didn't have to be a fight for us. When we went to receive Airr's birth certificate, I mentally prepared myself for a form that said "Mother" and "Father." My lips curled up into a smile as I looked at the spaces marked "Parent" and "Parent." It was such a simple paperwork shift, and something that I'm sure many people have rolled their eyes at. But what feels "over the top" or "aggressively inclusive" to someone is exactly what another family needs to be reminded that families come in so many shapes, sizes, and formations. Some children have no mother, others have no father; some are raised by two parents, others live with grandparents, aunts, uncles, or older siblings. Some people conceive their children without much effort at all, like Shelden and I with Lailaa, and other parents go to great lengths to make their families complete, like An and I with both Airr and Hartt. In each of these situations, children are a blessing. I don't care how my three babies found their way to me, I'm only endlessly grateful that they are here exactly as they should be.

The blended family that Anya and I have built is a family of multitudes. I joke often that we could be the United Nations version of the sitcom *Modern Family*: Black Americans, white Americans, Russians, Indians, Koreans, and Puerto Ricans. So many other beautiful ethnicities and nationalities are all reflected when we look around at family gatherings. By being around differences, it actually challenges and opens your mind to the idea that there is more than one way to love, create a family, celebrate life's big events, and cook food. Together, Anya and I have mastered celebrating our family's full range of cultural traditions. By actively celebrating, learning about, and honoring each other as whole human beings, instead of attempting to look past our differences, we've made concerted efforts to show up for each other. Doing so has opened us both up to a love that is deeper and more fulfilling than any we've known before. Nothing is more indicative of this than the way we close out each year.

Every December, my extended family comes together for a typical Black American Christmas. Movie marathons and dancing. Games and drinks. And of course a seemingly never-ending feast of soul food: turkey, greens, pork, mac 'n' cheese, sweet potato casserole, corn pudding, stuffing, homemade gravy, corn bread, and plenty of dessert. Each December, I devour everything on the table except the pork. (Ever since we got a pet pig, I haven't been able to eat it.) Our family recipes have been passed down for generations. I can remember making cinnamon rolls with my great-grandma Duke, sugar cookies with my Mimi, and my mom with her delicious chocolate pies.

Anya learning the Parker family traditions was amazing. We watch *National Lampoon's Christmas Vacation*, and we decorate cookies for Santa. The kids go to bed, and the real work begins. I go overboard when buying presents for our kids because I can remember the magic of waking up and seeing all the presents under the tree. Every year we "adopt a family" and commit to gifting them a little Christmas magic as well. Christmas day, we lounge in our pajamas, open gifts, and watch NBA basketball all day!

Then a few days later when it comes to usher in the New Year, we celebrate Russian style! The history buff in me can't help but give you some background: When Russia was part of the Soviet Union, holidays like Christmas were abolished due to the state policy of atheism.

Novy God developed as a secular New Year's celebration with shared traditions with Christmas, like gift giving, ornate decorations, and activities for children. On that day, Anya leads the way as the whole family buzzes around assisting our head chef with her ambitious and always scrumptious menu of what I call Russian soul food. She cooks all day long, preparing special dishes of Оливье (oliv'ye, potato salad), Борщ (borscht, classic beet soup), Кулебяка (kulebyaka, an elaborate and enormous pie stuffed with salmon, rice, and pickled chard), and Селедка под шубой (herring under a fur coat). As An cooks everything from scratch, we laugh and celebrate over rounds and rounds of vodka shots and caviar.

The first year of this tradition, my family and friends were a bit skeptical to try the dishes, but now, years later, my friends and family fight over the delicious borscht and herring. My heart smiles to see my wife so excited to share her culture and traditions with many people who have never been to Russia or tasted Russian cuisine. She beams as she describes dishes and their ingredients and how they are served back in Moscow. I am grateful for our people understanding that their willingness to try the food and ultimately enjoy it does more for Anya's soul than they know.

Just before midnight, we begin the preparation of writing our wishes for the New Year on pieces of paper. As the countdown happens, we prepare to burn our wishes and place them in the champagne before toasting and drinking our bubbly. Anya delivers an elaborate toast in a mix of Russian and English and everyone cheers; Anya and I stare into each other's eyes grinning. We lean in for the first kiss of the New Year, and I silently express my gratitude for everything that got us to this moment. I look at An and want to look at her like that for the rest of my life. I want to look at her the way that my Mimi continued to look at my B-Paw. The care in her eyes was always palpable. Those are the only relationship goals I could ever ask for.

PART THREE

Negativity

NINE

Different Isn't Always Bad

We live in a wonderful world that is full of beauty,
charm and adventure. There is no end to the adventures
we can have if only we seek them with our eyes open.

—JAWAHARLAL NEHRU

efore the WNBA came on the scene, the main opportunity for women playing professional basketball post-college was abroad in professional teams or representing Team USA in the Olympics. An entire different style of play lay across the waters abroad. The international game was different than in America—more physical, different rules, and, at the time, a trapezoid lane as opposed to the rectangular paint. I had always dreamt of testing out my game versus some of the best overseas players. When I was fifteen years old, an opportunity presented itself to compete in an international tournament with other girls from across the USA in Reze, France.

When our plane landed in France, my eyes widened in awe and didn't really go back to normal until the trip was over. The trip coordinators paired two players up and placed us all with homestay families, where our time spent away from basketball could be with locals. Fully immersed in the culture, we lived as the French did. The family I was placed with had two younger children and I got to see how other kids grew up countries away from Illinois. I'll never forget our first breakfast in France. I didn't know what to expect, but was hoping to try out a buffet of French pastries and maybe even French toast. Imagine my surprise when my homestay parents sat down at the table and presented us with bread, butter, jam, cold ham, and boiled eggs. No pancakes, bacon, ham, sausage, cereal, oatmeal, grits, waffles, French toast, or anything?! When I asked if they had ever heard of French toast, they were unsure what we were talking about. Though we were only teenage girls, we were athletes above all and a slice of toast wouldn't suffice for the appetites we had. I'm pretty sure we ate the entire loaf of bread and still wanted more!

My parents tagged along on the trip, staying at a nearby hotel and traveling to the gym where games and exhibitions were being held. One morning, they took me to Les Invalides, a number of buildings and monuments that chronicle and honor the military history of France. My dad and I walked through the museums for six or seven hours, slowly moving through each room, reading every plaque, and stopping to stare at every artifact, painting, and sculpture. Ever since I was a little kid, my dad and I shared a love for history. Countless nights we spent back home on the couch, watching World War II in color on the History and military channels. We would debate, discuss, and listen to each other as we compared and contrasted American history versus what we were learning there. My mom hung with us for the first few hours but became so bored by our glacial pace that she left to grab coffee and do some shopping. When she returned, Dad and I were still making our way through the museum. She had to pry us out of there and I promised to return one day.

I loved immersing myself in French culture, I was mesmerized by the cacophony of new sounds, smells, food, and sights. For so long, playing basketball and going to the Olympics had been exclusively about what I'd do on the court. For the first time, I realized that basketball could grant me more moments and opportunities like this. I wanted to see the world and the places that I was reading about in textbooks. When I realized that basketball could be the key to that, too, it lit another fire in me. On the court, I dominated. I left that tournament leading our team to the championship and taking home the Most Outstanding Player against other countries' junior national teams. We competed against Latvia, Lithuania, France, Russia, and many more talented up-and-coming athletes. This trip added to my growing confidence in my abilities—if I kept working hard, I could one day be one of the best in the world. For years, I kept in touch with many other players who I competed against at that tournament. Traveling enabled me to meet so many different people. We exchanged letters in the mail and I would smile at their attempt to write in English. Months after the tournament, some of my new friends would forget the time change and call our house phone at 2:00 a.m. My parents would act upset but would smile at my newfound international pals! I realized that I absolutely loved learning about, and learning from, different cultures, people, and places. I immediately knew I wanted to travel and learn about the world—and through basketball, that was possible.

Traveling also opened my eyes to the realities of the world and what it meant to be a female basketball player in America. In 2004, while playing in the McDonald's All American Game, I met Dwight Howard. He was a 6'10" center out of Atlanta, Georgia, and was the projected number one pick and led an impressive 2004 boys' class. At the time, you could jump from high school straight to the NBA. A number of the boys at the All-Star game were projected to go as lottery or first-round picks in the upcoming NBA draft. I was ranked number one in a heralded girls' class, but my future looked a bit different. I was preparing for a freshman year at the University of Tennessee while Dwight was gearing up for a professional career with the Orlando Magic. Our time at the games was brief, but Dwight and I walked away with each other's cell phone numbers and AOL Instant Messenger accounts. After talking a bit over the next few months, we arranged for Dwight to accompany me to my senior prom.

Our "relationship"—if you can even call it that—was short-lived. But because of when and how we met, the contrast between how our lives changed after the McDonald's All American Game couldn't have been starker. Dwight went straight into the NBA from high school and immediately signed with Adidas and launched campaigns with McDonald's and T-Mobile a few years later. I specifically remember reading an article not long after prom that detailed earning projections and talked about Dwight as a mogul in the making. The WNBA, due in large part to low salaries, has a rule barring players under the age of twenty-two or who didn't graduate from college from entering the draft. Despite the excitement around my game, I was headed to college in the era before name, image, and likeness deals, meaning my ability to make money was somewhat stunted for the foreseeable future.

As time went on, I started noticing that this world was made for men to succeed. Whether it was in the business world or just earning power, women could do the same exact job and be paid less. I wanted to be happy for Dwight, I did. But as I watched the red carpet roll out for him, I couldn't help but think about our parallel trajectories and how our careers were advancing at different paces. Dwight was and is an incredible athlete, but at that time, all I could think about was that my left hand was way better than his and that my mid-post game was more complete. Dwight was six ten and athletic and could jump out the gym. He was also a man in America entering an established league and half a century's worth of cultivation waiting for him. It wasn't fair that he had an opportunity to choose his path and monetarily capitalize on his abilities and skills, while I would have to wait. And even when I was in the WNBA, that wouldn't come with the same compensation that being an NBA player brought.

That juxtaposition is what frustrated me so much about playing abroad when that time came. I had set a tone in high school just like many of the NBA peers I'd come up alongside. This was the time before social media was hot and to use Facebook you had to have a

.edu email address to sign up. At this point, in 2004 and the buildup post–McDonald's All American Game, I had become somewhat of a household name. But none of that seemed to matter. Why did men get to build careers and fan bases right here in the United States while I had to go to four years of college, play in the WNBA, and then fly halfway around the world to receive reasonable pay? I'd sold out arenas, seen my jersey number everywhere, taken the time to do photo shoots with *Sports Illustrated, Slam, USA Today, Time,* you name it! And, yet, I still had to wait to earn a living from basketball. I thought I was angry at Dwight, but really, I was upset at the systematic exclusion of women athletes from the vibrant sports industry I'd come up loving. As of the 2020s, more than half of all WNBA players play abroad during the WNBA off-season. Women could be entertaining to watch, but the lack of visibility, and thus a real chance to succeed, meant that we were stuck taking what we were given and living in the reality that things were not going to change.

We led the nation in attendance every year while I was at the University of Tennessee, and it was a thrill to go on the road as the marquee game on every away opponent's schedule. I remember there was a time after a game versus Notre Dame when I was leaving the court and additional security had to be called as a result of the swarming crowds surrounding the pathway to the bus. From that point on Pat demanded I had security with me at all times. After I blocked an opponent's shot into the stands and exclaimed, "Are you serious!?", I saw my words appear on T-shirts sold at local arenas. Meanwhile, I was still in college eating Papa Johns for pregame meals. Once I entered the real world, I understood that talent and work ethic weren't always going to be enough. The rest of the world seemed as if it was on the sideline, insisting on what girls couldn't do, what lanes would be closed, and the opportunities that would only be extended to their male counterparts. Despite sold-out arenas and kids everywhere rocking my jersey, it didn't matter, they refused to believe it could carry over to the pros, where players like me could actually earn a living for tickets sold and gear purchased. No matter how hard girls and women fought for a shot, no matter what we were able to prove, the opportunity wouldn't be extended. If it didn't work in the past, no female in the future would be able to accomplish or be given a chance to prove its possibility, and we should just be grateful for what we have. My career was forced to look different not based on what I could or couldn't do but on what society thought I could handle. I wanted to continue to build my career right at home where my parents, brothers, nieces, and nephews could be present for it all. I wanted my nieces and nephews to see what's possible through my journey, and that girls should have just as much access and opportunities as the boys.

I was a little girl when I first became cognizant of the gendered double standards I'd find myself subject to over the course of my career. At home, it was different, but at school, the disparities jumped out everywhere. We had hand-me-down jerseys for the girls' middle school basketball team while the boys got new ones. Our girls' team attracted a lot of people to see us play, but we were still forced to play before the boys as if they were the main attraction and we were the opening act. In gym class, the girls were always picked last, and the boys rarely (if ever) passed the ball to us. The first and only time I was ever not picked first was in that middle school gym class; talent had nothing to do with it as the boys only focused on their own whims. Boys would overpower, exclude, and exert their dominance over gym-class games and were not only allowed to but actively encouraged to by the adults around us. It was like the system was training future chauvinists to carry on the cause. As we got older, the expected became reality: More girls lost interest and confidence in their abilities. The majority of girls drop out of sports around twelve or thirteen years of age as a result of lack of accessibility, opportunity, and confidence.

By the time I was actually headed abroad for the first time professionally, I was a young mom, wife, and professional athlete. Though I was still critical of inequity in sports and how the world still defaulted to the idea that boys and men were better, I also had a lot more life experiences under my belt and more responsibilities to bear. If Russia and other international teams were better positioned to compensate me at the level I knew I deserved, then who was I to look down at the opportunity before me? It wasn't just about me anymore; in order to provide the life I envisioned for my daughter, I had to roll up my sleeves and board the flight, so that's exactly what I did.

Over the next decade, I spent six seasons in Russia, two seasons in China, and one in Turkey. During that time, I often made more than twenty times as much as what I was making through the WNBA. In addition to bringing in compensation that wasn't yet possible playing basketball in the United States, I often played for teams that granted me a lifestyle that was a lot more lavish than what we had back home in the WNBA. Chefs, drivers, expensive watches and diamonds for my birthday, and bonuses when we won. International basketball made providing for my family light-years easier and gave us some once-in-a-lifetime experiences along the way. But being overseas, I was also diminishing my brand in the States because I was not present and visible. I couldn't shoot commercials or do photo shoots. There were trade-offs everywhere, and I didn't love that I was forced to choose, but I had to constantly calculate and evaluate what was best for us.

Lailaa and I were abroad just as much as we were "home," and we learned to build community wherever we were. Playing abroad was life-changing for us. What happened once we embraced the chance before us was magical. I am always grateful that, despite my doubts and anxieties, we boarded that flight to Russia. I sometimes stop and think of how playing overseas brought me not only the ability to take care of my family, but also allowed me to meet the love of my life, travel the world, learn about new cultures, establish lifelong friendships, and make priceless memories with Lailaa. And the best part is that my daughter got to be a front-seat passenger for it all. The world was her playground.

Becoming Global Citizens

I didn't just play abroad. I lived abroad. Especially having a daughter,
I couldn't compartmentalize my time "away" when it was just as significant in the eyes of my child. She had no concept that home was
often defined as one stationary place or about the guilt that tugged
at my soul whenever we would board the long flight across the water.
If you asked three-year-old Lailaa, she would have told you she lived
in Russia, and after counting perfectly in Russian, "*Odin, dva, tri,
chetyre, pyat,*" sometimes she would exclaim that she *was* Russian.
That's where she went to school, grocery shopped, went to playgrounds and museums, made friends, and hung out with her mom
and grandma. By the time she was eight, we'd lived in three countries
together, and she was able to remember and soak in even more about
the places she was hopping around.

I had to get over not giving Lailaa the childhood I was afforded. I
spent most of my young life in the same place with the same neighbors, friends, and classmates. I went to kindergarten through senior
year in the same school district. Most of the meals we ate were centered around our kitchen dinner table. The first time I traveled on
a plane—that I can remember—was when I was eleven. Traveling
most of the time meant we were taking a road trip to Des Moines,
Iowa, to visit my grandparents. Lailaa's childhood was anything but
constant. Or, rather, the only constant in her world was change. We
traveled often, and she became accustomed to boarding planes, packing, unpacking, starting over in new places, trying new cuisine, and
entering classrooms that spoke a different language than she did. The
entire time, I was navigating near-crippling mom guilt.

I used to beat myself up about what I was "subjecting" Lailaa to.
I'd lie awake, fearful that I was somehow ruining her childhood or
that I was a terrible mother. I would hear comments from friends
and families about "poor Lailaa." They felt bad for the fact she was far

away from the USA and her family. I used to allow these comments to impact my feelings about me as a parent, it increased my mom guilt. I was so scared about protecting her from a life overseas, far different from my own, that I didn't stop to realize maybe she didn't need protection. My family and friends meant well, but they weren't Lailaa's mother and weren't privy to her joy and excitement. A lot of the individuals making these comments had never left the USA in their lives. Waking up in a new place next to the constant love of her mother was all the stability Lailaa needed, and in fact, these experiences were actually teaching Lailaa things she'd never learn in a classroom.

I imagined when I became a mother that I would be teaching Lailaa all these lessons, but watching her abroad, tackling new experiences with grace and childlike curiosity turned me from the teacher into the student. She taught me that different doesn't mean bad and that differences are beautiful. Culture, cuisine, people, etc. I am better for experiencing it all. I was raising a daughter wise and empathetic beyond her years. So often we try to emulate exactly our positive experiences in childhood and steer clear of things we didn't like with our kids, failing to realize that we were raised in a different world. And just because this is a new experience doesn't mean it is bad.

Raising Lailaa all over the world is nothing like the stable, constant upbringing I had in Naperville, but that doesn't make one of those experiences bad. Only different. We both learned to be confident and sure of ourselves. Lailaa learned it from being the only Black American girl in her Russian preschool class, and I learned it many times as the only girl competing with and against the boys on basketball courts growing up. We both were able to experience adversity and come out on the other side with confidence and similar morals and values from two completely different upbringings. Lailaa was my priority no matter which country we were in. Instead of second-guessing my choices as a mother, I decided to stop framing our time abroad as something to get through versus a chance to teach my daughter open-mindedness through genuine cultural exchanges around the world with my baby girl. There was no reality for my daughter to compare her situation to. This was all she knew and loved. Comparison is joy's biggest thief, and I realized that scrolling through social media and looking at my friends' children's childhoods back in the States. I saw them at pumpkin patches and going to play places, going on field trips at school. But then I also saw the joy on her face as Lailaa made angels in the snow, learned to ice-skate, went to the circus, and begged for an after-school treat at McDonald's. I had to stop feeling bad for Lailaa's circumstance when there was clearly so much beauty in it. Childhood goes fast as it is. I was wasting so much time in dread, living to get back to the States that I was missing, instead of enjoying the precious moments of Lai's childhood.

Russia was the country where we lived the longest while abroad. During a lot of the earlier years, Lailaa was so young that without pictures and stories, she barely remembers living there. But Russia still holds a special place in my heart. It's where we first got the hang of our time abroad and learned to trust each other through exciting times and challenging ones. Children are so innocent and unfiltered because they haven't been taught to sugarcoat their words. In some instances, their unadulterated honesty is refreshing, but in unpredictable environments it can be nerve-racking. I've always wanted my children to be considerate and kind, and life abroad provided countless tests of just how much my sweet Lailaa could roll with the punches without saying anything offensive to our international friends.

Because Lailaa was so young when we went abroad, I wanted to be proactive about encouraging her to not be judgmental. We set some ground rules:

"We're not gonna say what we don't like until we've tried it," I told her early on. Whether it was a new food, place, dance, song, or tradition, it costs nothing to be courteous and see the world through someone's eyes. Most times, something you didn't expect to enjoy surprises you, and if not, the worst that can happen is that you tried something new and decided not to do it again. I couldn't be mad at that, but I wouldn't stand for my daughter turning her nose up at the world. Not with so much beauty around us and cultural differences to learn from.

"We will listen and learn how others in other cultures do things and not just think that it's America's way or the highway." After all, we were foreigners and in another country. American exceptionalism is real and can breed condescension in people of all ages. Different doesn't always mean bad, and there's more than one way to do things.

One of the first ways I modeled for Lailaa the effort and intentionality we'd bring to life abroad was in hiring a translator and taking Russian-language lessons. It was difficult to learn an entirely new alphabet and contort my mouth into new positions to make sounds I'd never had to in English. Russian is a complex mixture of rolled *R*s, smashed vowels, and melodic intonations. Nothing like the Romance languages I'm used to speaking or hearing back in America. It was incredibly difficult to step into such a distinct and new experience, but I wanted to demonstrate to Lailaa that I was going to lean in and fully immerse myself just as I expected her to do. It was also a reminder to myself that being a novice is a humbling and refreshing experience. We take for granted that we will be able to communicate with the people around us, so needing to put in real effort to understand and be understood made me feel small in some ways. Rising to the challenge reminded me that mindset makes the impossible possible. Though I never became fluent, I can still read Russian, even now!

When Lailaa was around three years old, she attended a Russian preschool where most of the other students didn't speak any English. I sent Lailaa to school reluctantly and scared that she would feel alone. I wanted to shield her from the language barrier and from feeling different. What if she had to go to the bathroom and couldn't communicate that? What if the teachers didn't notice she wasn't adjusting? I was wary of their schools and teachers. Were they up to my standards? I thought the American school system was better intrinsically and that there was no way I could trust a school in another country. But Lailaa needed to be around other kids, to have a schedule, to have somewhere to go play on a daily basis. I finally decided to practice what I preached, and it was the best decision I ever made. Children are children no matter where they are; their language becomes universal as they learn to smile and play with any and everyone. Lailaa played with her classmates through charades-like interpretations, common interests like dolls, and games everyone can enjoy. She even ended up teaching most of her classmates a bit of English. Besides, at that age no one is listening to anyone else that much.

Lailaa came home one day excited to set up a playdate with her new friend outside of class, thanks to an invitation from her friend's mother. My mom and I were a bit nervous about how this would play out, considering we spoke only enough Russian to get by. The team provided us a full-time translator to help us whenever we needed it, but I was extremely adventurous, and at times I loved the thrill and excitement of trying to figure it out ourselves. This was before the world of immediate Google Translate and the ease in figuring out how to navigate. It was important to me that I offer her a normal childhood of friendship and playdates, so to the friend's house we went.

It was normal in Yekaterinburg and in Russia in general for the apartment buildings to look lackluster on the outside. Oftentimes the buildings dated back to the early eighties, while some date back to Stalin-era Russia in the fifties and sixties. Even our apartment wasn't the most beautiful on the outside, but a luxury two-story apartment was nestled inside the tattered and beat-up building. It was very hard to tell what an apartment would be like from the building's exterior. The apartment building of Lailaa's friend was no different, the hallways were dark and narrow with light bulbs flickering and dim lighting. Grim to say the least. We walked up to the friend's home, knocked on the door, and waited for our hosts to greet us. When they opened the door and waved us in, I quickly saw that the interior was even more dilapidated and bare than the exterior. There was absolutely no flooring. Only compact dirt and concrete below rugs forming the foundation we stepped on. The one-room home was a mixed-use space for eating, playing, and sleeping with a small heater warming the area in its center.

As soon as I scanned the room, I wished I could have primed Lailaa. There were so many things I wanted to say, and above all, I didn't want her to make her new friend feel bad about herself. But there was no time to stop my three-year-old from running inside to her friend and blurting out, "Oh my gosh!" *Here we go*, I thought, cringing in anticipation before Lailaa continued, "Look, Mom! There's a dollhouse!" Lailaa and her friend beelined for the toys in a corner of the room and began playing with the dollhouse without batting an eye. My worries were completely unfounded and I was so proud of my girl at that moment. For not being consumed by the material world and still being able to enjoy the company of a good friend, no matter what they did or didn't have at their disposal. Lailaa always saw the positive and moved through the world full of grace and joy. She embraced everything thrown her way. A lot of her demeanor was shaped as a result of her experiences abroad.

In Russia, our weekends were filled with going to IKEA and looking around the mall. At this mall they had lots of indoor playgrounds, and for a snack, Lailaa loved the Cinnabons. We would walk through the different grocery stores in awe of the fruit, vegetables, and brands that were at the store. The toy store was always a hit, and so many times she would pick out Russian-speaking toys. She fell in love with *Másha i Medvéd'* (*Masha and the Bear*), a Russian cartoon that she watched while eating breakfast. The cultural exchange, open-mindedness, and ability to see the world with my baby girl proved that we could do hard things as long as we had the right productive mindset.

Living in Istanbul was Lailaa's personal favorite and where she had the most fun, likely because she was old enough to remember so much more of it. Though we were only there for two months, she was old enough to be more independent and explore her own desires. There was a coffee shop that she particularly fell in love with, and we truly became regular fixtures there. Lailaa would bring her homework and post up at one of the standing tables, ordering croissant after croissant.

In Istanbul, we explored the fish market, Turkish teas, and mosques. We went to the bazaar and shopped. Turkey was also the place where we built our most expansive community. There were so many different teams clustered and hubbed in Istanbul, which meant a lot more familiar faces and families in the same city. It made for some beautiful convenings and adopted family friends. Turkey taught us that we could fall in love with a city on the border of Europe and Asia just as much as Los Angeles, Chicago, or Las Vegas. I'm grateful for my teammates who welcomed my daughter with open arms, loving her and playing with her like she was their own. That support meant everything.

Pushing Through

One of the many challenges of being overseas was navigating celebrations and traditions when away. Normally, our time overseas was set up perfectly so that we were always back in the United States for Lailaa's birthdays, and she could be with family and friends. While I was in Turkey, the timing didn't line up, and we were set to spend her birthday in a new place for the first time. Lailaa decided she wanted to go back to the USA for her eighth birthday, and I was torn on what to do. As her mother, I wanted my baby girl close no matter what, but I couldn't be selfish. I had to respect my daughter's wishes. She made so many sacrifices for my career and my journey, I owed her some leeway when we could allow it. Off to the States she went while I cried all day at home missing my baby girl on the first birthday she spent away from me. I felt awful in that moment, asking myself what a career meant if it kept me from my little one on such a big milestone. When the photos from Lailaa's birthday party came in and I saw the smile on her face, I knew I'd made the right decision.

As with most areas of life, playing abroad was never black or white. We shared some amazing experiences that made up for the sacrifices we were making to be there, but it didn't mean those challenges were nonexistent. While abroad, I often had only Lailaa, my mother, and later Anya with me. Family and friends sometimes came out for a week or two and got the chance to watch me play, but by and large, I was fairly isolated while abroad—from loved ones and fans alike.

The first time I went abroad to play, Lailaa was seven months old, and my then-husband was playing for the Boston Celtics. Being a new mom in a completely new place is overwhelmingly all on its own, but being in a new place with a baby was a hazing process. For our first trip, I brought ten suitcases full of clothes and gear but also diapers, baby food, wipes, toys, books, and everything else I needed to parent. There was an entire nursery tucked away into our luggage because I didn't know if they had everything I was accustomed to like the brands I knew worked well for my baby. Arriving with our parade of artillery, arming us for the next few months, I was more terrified than I'd ever been. It's one thing to sign a contract from my cushy Los Angeles home, but now I was actually in Russia with a newborn, my mother, and the crushing reality that this was it. Outwardly, I felt the pressure to make sure both Lailaa and Mom were good, but inside, I felt as though we should turn right back around and call the whole thing off.

Even with my mom there and my translator's support, I often felt like I was wading through sludge to get through the day and week. Practices and games were followed by breastfeeding, co-sleeping, and catching up on all I'd missed while away. It took some time to get into a rhythm and enjoy the place we'd be spending the next few months and years. I couldn't always lean on American conveniences that Lailaa had access to for half the year. Some days, we turned on the tap water in Podunk towns and had to let the yellow liquid run until the rust was gone and we could enjoy clear water for a shower. In some of the places we've lived, the food didn't agree with us, and we survived off crackers and snacks we brought or packed lunches. That hardship brought us closer together than I would have ever imagined because we learned to lean on each other. It required creativity and a solutions-oriented mindset to do more than just survive, but to live no matter where we were.

Little by little, we acclimated to life abroad and embraced the newness of each day. I'll never forget celebrating Halloween with Lailaa there. When we first arrived in Russia, she was hardly old enough to participate, let alone remember anything. But by the time Lai was in kindergarten, I really wanted to make the day special for her and give her those core memories of trick-or-treating and getting dressed up in costumes. Taking traditions from the States and transporting them abroad required early planning like picking and packing a Halloween costume in early September, taking egg-dying kits over for Easter when we left the States in January, and shipping Thanksgiving or Christmas decorations from continents away. Our club at UMMC Ekaterinburg threw a Halloween party for all the players and their families, which brought a communal American experience to an international group of people. The party had cotton candy, music, and goody bags full of treats. It became such a core memory for us both that even when she went trick-or-treating in the United States, we'd compare it to Halloween in Russia. Even now, we still make a big deal of Halloween to keep the spirit alive. We usually throw a huge Halloween party at our house for family and friends with joint costumes, loads of pictures, and a spooky dessert like eye Jell-O or Oreo-cookie spiders. It's an extension of the magic we first unlocked in Yekaterinburg.

During my second season in China, I was playing in the northern part of the country, so far north that it was close to the border of Russia. It was cold, smoggy, and dark a majority of the time. Early in our time there, Lailaa and my mom became very ill. Lailaa's fever one night spiked to 104.4. We went to the hospital and were quickly seen. It's scary enough in the comfort of your own country and language when your child gets sick. But trying to get answers, make them feel better, and make decisions in an unfamiliar place is the worst. We had significant challenges figuring out what exactly Lailaa was sick with. Tests that would be second nature in America, we quickly learned how unreliable and tainted the cultures could be in China. After a couple of days, we found an English-speaking doctor from America. He informed us that, even if the cultures came back positive, they could very well be negative or inconclusive. The medicine that he prescribed might not be attainable, either. Depending on the pharmacy chosen, some sold placebos. Luckily, after a few days of Tylenol and Motrin, her fever broke and both she and my mom began to feel better. But, the realities of having my family overseas stuck with me. The differences in health care varied by country and I felt for each parent going through a similar powerlessness of watching your child be sick. These lessons shined a light on how opportunities and your place of birth significantly impact your way of life.

Our first season in China, Lailaa came to my first game and sat next to my Chinese translator. I felt a tap on my back and a little voice that asked me if she could go to the restroom. I motioned that it was okay to take her and that Lailaa was old enough to go into the stall on her own. The two were gone longer than I expected, and naturally, I was watching the door like a hawk. Finally Lailaa walked back into the arena with a ghostly look on her face. I checked in with her afterward to see what had happened and make sure she was okay. "Mommy, the toilet was a hole in the ground," Lailaa replied. I couldn't help but laugh. Our team-sponsored housing had many fixtures she was used to, including in the bathroom. But most toilets in the region required you to squat above the hole and handle your business. Lailaa, in her innocence, was confused and startled by the lack of a toilet seat or space to flush. With time, she learned not to bat an eye and do as the locals do.

Though our season in China wasn't as memory filled as our extended stretch in Russia or our cozy neighborhood in Turkey, Guangdong was still a beautiful part of our story. We found normalcy in the very out of the ordinary, like when we informally adopted a few stray dogs who always lingered outside the gymnasium. Lailaa noticed them first, behind the door we always used to exit, and before long we couldn't seem to get rid of them. We began bringing them water and food to be sure they were taken care of, and it was nice to have pets to take care of, a reminder that even when you seemed worlds away, some things were universal.

Life abroad was full of moments like those. Learning on the fly and putting on a brave face. Adapting to a foreign country is constantly finding new and different ways to do things. Our second stint in China was in northern China, closer to the borders with Mongolia and Russia. Guangdong's climate is a lot warmer, which makes sense considering its close proximity to Southeast Asia. The Xinjiang region where we were based was much farther north and experienced incredibly frigid winters. And lucky us, our time there coincided with one of the coldest winters in history. Some days were so cold with temperatures dropping to negative thirty degrees Fahrenheit. The sun didn't rise until close to 10:00 a.m. and it was dark by 3:00 or 4:00 p.m. The buildings couldn't be warmed up enough to counteract the subfreezing climate, so I practiced in a North Face coat and gloves. Even indoors there was no escaping the icy cold.

On top of the glacial winter we were enduring, this part of China was fairly isolated from other, more touristy parts of the country and home to industrial factories like coal-mining and power plants. This isolation not only meant meeting fewer people who spoke English but also meant the area was chronically polluted by chemicals and emissions. The air in Xinjiang was muggy and had a hazy brown-gray shade. It was common for everyone in the area to wear masks outside, long before COVID-19, simply to filter the air and breathe better. I had to take even more precautions for my health and to protect my basketball future.

Though the team I was playing with paid very well, the benefits beyond that were minimal. We were housed in a hotel room with no kitchen appliances or separated spaces to settle into and make ourselves at home. Our VPN for accessing American websites and TV shows barely worked, either, so in-room entertainment was hard to come by, as was a consistent connection for FaceTime and Skype. Talking to family was my lifeline in those cold and lonely months away. On top of that, every trip to a grocery store felt like we'd been transported to another place and time. The grocery stores were full of animals and foods that we weren't accustomed to seeing, like whole frogs out in the open with cut tendons to keep them from jumping and types of fish I had never seen before.

The language barrier was also the most difficult one we'd navigated yet. Each country I've played in has enveloped my family and me in a new language, from Russian to Turkish, but in each country we traveled to, a mix of simple sentences and charades could usually work in our favor. We always took the time to learn basic words in our host country's language and had benefited from the fact that English is so globally recognized that most people we come across can fumble through a conversation with us. In the northern part of China where we stayed, it was a completely different story. There, it seemed like there was an unwillingness to play along, and even common words weren't understood. From the "and um" words that sounded like the N-word in English to the way that all the leftovers from dinner were served at breakfast in our hotel the next day. We became accustomed to communal food with a dinner table turntable—or what we call a lazy Susan here in America—where the center of the table spins and everyone dips their chopsticks into the food over and over again. Everything felt daunting and out of our comfort zone.

We didn't get out much or have many adventures during our time in Xinjiang, but we still made the best of it knowing that we had one another and that one day we'd laugh about it all. A lot of times we ate downstairs in the hotel, which still proved challenging. The food was a completely different cuisine, and even the way chicken was cut was difficult because of all the bones. They didn't cut it the way we were used to, like breast, thigh and leg, and wing. It was just as the knife laid. An, who we were lucky enough to have with on this adventure, was especially resourceful when it came to ensuring we had our comfort foods, and she wasn't working with much. But when there's a will there's a way, they say, and Anya had will! She bought an electric skillet and would plug it in in the living room to chef up the best meals we'd had in months. It made our remaining time there a lot more enjoyable knowing we had her concoctions to look forward to each night. If I did have any remaining questions regarding our relationship, I felt even more steady after China. It's easy when things are great and familiar and in a routine, but with our family being across the water thousands of miles away, I saw the way we showed up for one another. Seeing my daughter find joy in bubble tea and bubble waffles, Anya found ways to make pancakes and coffee. We played games and tried to make the best of things. As a result of the internet working only certain hours of the day, we had some of our most intimate moments and conversations together as we piled into the bed and just talked about whatever was on our minds.

It was Christmastime while we were there, and I was grateful that my team made an effort to make it exciting for Lailaa. My teammates were always the highlight of my experiences abroad, and my time in China was no different. We built incredible bonds and my teammates went out of their way to make my family feel welcomed, oceans away from home. We had a team dinner and a game. Lailaa was so excited for Christmas and woke up at 3:30 a.m. to open gifts. At first I was upset, knowing I'd be exhausted by the end of the day, but then I realized I used to do the same thing, and she couldn't care less about my game schedule when Santa came!

Often we missed home tremendously. Lying awake thinking about the first thing we were going to do when we got back to the States. What got us through the moments and difficult times were one another. I felt grateful for my family, and I felt like I wasn't at this alone. My mom and Anya and Lailaa lifted me up when I would get frustrated and overwhelmed. I really felt sorry for the countless Americans who went overseas to play alone without a support system. No matter how challenging our time abroad got—even when navigating militarized cities, food we didn't love, harsh climates, limited Wi-Fi, and immense language barriers—we still had one another. There were stressful times where all we could do is look at one another, laugh, and mutter, "This will be a funny story one day!" Whom you surround yourself with makes all the difference when times get really tough. They not only cancel out the noise, but fill the space with joy and laughter. If I approached living abroad as a hurdle to leap over or a sentence to carry out, I would have missed the once-in-a-lifetime opportunities all around us. How many people can say they speak some Russian, have a favorite coffee shop in Turkey, and have visited more countries in their first ten years of life than some people do in a lifetime? Lailaa can, and her mom's international basketball career made that possible.

TEN

Better the Hard Way

Nobody in rap did it, quite like I did it.

—JAY-Z

People often ask me about which win stands out the most. Was it bringing home two NCAA championships with Pat Summitt and the Lady Vols? Was it Olympic gold? Was it any of the WNBA championships? Each of those accomplishments and triumphs holds a special place in my heart, but more than any win, I remember every loss. The losses creep into our bodies and settle. . . . We feel them in our bones for many seasons after. They haunt us in our sleep and taunt us while we're awake. Losing is definitely a more intense feeling. The wins are represented with rings and banners and are celebrated for years to come. The funny thing with winning is it's usually only satisfying for a little while. Then you want more. Winning feels incredible in the moment, then the next season you go back to wanting another championship, another medal, another ring. But the losses represent regret, what if, if only. Those feelings are difficult to process, but over time can turn out to be good lessons that get you over the hump. Wins are what everybody is heralded for. To be a champion is to be among the select few who can honestly say they battled the hard stuff and overcame it. Losing sucks. There's no way to describe the feeling and emotion involved with it. Losing challenges you to look in the mirror and ask yourself what you could have done better.

Even the GOATs and the best of the best lose more championships than they win. Tom Brady had seven Super Bowls and fourteen seasons where they didn't make it all the way. As great as Michael Jordan was, he won six NBA Championships but lost nine. I remember the first time I set my mind on winning a championship. I was a freshman in high school and had tasted a bit of success leading our NCHS team to the game before State. We were far exceeding our expectations, but that experience made me want to go all the way, to be one of the eight teams left playing in the state of Illinois. The state tournament was televised, and there was a pep rally and celebration; it was a big deal. I tasted what winning could and would bring and I would often dream of how rewarding it would feel. It made me want to get up and go work out on weekends and stay late after practice to get better. I knew this was my passion because it would wake me up at night from my dreams. Some were us hoisting the trophy and what that would feel like, and another I would have big tears in my eyes and a lump in my throat because I had felt the loss and my dream deferred again.

High school and my younger years taught me how much passion means and when you want something, don't waste time, work to go get it. We won back-to-back state championships my junior and senior year. In the closing minutes of the championship game against the number one team in the state, I pictured another offseason of disappointment. I thought in the time-out about that feeling I had last offseason after we fell short. The feeling the losses unleashed motivated me to fight to avoid that feeling ever again. At some point it isn't about working hard and learning and gaining skills in the offseason to reach your goal; it's about using all those skills and work ethic you learned when you actually get there. Trusting your preparation. Digging deep in the moment is the separation from winners and losers. Finding it when it counts. Trusting the skills you acquired and worked for in the offseason and tuning out the doubts and fears. It's leaning into your teammates and pulling confidence, strategy, and will out of them. Making them trust and know that you will lead them where they need to go.

My WNBA career began with the devastation of a last-second shot that cost us a trip to the finals. Having just won two out of the three NCAA championships I'd played in during college and grabbing gold at the Beijing Summer Olympics, I was on a winning streak that seemed cosmically designed. I needed a WNBA championship to complete my trifecta (or a triple crown, as I called it) and add new hardware to my trophy case. I foolishly believed working hard and wanting it badly was enough. Two of the last three championships I had been a part of were national collegiate championships, and in high school we won back-to-back to end that career. Winning was expected at this point, and I approached this new adventure and challenge in the WNBA no differently.

We entered the Western Conference finals with a home game that we easily won and were set to play the next two games in San Antonio. That season San Antonio had won all but two home games throughout the season. We were the team with a stacked roster and big dreams for what Lisa Leslie and I would accomplish together. We knew in the playoffs that road games are a grind, and this was no different. Though we held the lead most of the first half, we went into the third quarter down by three and never really regained our confidence. We were missing shots left and right, and the entire fourth quarter was a volley back and forth.

With less than two minutes to go, San Antonio point guard Becky Hammon missed a layup, and Lisa Leslie rebounded. On the next possession, I knocked down a crucial jumper and secured another lead for us that we tried to hold on to. With 11 seconds to go, Sophia Young made both of her free throw attempts, retaking the lead for San Antonio and keeping their hopes alive to extend their season. The following trip down the floor, my teammate DeLisha Milton-Jones snagged a big offensive rebound put-back to give us the one point lead once again! With 1.3 seconds left on the clock, San Antonio called a time-out.

I gazed up at the clock entering the huddle, I pumped my fist, slapped high-fives, and exchanged smiles with teammates. *We got this!* With little more than a second on the clock, Vickie Johnson inbounded the ball to Sophia Young, cutting away from the basket. I turned my head as Sophia went into her turnaround jump shot in front of my teammates' outstretched arms. Time stood still.

The ball hit the backboard before falling in right at the buzzer. My heart sank as I involuntarily dropped down to my knees. The Silver Stars celebrated around me on the baseline as I tried to compose myself. This game should have been ours. My stomach tightened and my fists clenched. "What if?" scenarios already began to replay in my head. Why didn't we put our 7'2" center Margo Dydek in the game to guard the ball? Should I have jumped and contested Sophia? Maybe we let our guard down a bit? Would've, could've, should've . . . DIDN'T! There was a deafening silence in the locker room as we showered and did media postgame. No matter how hard I tried to switch gears, suggest that the last possession didn't decide the game, and remember other crucial moments of the game, that last possession played on loop over and over in my head. When we got on the bus, our coach, Michael Cooper, sat staring into space. I walked past him on my way to my seat in the last row. We arrived at our hotel and I was the last to get off the bus. I tapped Coach on the shoulder and offered him reassurance I hadn't even yet offered myself. He looked me square in the eye and yelled, "When you have a lead on someone else's home court to go to the finals, you don't blow it. You don't miss opportunities like that!" Though I understood Coach's frustrations, I also felt as though he was prematurely conceding. We had another game to turn things around and still come out on top. We didn't rise to the occasion in that moment, but there would be other opportunities.

Michael Cooper is a Hall of Famer and one of the greatest defensive players of his generation. During his twelve years with the Lakers, Coop secured five championships and was an essential part of the Showtime Lakers dynasty. He knew from his time in the midst of the Lakers-and-Celtics rivalry how hard it is to win. He knew all the feelings that I would experience over the next nine years in fighting for that elusive WNBA championship. Year after year, loss after loss, my glazed-over gaze on the bus resembled Coop's. I always thought back to that moment on the bus and now "get it" even more. Rarely does the end of the game come down to X's and O's or plays; it comes down to rising to the occasion. The true definition of a champion usually shines brightest in those pivotal moments as the time ticks down.

A last-second shot like that breathes fire and passion into a team. While we were attempting to reignite our team morale, San Antonio was poised, confident, and ready for game three. When we battled them again the very next day, we could feel the difference. Becky Hammon went off, scoring thirty-five points in thirty-eight minutes. She single-handedly led the Silver Stars to victory. Despite her 5'6" frame, she was the best player on the floor. At that point, San Antonio was playing with house money. We had given them an opportunity, and as a result, they played loose, free, and determined. Every screen Becky came off of, no matter how we defended her, she let it fly and was unconscious from the three. Becky and Sophia combined for 53 of the team's 76 points. We had given Sophia a revived confidence and Becky proved to be a leader who was primed to show up for her team when it mattered. We ended up losing 76–72. As I watched the fans erupt and the Silver Stars celebrate on their home floor, I looked at Becky Hammon in admiration. Undersized, underdog, on the ropes, and undervalued at times, she had single-handedly beat us.

I have never been the most patient person, and at times, much to my detriment, I have had to keep learning the same lesson over and over. The years ticked by where we would advance to the playoffs and fall short. That 1.3 seconds could have changed the trajectory of my career, I often thought. Sometimes mojo is more important than skill, and luck is more important than experience when it comes to forming the right mindset. That loss, if I'm being honest, took a little bit of my confidence away. It had rarely taken me more than two years anywhere—whether high school or college—to climb the mountain and be on top.

In 2013, I won MVP of the regular season, and it was a personal statement to the league that I was healed and ready to make good on my promise from all those years ago. When I first entered the WNBA, I was asked how many championships I wanted to win, and I greedily answered, "Nine or ten." Well, there I was in year six and still nothing, not even a finals appearance. By 2014, my seventh year in the WNBA, I could hear the mumbles of fans and media, questioning why I hadn't yet earned a ring. I put a tremendous amount of pressure on myself to deliver. I was finally healthy after pregnancy and various injuries. After years of playing through pain, I wasn't limping or at 75 percent; I was at full throttle. I wasn't a rookie anymore, either. My experience in the league showed in my game. I had the skill set and had mastered playing at my own pace, dictating action instead of reacting to it. But, in the brightest, biggest moments, I could feel my body tense up and brace for what lay ahead, almost anticipating things not working out. *Here we go again.* Just six short years before, I loved those big moments, I relished the opportunity to make big plays down the stretch, I expected to prevail, I wanted the ball in my hands because I knew I would deliver. Every time we fell short, my belief in those moments shrunk. I deserved to win, I thought. Was there a way back to that young twenty-two-year-old energy and confidence?

I dedicated my offseason to lifting weights, staying in the gym, and watching film—even while playing overseas. I picked the brains of people I respected and who had been through what I was now experiencing, like Kobe Bryant and Kevin Garnett. I leaned on their advice in my pursuit of a title, remembering that dedication to the process married with relinquishing results would come through for me. It wasn't always easy, especially for someone so competitive and laser focused. How can I relinquish the results if the results are what are keeping me from the championship I so desired? I had to fight back the creeping thoughts that even if I do everything right and even when I train in the offseason, I could still come up short. Learning to win on this level required the realization that, at any point, I could fall short. That's not to say I should be waiting for the other shoe to drop or live in fear. Quite the opposite actually: Worrying about the future doesn't actually change the future. It just takes my focus away from the moment and diverts my confidence that was built on all the preparation and time I put into being ready for those moments.

One of my problems was that I was thinking about wins and losses as things that had happened to me, not *for* me. At some point, my mindset shifted and, instead of being on the attack and fearless, it seemed time and time again I just braced for impact. I was operating like a damsel in distress waiting to be saved, instead of learning from what was being thrown at me and taking control of my path. I've always felt, as the novel *The Alchemist* describes, that the universe conspires to help good people achieve their dreams when their intentions and motivations are pure. I still believe that to an extent. Questions swirled every offseason: Did I even deserve to win anymore?

It was as though I was playing under a dark cloud. No matter how hard I worked, the result remained the same. I became superstitious, walked on eggshells, read self-help books, and dedicated myself to identifying my weaknesses and working far past exhaustion to improve them. Over time, that cloud stayed with me like a weighted vest. It burdened me and made me feel heavy with self-doubt and worry. It made me move with hesitation as I felt my purpose drained out of me. Trying to accomplish things with regret tied to your foot like a ball and chain is nearly impossible. I was magnetizing negativity toward myself by believing the lie that losing was inevitable. It was inexplicable and eating me alive. I began to question my identity and self-worth. One missed basket or faulty drive could send me spiraling, and I started to see that my inner voice had become my harshest critic. How could I expect to win with that cruel feedback ringing in my ear?

For a while there, I'd convinced myself that I simply couldn't win a closeout game. Oftentimes we would get out to a solid game-one win but fail to capitalize on the momentum to keep the lead and close out the series. In 2012, I was scoring and dominating. In our two games against the Minnesota Lynx, I had 25 points, 11 rebounds, 4 assists and 33 points, 15 rebounds, and 5 assists with 4 blocks, and it didn't make a difference. We lost both games in a clean sweep for Minnesota. I didn't understand what more I had to do to get the win. Time and time again, the results kept telling me it wasn't about stats. Again, the game came down to a last-second possession that we failed to score on. It seemed as though no matter what I did, time and time again we came up short on the final play. I kept asking myself what would get me and my team over the hump of losing. Devastation became synonymous with the closing minutes of games. I stopped believing in our abilities and resigned myself to the idea that, no matter what, the ball would not bounce our way. That somehow I had bad luck, and there was nothing I could do. I remember watching the movie *Like Mike* with Lil Bow Wow where a pair of sneakers allowed him to hoop like an NBA player. Whenever the small teen was wearing the magical sneakers, he could suddenly hit half-court shots and fly above his opponents, but without them he lost all his powers. I felt like my whole life I had the sneakers and, suddenly, my winning ways were snatched from me and transformed into terminal last-second-shot heartbreak.

Saying the start of 2016 was tough is an understatement. I was cut from the Olympic team, my husband and I were separated, and

Pat passed away in June. Suddenly, a championship seemed like the least of my worries. That year was heavy, and it was challenging to balance my emotions daily. The rush of anger from being cut from Team USA, anxiety regarding the decision to separate from my daughter's father, and grief because it didn't seem fair that one of the best humans I knew was no longer here. The heaviness from all the emotions off the court only seemed to lighten when I stepped in between the lines. I leaned on basketball and my teammates a great deal during this difficult time. Playing basketball that year became a game again. Life was serious and my escape was falling back in love with basketball. I stopped worrying about results, championships, and pressure and just played. I didn't have my best year statistically, but I showed up every day as best I could. For the first time, I gave myself grace. The regular season flew by and as a result of our focus, attention to detail, and the stellar season MVP Nneka Ogwumike had, we ended the regular season number two behind the Minnesota Lynx.

Just as we had in the past, the early rounds of the playoffs were anticlimactic. We took care of the Chicago Sky in four games and advanced to my first ever Finals Appearance in my nine-year career. All those years before, I was naive to think that opportunities and chances grow on trees. My twenty-two-year-old brain, coming off of back-to-back college National Championships and a gold medal, could never fathom I would be thirty before I would finally advance to the WNBA Finals. Yet, here I was . . . finally. It felt surreal the entire time. During the playoffs, the first thing I thought of in the morning was a championship and the last thing I dreamed of at night was a ring. The stage was set and the ball was tipped in Minneapolis's Target Center in front of a packed arena, most of which was cheering against us. The 2016 WNBA Finals were underway.

In game one, we found ourselves back in the same position we had been my entire time in LA: another to-the-wire closing moment. The game was all tied up, and we wanted to win it or go to overtime, with no chance for them to shatter our hearts in regulation. Chelsea Gray dribbled the clock down, and as she attacked the right side, Maya Moore showed help, leaving Alana Beard open. All year, our team had made the right play, and in that moment, Chelsea was primed to do the same. Trusting Alana, Chelsea passed the ball as the clock ticked down. I was under the basket with a clear view of the shot as it left Alana's hand. I exhaled and fought for position, knowing there wasn't going to be enough time on the clock for an offensive rebound. The ball went clean through the net, barely touching the rim. My eyes widened, and I was in disbelief. Everyone rushed Alana and tackled her on the baseline, but I was slow to react. In disbelief, I checked every possibility of something happening. Did she get the shot off in time? Was there a whistle? Did the time actually expire? If you look back at the video you can see me walk hesitantly to the bench to circle up for a time-out and another Lynx possession or an overtime that I was sure to come. But after a few moments of the referees reviewing the play, the game was called. We had won. We had actually won on a last-second shot! We beat the Lynx in game one on *their* home court.

I remember sitting at my locker with my head in my hands. If you didn't know the results, you would have thought I was wallowing in defeat. But I knew this was the moment I had to quiet my mind, level all emotions, and lead this team through the storm I had been battling since 2008. We couldn't be satisfied with this victory. I sat there for about an hour with ice on my knees and just stared straight. I didn't want to look at my phone and succumb to the many messages of congratulations that were sure to be on there. Kobe's voice was echoing in my head saying, "Job not finished." If I allowed myself to relish the victory, ultimately letting my guard down, I would lose the focus needed to win the next few games. I decided that I would act as if we'd lost. Losing myself in the what if and the emotions of being down. The mistakes are more glaring when you lose. But it's extremely hard to manifest that emotion without actually going through it. I heard Pat's voice: "Handle success like you handle fail-ure." Is this what she meant all those years ago? This is the test she challenged me to pass every year at Tennessee.

Going into game two, I did what I had done so many times before: I tried to control the outcome from the first tip. But I was awful. I scored just 6 points and had 4 rebounds. I shot 3–12 from the field. We lost by nineteen points, and the Lynx evened the series out. I asked myself why my energy was the way it was in one of the biggest games of my career. How did we show up in the manner we showed up with a championship on the line? On the flight home, I beat myself up. I didn't look at the shots I'd missed; I looked at the drive I'd played with.

Game three was pivotal, and we knew it. Back on our home court after stealing the home-court advantage in our game-one vic-tory, which meant, if we did things right, we wouldn't have to win another game on their floor to win the series. We could close this out at home. I told myself one thing before game three. I didn't over-analyze or think too much. I simply said to myself, *I am going to bring the energy. Everything will not go perfectly, but my will and extra effort can end some of the not-so-good plays in a positive way.* Often when I looked back at film, I could see myself mid-play second-guessing or seeming disappointed in a shot instead of going after the offen-sive rebound. Kevin Garnett has one of the best reflections: "Your job as a competitor is to grow your opponent's doubts." All those years prior, my opponents had done their job. They had grown my fear. There's a balance between being overly confident and Gregg Popovich's appropriate fear where you know you could lose so you don't get too cocky; that's about honoring the fact that when you get to the finals, the separation between your team and your opponent is slim. Any type of edge can prove to be the difference. But I had fallen into the fear of losing. And operating out of fear is never a recipe for success. Today couldn't be that kind of day.

My game-three performance wasn't perfect, but I definitely brought the energy and effort. In the words of Mike Tyson, "Everyone has a plan until you're punched in the mouth." We came out, punched first, and took a 32–17 advantage after the first quarter. We were the first to loose balls and rebound and had a pep in our step defensively. We imposed our will on them. For the first time, I was seeing firsthand that most of the time a game comes down to enforcing plays and putting your opponent on their heels. We took game three not because of strategy—X's and O's or adjustments—but because we played harder than they did. In my postgame interview with LaChina Robinson and my daughter on my hip, I took accountability for my previous two games in the series. I needed to be better than I was and, as a result, we were one game away from a championship.

Despite telling myself to stay focused and not look ahead, I remember right before my pregame nap dreaming of jumping on the scorer's table à la Kobe and yelling into the stands as the confetti fell. I couldn't help but dream of actually winning a WNBA title. What it would feel like, what I would do, whom would I hug? Those thoughts made my mind race. It was hard to not drift to the prize when we were so close.

During game four we were home playing in front of our fans and so many other hoopers and celebrities. We were up 2–1 in the series with a chance to seal it on our home floor. This was the way the story was supposed to be written, I thought. My first title in LA with Magic Johnson, part owner of the Sparks, front and center along with Kobe Bryant and his family all there to watch us hoist a trophy. Or so I thought. This time, Maya Moore put us on our heels. She was relentless, pouring in 31 points, 9 rebounds, and 4 assists to single-handedly carry Minnesota to victory. We played the game seemingly in a daze. We woke up toward the end and gave a valiant effort to close the lead in the final minutes of the game, but it didn't make the difference we needed. Yet again, the whistle didn't go our way as the referees missed a blatant backcourt violation that would have given us possession back and a chance to take the lead. Kobe nodded his head in disbelief as Maya put on an offensive clinic with step backs, fadeaways, and pull-up threes. Kobe was giving his nod of approval at her skill set and her ability to take over. On *my* court.

In the locker room after the game, I was devastated. Instead of champagne and celebration we were given our itinerary for the trip to Minnesota in the morning. Magic came in and tried to revive our group with a pep talk, but to be honest my gaze barely left the floor. Pregame we had the championship in hand, and now we had to get back on a flight and travel to Minnesota to face them on their home court. Michael Cooper's words from way back in 2008 rang in my head. When you have the chance to take care of business and close a team out, you do it. Well what now? Give up? We still had one more shot at it. The next twenty-four hours were a blur, but somehow through the haze we ended up back in the familiar hotel in Minnesota.

The night before game five, I called my brother Anthony to vent about the referees not calling an eight-second violation on Minnesota. "Just once, I want a call to go our way," I said exasperatedly. There had been so many on-the-fence calls that leaned against us, and I could feel my angst rising up in me.

Talking to Anthony, feelings of defeat began to creep in. That year had been a tough one and still I'd worked my ass off to make it to this point. If we lost in game five, it would have all been for nothing. There are few things more exasperating than being inches away from something you've wanted your whole life, only to be rolled down the hill to begin the trek again. It was less about wasted time and more about all the time that I knew I'd have to put in the following season just to have a chance to be back at the same place. Staring up at the figurative mountain ahead of me—remembering the aches and time away from family—I realized this couldn't be the end. I wanted to be Becky Hammon, Maya Moore, MJ, Kobe, Kevin Durant, and the list goes on. It was my time to stop feeling sorry for myself and be what I knew I could be.

Anthony refused to let me wallow in my misery when I still had time to do something about it. "Do you know why golf balls come so dented instead of smooth all over?" he asked. It was the most random interjection, and I wasn't quite sure what it had to do with me or game five. He continued on, telling me that golf balls are dented on all sides, but they used to come perfectly smooth and spherical. But these smooth balls were unpredictable; you couldn't direct them through the wind or get the balls to go exactly where you needed them to land. With time, someone noticed that the more you played with a golf ball, the more dented it would become. With each new dent, the ball traveled with more ease and the golfer hitting the ball could not only hit the ball farther, but with more accuracy to the left or right. With lots of dents, the golf ball could curve when prompted and glide through the air. We were those golf balls. We were imperfect and bruised by losses, disappointments, attempts, and misfires. But each swing left us better prepared for the next drive. We just had to be willing to take the next swing with confidence, with the understanding that each dent had its purpose. At the end of our conversation, Anthony reminded me that I had shared the book *Chop Wood Carry Water* with him. That story came from that book. I had all the necessary skills, I had put in the work, and I was ready. I just had to shed my own doubt.

I barely slept the night before game five. Overthinking and worried about the outcome yet again. Before closing my eyes, I sent a text message to my teammates. I knew we were all in our respective hotel rooms reflecting on our last game and what was ahead of us. I wanted us to be on the same page about staying hungry and letting our confidence carry us home with the championship trophy. To motivate each of my teammates, I shared Anthony's story about the golf balls. As soon as I pressed *Send*, texts and reactions began pinging in response. Everyone was buying in and locked in. With that, I had one more job to do. I did a quick search and found the cutest puppy. *Either I'm leaving here with a puppy and a championship or just a dog*, I thought to myself with a chuckle. No matter what, I'd be leaving the state of Minnesota with something good.

The next morning at film before shootaround, Coach Agler asked the group a question: "If at the beginning of the season you were given one game to win a championship, would you take it?" That question hit different. I'd never thought of it that way. Hell yeah, I would have taken that even if we had to travel to the moon and play basketball. My gaze had been low and my words few since our defeat in game four. I realized that the leader I knew I needed to be couldn't just step up when things were going right. If anything, the team needed me more now than ever. I looked up at Coach, and my mindset shifted from we have to play a game five to we *get* to play a game five.

It takes a different mentality to win on the road during the regular season, let alone to win a championship on someone else's home court. Before lying down for my pregame nap, I heard my phone ding. A message popped up from Kobe Bryant. "How you feelin'?" I questioned how to answer that. I landed with "I want this so bad." He said, "Don't worry about the end result. It will come. Just play." The next message came right after: "Do it the hard way. It always feels better that way anyway. Live with you or die with you. You can't die in a gunfight with bullets in the chamber." The same message after all these years, but delivered in different ways over and over. I'm stubborn, but even I knew it was time to lean into everything I had learned and that required me to truly relinquish the results and focus on performing my best.

Right before game five, I stood in the middle of the court and blew into my hands during warm-up. I looked around; 19,423 fans all packed into the Target Center. Most of them were in green, heckling, yelling, taunting our team. It was our team and a small group of fans against this entire arena and city. Nobody there in that building wanted us to win. Secretly, I used to love playing away games as a kid. The boos when I had it going motivated me far more than the cheers. I shifted my mindset back to that fearless little girl who just played basketball.

The first two minutes of a game of this magnitude, I don't care how in shape you are, you are completely out of breath in those first couple possessions. The excitement, the nerves, the atmosphere all cause teams to play superhard and superfast the first few times up and down the floor. Before long, we had settled into the game. My first bucket, I got to the paint for a nice right-hand layup in front of the rim. It always feels good when your first bucket goes down. I was engaged on every play, on both ends of the floor. I kept telling myself and the team that we never know when that championship play is going to come. Let's be ready to make it.

We fell behind at halftime by six points, and coming out for the third quarter we knew we needed to be ready to counter as they were a dominant third-quarter team. I could hear Pat's voice in my ear saying, "You can't control if shots go in or shots don't, but what you can control is defense and rebounding." We held our own. In a game that had twenty-four lead changes and eleven ties, every possession was valuable.

I truly got lost in the game. Not looking forward, not looking back, but staying in the moment. The third quarter I remember playing so free. I was deliberate and not rushed. Hesitation had paralyzed me in previous games. Not today. I was just hooping. Kristi Toliver bounced me the ball on a pass, and I pumped fake, drove the lane, floated to the left side, and finished a layup with my off hand over and around Sylvia Fowles in what should have been an and-one.

The key to tight end-of-game situations are the little things. Boxing out so that your opponent doesn't get a second chance at a shot, setting good solid screens, keeping your spacing on the floor, remembering and being deliberate in your defensive schemes. But it's also important to remember that basketball is a game of runs, and it's crucial to keep your mind present as the possessions wind down and the clock ticks to zero. Finally, the last ten minutes rolled around, and we entered the fourth quarter down one point. It was back and forth for quite a bit early in the quarter, but after eleven straight points by Chelsea Gray, a Kristi Toliver fading-left three-pointer as the shot clock expired, and a layup off an offensive rebound by me, Minnesota was forced to call a time-out to stop the momentum. We were up 71–63 with 2:58 left in the game. It was hard not to taste it, but we knew the Lynx weren't done.

Coming out of the time-out on the first possession, I went to double the post, and the referee decided at that moment to call a defensive three seconds. This effectively meant that the Lynx got one free throw and the ball back. I remember turning around in frustration; yet again, the refs. But quickly, I refocused, knowing all we had done to get to this point and that this wouldn't derail me. Maya knocked down the free throw and then the same possession came off a baseline triple screen to hit a catch and shot three. The lead we had quickly shrank to just four points.

Before we knew it, after a bad offensive possession and a turnover, the game was tied. Just that quickly. We had the ball and got it into the post to Nneka, who turned around and shot a jump shot as the shot clock hit zero. It was questionable whether she got it off in time, but the game resumed, and the referees never stopped play, and the rules state that the game must stop right then and there or it can't be reviewed later at a dead ball. The Lynx came down in flow, and Seimone Augustus knocked down a pull-up jump shot. The game was tied again with 35 seconds left. Minnesota called time-out and asked for a review of Nneka's previous shot but the referees, due to the rules, weren't able to look back.

The corners of my mouth turned up a little bit. Did the referees finally mess up in our favor? Everyone always says calls are part of the game, but it's hard to truly believe that when it felt like every missed call is against you. But, that blown call definitely gave us a bit of an advantage!

Rebound, I thought to myself thinking of Pat Summitt's strategy of not allowing us to dwell on our mistakes. Plays aren't going to make themselves; you have to stay in the moment. Rebekkah Brunson knocked down one of two free throws after she was fouled on an offensive rebound and I responded by cutting to the basket and scoring a layup. We were up one point and desperately needed a stop. Everyone in the arena, and those watching on television, knew where the ball was going. Maya Moore got the ball on the left side and drilled a jump shot over Alana Beard's outstretched hands. The Lynx took the lead once again by one with less than twelve seconds left in the game. Neither team had a time-out remaining. Chelsea Gray got the ball, went the length of the court, and shot a turn-around jump shot that came off the rim. Out of nowhere Nneka Ogwumike grabbed the rebound and quickly tried to put it back. Sylvia Fowles blocked it back to Nneka and, fading backwards, Nneka shot it again.

There have been so many situations where I have had a front-and-center view of last-second shots. I looked up through the cylinder, knowing that our championship aspirations came down to this. The ball fell through the rim, barely grazing the net. We didn't celebrate, instead running back to defend the Lynx with less than three seconds left on what would be the last possession of the game. We were determined to play until the clock hit zero. Experience had taught us that stranger things have happened, and we weren't going to let our guard down.

I got up, ran down the floor, and was ready to battle defensively. I was a machine. The ball was inbounded to Lindsay Whalen, and she heaved at the buzzer from half court. I tracked the ball the entire way. It shot off the glass as time expired, and I grabbed it, racing toward center court. I couldn't believe it. I could finally say it: *We won!* 77–76. This was the elusive championship that I had dreamt of since I'd stepped on the WNBA court, and its absence had become a nightmare. I was in disbelief. I tackled Kristi Toliver at mid-court, and I cried as we embraced. I remember being exhausted. Not from the 28 points and 12 rebounds, but from the focus and emotions to compete this entire season, the playoffs, this series, and especially in a game-five situation.

Holly Rowe found me on the court for a postgame interview and asked what the moment meant to me. With tears in my eyes, I exclaimed, "This is for Pat," and gulped down the sobs I knew were waiting to be unleashed. This was the first championship I had won since Tennessee. Since Pat. It all felt so heavy. I was able to bury myself in basketball and feel closer to her through the game after she passed, but now, standing in this huge moment, I couldn't help but feel a bit empty. She should have been there. Not in spirit as I know she was, but physically. I cried a mixture of happy-sad tears that turned to sobs. I couldn't finish the interview and walked away holding all my emotions with me. I couldn't help but feel Pat was there. I chuckled to myself as I remembered her often saying, "Offense sells tickets, defense wins games, and rebounding wins championships." We won on Nneka's offensive rebound!

The postgame trophy presentation was a blur. I ran to the stands, and my daughter jumped in my arms and exclaimed, "We did it!" There are no words to describe what it feels like to share experiences like this with your child. Everyone sees us hoisting the trophy and scoring the points, but few realize how much the families and support systems are a part of helping us accomplish those dreams. Lailaa sacrificed and supported me in my dreams more than anyone. She knew that we'd always been a team and always would be.

After winning that trophy, the celebration, the champagne, and being named Finals MVP, we returned home back to Los Angeles. A couple of nights later, I drove to the airport and picked up my puppy. I got the championship *and* the dog!

ELEVEN

When to Hold Them, When to Fold Them

*There's a difference between quitting
and strategic disengagement.*

—BRAXTON BAKER

*T*he Alchemist introduced me to the idea of a Personal Legend, which is a person's destiny or deepest desires, which you can only achieve by rejecting comfort and dedicating yourself to a given journey. Sometimes the forces behind a Personal Legend may seem negative or particularly challenging, but it's all preparation for where you are going. If you achieve success without having done the work and learned the lessons, you'll squander it. But when you really want something and you've identified your mission on Earth, then you have to believe in yourself so much that no one or nothing could deter you.

Reaching the pinnacle of women's basketball has always been my Personal Legend. What exactly the pinnacle would look like has shifted over time. I don't believe that success can be defined at the start of one's career. Success comes through obstacles, negativity, and rising above, and it looks unique to different people. Everything isn't equal, and we each navigate our own starting blocks and circumstances. I didn't always understand the trials put before me, but time revealed that overcoming difficulties was a necessary part of my journey. For so long, I focused on others' journeys and why they didn't have similar challenges as me or why my circumstances seemed so much more trying than theirs. Soon I realized that sometimes the battles people are fighting are unseen. Perspective keeps us from truly understanding one another's journeys, so we assume we're the only ones pushing through pain. The lesson we all learn in school— keep your eyes on your own paper—holds true as an adult. Keep your eyes on your own journey. Spend time leaning into that and pay less attention to what everyone else has or is doing. If success in the WNBA came to me too easily, I may not have appreciated that there's so much more to basketball than being physically dominant. The politics and behind-the-scenes struggles were also part of the package and taught me a lot about myself, my mission in life, and how to let my process play out. Sometimes we exert too much time and energy into trying to show people who we are, and we become somebody completely different in the process. But you don't always have to tell your story. Time will.

As the number one draft pick coming out of college in 2008, my main focus was winning. I wanted to win multiple championships in the City of Angels. In the past, the teams I had been a part of had great people, solid leadership, experienced veterans, and a culture that was built around communication, accountability, and working with and through people's strengths and weaknesses. Every solid culture begins with solid leadership. Ever since I was a teenager, making it to the WNBA was a dream of mine. I had focused on bettering myself from a basketball-skills standpoint and the elevated standard of play. But what I had heard over and over from Coach Summitt was "You win in life with people." There's a certain standard that both winning people and winning organizations have to have that is only glaring when it's missing. During my nine years of fighting on the court for a WNBA championship, I was fighting off the court, as well.

The environments that I operated best in were those that encouraged and amplified competition, made me feel heard, and were willing and able to understand that my questions were not a threat, but simply a way that I better understood concepts. Every coach I have ever played for has established a relationship and passion to try—not always agree but try—and meet at a place of understanding. This doesn't just happen or appear one day; it takes time to cultivate, gain trust, navigate, and learn your way around each other on any team.

I was surprised when I first arrived in LA. In some ways, I blame my dad and Coach Pat for setting the bar so high. I went into the WNBA expecting to find a home like I had at Tennessee. I was searching for camaraderie with my teammates, care from my coach, and cultivation by the general manager. We didn't necessarily need to be best friends, but winning with people and leaving an indelible stamp on basketball as a sport are team efforts. Chemistry and community are just as critical to good basketball as skill and stamina, but I struggled to get my footing within an organization that prioritized wins and championships over people and purpose.

Although I took home WNBA Rookie of the Year and MVP, it wasn't easy on or off the court adjusting to not only the physicality and pace of the game, but the culture. For the first time, despite all this individual success early on, I felt unsupported. I never was the type to internalize outside noise from fans, media, or opponents, but I really cared, whether I liked to admit it or not, about what people within the industry thought. I had heard whispers from veterans regarding the franchise here and there. The echoes of "the professional lifestyle is different," "be careful who you share anything with," "this is a business now," and "everyone has their best interests at heart." I listened but quickly realized that true colors come out when things don't go your way. The first couple of years, things were all right. I won't say I was at my best, but I wasn't at my worst. The year 2012 was the start of the gap that had been growing between me and the organization, with things reaching a boiling point in 2014.

It started out with small miscommunications and meetings that ended with unaddressed emotions and endings with few solutions. In positive environments, meetings between players, coaches, management, and ownership don't just occur when something needs to be fixed. In the teams that I played for, I was accustomed to having consistent check-ins throughout the season and offseason. You can't only talk when things are bad. That's not the best time to really learn about people. It only got worse from there, with fingers being pointed and no agreed-on solutions. Words were exchanged, trust was lost, and now we were operating from a place of wariness and hurt in every circumstance.

While the years stacked up, so did life. Through pregnancy, injuries, and surgeries, I felt myself withdrawing and communication becoming harder and harder. I felt more unsupported through off-the-court circumstances, which made me carry a distrust on the court, as well. Instead of leaning in with trust and confidence, I retracted and withdrew with stubbornness and immaturity. Everyone plays a role in a relationship, and I can admit that, at times, I didn't uphold my end of what comes with being a franchise player. Both sides wanted to win, but how we expected to go about accomplishing that feat was far from the same.

When the 2012 playoffs rolled around, we had high expectations, and I finally felt and was playing healthy. We were in the Western Conference finals versus none other than the Minnesota Lynx. We lost game one in a best-of-three series and were back home to try to stay alive and force a game three. I dominated from start to finish. I had thirty-three points, fifteen rebounds, and five assists. We were down by one on the last possession of the game. Our coach drew up a play for me to set the screen for Alana Beard to go to her right to the basket to win the game. We lost 80–79. Walking off the court, I was pissed. I wanted the ball, I deserved to have the ball, and just as they rode my play that entire game, they should have allowed me that opportunity. I felt disrespected.

My family and friends turned to Twitter to question the decision-making at the end of the game. Not only did that cause tension between me and our general manager, Penny Toler, but it seeped into the team chemistry, as well. I wasn't the one who posted that tweet so, initially, I didn't feel responsible for their words. I went into that offseason without addressing, talking to, or communicating with anyone from the organization. Heading overseas, instead of realizing the need to close this chapter before we could successfully build the foundation for our pursuit of a title, I put my head down, focused on what I needed to do in between the lines to get better, and became even more distrusting of the entire organization. In hindsight, I can understand the big picture: Nobody wins when the family feuds. And when you leave problems up for interpretation, it's never good for a relationship.

The following year, 2013, it only got worse. Despite coming away with my second regular MVP, yes—surprise—we lost, to Phoenix on a last-second shot, a turnaround baseline over my outstretched hands. That was salt in an already open wound. Throughout the year, I had focused on my on-court performance. In the very little communication that happened between me and Penny Toler, I asked for specific personnel to complement my skill set and enhance our team's ability to create more space on the offensive end. I wanted, needed, and demanded to be surrounded by more shooters, but changes were made in a different direction, and I would find out about trades and acquisitions like the fans, from the press releases. Even though I won regular-season MVP again and felt like I had done what was necessary in the offseason to get better, it hadn't translated to success as a team, and I couldn't help but wonder if the organization and our differing views would ever allow us to win. With my needs not being met, I was harboring so much animosity toward the entire franchise.

At this point, I was frustrated with our inability to get over the hump. Emotions and tempers flared in our exit meeting that followed several days after our disappointing finish to the Phoenix Mercury. I entered Penny Toler's office calm after giving myself a pep talk. *I am not going to get emotional, I told myself. This is transactional, and I will keep this quick and painless.* My pep talk was already off to a bad start because I had failed to remember that this was me I was talking to. I am emotional and not naturally transactional in how I relate to others. All of us have been there, where we try to fake the funk, but I am not good at it. Before I knew it, only moments into my meeting with Penny Toler, a barrage of *fuck yous* were being shot back and forth, each one returned quicker than the previous one. At one point, I felt like it became a competition, neither wanted to let the other get the last one. Frustrated, I finally relented and walked out of my general manager's office.

I quickly got a text that informed me that my meeting with my head coach, Carol Ross, was canceled. Stubborn, frustrated, and irritated, I went, anyway. Coach Ross was definitely surprised when she saw me stroll in. I had calmed down on the journey over to the meeting but walked in with a heavy heart. All I wanted was to win. Driving an even bigger gap between me and the front office and digging my heels in even more was counterintuitive to what I said I wanted. When I saw Coach Ross, she asked me if I wanted to be there. I had to gain clarification because she could not be talking about what I thought she was talking about. She meant what I thought; she asked me if I wanted to be traded. Clearly she had spoken with our GM, and I was disappointed that she didn't even wait to hear my side of things. In the offseason, I pointed the finger at myself as I tried my best to improve in what the team needed me to do: get in better shape with extra cardio and lifting after every overseas game, become a better pick-and-roll defender, work on being a better support player to my teammates. In my head, I was doing everything in my power to win. But in my heart, I knew I wasn't. I knew as well as anyone that, to truly win, everyone from the top down has to be on the same page. That's what makes it so difficult to win: It's not just about the individual talent or personnel; it's about that talent and personnel buying in together. You can't win anything with your best player not getting along with the GM.

I am a person who wears my heart on my sleeve. In dealing with the people within the Sparks organization, I had the philosophy that I would be a reflection of whomever I'm around. I acted and operated in a way that reflected how I was being treated. When I felt disrespected, I aimed to treat any- and everyone in that same way. I was hurt, and hurt people aim to inflict that hurt on others. My disconnection with upper management developed into distrust, disconnection, and miscommunication with coaches and teammates. I was unhappy going to work every day, and every time something arose, instead of leaning in and operating from a place of open-mindedness, I retracted and became more distant and silent.

In that era, I truly became a product of my environment. The smallest remarks or comments would set me off. One time my coach insisted in film that I should have passed to a teammate on the break. Now, I pride myself on trying to always be in search of the right play, and I love to operate from a position of creating for myself but also setting up my teammates in the best way I know how. In that moment, the story I told myself was that the coach thinks that I am being a selfish player. The rest of the film session I could barely concentrate, I was fuming. I started looking at film not to improve and get better, but to point out the moments the coach missed calling my teammates out for not passing or moving the ball when they should have. Shortly after film, we went to practice, and I decided to take a page out of Kobe's book. I went the entire practice and did not take a single shot. I would break the defense down, get to the front of the rim, and kick it out to a teammate who wasn't ready to shoot even when I had an open layup! I continued this throughout the week of practice and even into games. I *over*-passed! This was the level I had stooped to. I grew into someone who I wouldn't want to coach, be a teammate with, or cheer for as a fan. The game became a job. Something I *had* to do. My joy was gone. I oftentimes would struggle on the drive to practice, asking myself why am I continuing down this path? All this was going on while still trying to compete for a championship!

By 2014, we were navigating yet another ownership change. This time Magic Johnson, Mark Walter, Stan Kasten, Todd Boehly, Eric Holoman, and Bobby Patton purchased our team in what could be described as a fire sale by previous ownership. It caught me off guard, as there were rumors that we were very close to being sold to Joseph Lacob and the Golden State Warriors. Uncertainty was high and communication was low—an even worse combination in an already bubbling situation.

The problem with suffering in silence was that fans, members of the media, and others outside the organization don't know the full story of the relationships and conflicts within. They don't see the heated locker-room discussions, the retaliation and pettiness, the being made an example of. All they saw was the final product: our performance, body language, stats, and wins. There were so many times when I'd be frustrated with leadership for how they treated players differently and pointed fingers instead of focusing on solutions. But if I allowed that frustration to shape what I did out there, it only reflected on me. Intentions and justifications only translated as excuses at the end of the day.

Our team ended 2014 with a first-round playoff exit to the Phoenix Mercury. We got destroyed in game two of a best of three series, and shockingly it was less of a blow because I knew we weren't good enough and the other team was better. We didn't deserve to win or to beat them. I went home that afternoon and as I was jumping in the pool with my daughter, I realized I couldn't keep going down this path. We geared up to go overseas in the next few weeks and I realized how unfulfilled I was. There I was during the prime of my career, just going through the motions.

That offseason, our general manager fired yet another coach and thus the cycle continued. Partly, I was hoping with the ownership change we could start completely from scratch, but once again that proved not to be the case. At this point, opening my phone and reading a text message about who our GM was hiring as our next head coach sent me over the edge. Not who we were hiring per se, but in the manner I found out. After taking some time and mulling over my options, I decided to sit out the beginning part of the WNBA season in 2015. I could not bring my best self to the organization and until I could do that, I felt that it was better I stayed away. Besides, I could use a bit of time to rest my body from the grind of jumping back and forth between the WNBA and overseas seasons. It never even crossed my mind to demand a trade from the Los Angeles Sparks. LA had become home and I loved the city! I had plans of never leaving and raising my children in the community and alongside friends who had become family since I was drafted in 2008.

The time away helped put things in perspective. Did I want to truly be a part of the Sparks organization or not? The answer was, I did. I was raised to finish what I start, and I had never been, up until that point, a part of an organization or program that had not won a championship. I wanted to make good on my promise of raising a banner for the city I had grown to love. If I let what was happening behind closed doors impact the way that I perform, then I'm only hurting myself and playing into the caricature being painted of me. That's something that I wish I would have learned long ago because there were so many times with the Sparks when you could tell I was reacting to things that had happened off court through my game-day performance, and it wasn't fair to anyone—myself included. Don't let others derail your focus and redefine who you are. Stand on who you are over and over and over again so that your intention is your reply.

With time I got better at not giving people the satisfaction of knocking me out of my place. I reverted back to who I was and what my role models had taught me. Instead of running away from my feelings, I leaned into being steady and consistent. I realized I couldn't only be great in environments that had leadership I was accustomed to. In spaces where that mentality and leadership lacked, I had to become what was missing.

Let the Work Speak for You

Taking time off in 2015 proved to be the break I needed. Professionally and personally I had the opportunity to take time away from the game. When I returned to the team, I enjoyed learning the new system that our new head coach, Brian Agler, implemented. He would lead us to a championship and back-to-back finals appearances. He took control of the locker room and implemented a system on offense and defense. Things for the first time made sense. We had accountability, rules, and a system. The greatest thing Coach Agler did was create space between our front office and the players. We no longer had to endure irritating postgame locker room speeches by our GM after poor games and performances. But what was crazy was, there weren't many poor performances in the 2015–2017 seasons, but in 2018, we lost in the first round of the playoffs. Penny Toler fired Brian Agler following that season.

By the time I hit year twelve of my tenure with the Los Angeles Sparks, I'd had six coaches, and in 2019, Derek Fisher became the seventh. Then GM Penny Toler boasted about the decision, going so far as to suggest that she only ever considered Fisher and didn't interview any other prospective candidates. Pretty confident for someone with ten coaching transitions under her belt.

I'd known Derek before he joined the organization because of our work at NBA TV and Spectrum SportsNet covering the Lakers. He's a former Laker guard who played a solid role to help the organization win five championships alongside Kobe. We had a good relationship, but I was skeptical at first if he should be coaching in the WNBA. His recent stint as the head coach of the New York Knicks resulted in a 40–96 record. I was far from keen on the idea of hiring Derek because he was part of the Laker family and a former NBA player. In years past, there had been mixed results. Former NBA players like Muggsy Bogues and Dave Cowens had unsuccessful stints coaching. Michael Cooper and Bill Laimbeer who coached the Los Angeles Sparks and Detroit Shock respectively were outliers, each bringing their respective organizations two and three championships apiece. I hated the narrative that even in a women's league, just being a male gave you a leg up, no matter what your résumé or track record looked like. In women's basketball, the assumption is that any man can come in from the NBA and make us better, but it's hard to be an expert at something when you don't truly know the players or the way the game is played. Basketball is basketball, but our league, flow, players, and style differ from the NBA. Our game has its own nuances and distinctions. The vetting process could and should have been more rigorous because not every player can translate their skills to directing and leading others on the court.

There are always growing pains and bond building that needs to happen when bringing new pieces of a puzzle together, but the 2019 season only got progressively worse as time went on. Behind the scenes, many of us players felt that Derek still had a lot to learn about the women's game. Where we sought scouting reports and tools to help us with opponents, Derek was cautious and urged us to focus on repetition and "execution." When we asked to bring in male players for us to train against, a standard custom throughout the WNBA, he expressed discomfort and was reluctant to follow through.

When the season officially kicked off, we still hadn't found our stride as a unit. On top of that, hamstring and ankle injuries forced me to sit out of about a dozen games. As a result of my injuries, I was in and out of the lineup and in and out of practice. Yet even with all of that, I did my best to try and be out there, even if I wasn't 100 percent.

After winning two single elimination first- and second-round matchups, we advanced to our five-game semifinal against the

Connecticut Sun. We got off to a slow start in game one, and were down 21–14 to end the first quarter. It was slow, but we worked our way back into the game and by the fourth it was a one-point game. It was back and forth, and overall, we couldn't make shots when we needed to. Despite the effort and energy, we fell short. Game two was also played in Connecticut, and I had a really bad game. I wasn't the only one. We were outrebounded and outscored, and our morale was shot.

Here come the heels. I could hear that a postgame talk was looming. Our General Manager entered the locker room, and we all knew—this was going to be another postgame thrashing like we had experienced countless times before. It was hard to read between the *muthaf-ers*, threats, *sorry ass*es, finger-pointing, *pussy*s, and *N*-words, as to what she truly was trying to say. But I stopped trying after a while. We knew we'd lost, and to be honest, we knew we didn't play the way we should have. To some extent, sadly, these postgame harangues had been the norm throughout my career. We showered, changed clothes, did media, and went back to our hotel rooms.

An NBA executive would never be allowed to talk to his players like that because, whether the executive likes the players or not, money talks, and players are valued. These talks had become so routine that none of us players thought anything about it. A number of media members had heard the postgame oration through the walls as it carried into the hallways, and some brought it to my attention that what had transpired was not right. That no one should speak to us in that way, no matter how poorly we played. What's sad was I had become deaf to it, as if it had become something I expected and anticipated. As far back as I can remember, these types of locker room outbreaks happened many times. After years, I came to the conclusion that Penny was always going to be our GM, no matter what.

We were one game away from being swept out of the semifinals. There wasn't time to truly address the toxicity running rampant throughout the organization. In the one practice before game three, our priority was on regaining our momentum and advancing to the finals. To our dismay, Derek Fisher didn't have any fresh counters for how to outsmart the Sun's strategy. In game two, Chelsea Gray had been trapped against the sideline far too often. Derek was convinced we simply didn't carry out his game plan, and we felt like his plan wasn't specific enough to the team we were up against. We needed to play harder. Well, we said to ourselves, we definitely needed to rebound better. But we had followed a similar plan in game one, and we came up short with solid effort and rebounding. My one caveat was, can we try and make things easier for Chelsea? How can we help make it easier on our point guard? I shared an idea of possibly changing who screens. They were trapping Chelsea pretty hard with size and length in their front court. What if we had a guard set the screen instead? My question was met with silence, and I felt the tension in the air. After trying a second time, I finally dropped it as Derek's face proved it was pointless to continue the discussion. Derek insisted that we stick with the plan he'd drawn up for games one and two; so we stuck with it.

When game three came around, Derek sent an indisputable message to the starters. We were about seven minutes into the first quarter, and I had started off okay, with two buckets and one coming on a driving layup. It was a slow start for both teams, and the score was low but the game was neck and neck. Still, Derek subbed me out and benched me for the rest of the first quarter and the entire second quarter. Throughout the first half, Derek subbed players in and out, giving our team no time to get into a flow and regain our confidence. Going into the half, I was furious. One bad game and disagreements over strategy shouldn't have led to icing me out in such a critical game. Derek put me back in at the start of the second half and gave me all of four minutes before pulling me back out. We lost by more than twenty points, and there was no explanation for why Derek had made the choices he'd made. Again, I refused to give Derek the satisfaction of lashing out in postgame media and leaning into the difficult-to-work-with stereotype. When asked about why I sat out so much of the game, I redirected the question to Derek. My health had nothing to do with it, I emphasized. The choice to bench me was all Derek Fisher's.

"It was just about trying to do something different that would try and help us win," Derek said when probed about the reasoning behind benching me with so much on the line. It clearly didn't work out in our favor, and Derek was never truly held accountable for that.

After going back and forth, I finally decided to give it one more season. I wanted to play and be a Los Angeles Spark for life. I sometimes wish that I would have let go of that vision long before, instead of holding on so tight to a place that wasn't serving me. I wanted to stay and not feel like I'd quit this franchise that gave me my WNBA debut, but staying wasn't doing me any good. Sometimes you have to sacrifice to truly be happy and remember what's beyond your comfort zone. I could have ranted about what I did and didn't deserve from Derek Fisher, Penny Toler, and the Sparks leadership, but I was exhausted by trying to prove myself. The next season was my last with the franchise. I went out with a bang reminding Los Angeles of what they'd thrown away: the Defensive Player of the Year who led the league in rebounding, set a double-double record, and made my best field goal percentage in almost a decade. Penny Toler's contract was not renewed following the 2019 season, and after a season with interim GMs, Derek Fisher was promoted to GM and head coach. That was the last straw. Walking off the court in 2020, I had an eerie feeling as I took off my jersey and got dressed. Maybe this was the last time I would play in a Los Angeles Sparks jersey.

"Chicago is where my family raised me," I wrote in the press release that went live, "where I first learned the game of basketball; and where I first fell in love with this orange ball . . . I am excited to continue the next chapter of my career where it all began. To my new teammates, my new organization, and my new fans: I'm home." That year, September 16 was declared Candace Parker Day in the city of Chicago. My heart swells with pride to remember what it meant to be called home to people who love you for who you are. When Mayor Lori Lightfoot thanked me for building up my teammates off court and setting an example for Black girls nationwide, it took everything in me not to burst into tears at the press conference. For so long I'd been begging to be seen and heard. There, in Chicago, I didn't need to plead anymore. The city showed me love at every corner, every stoplight, at the airport, back in my hometown of Naperville, and at Portillo's, and for the first time in a while, I was asked directly and candidly to lead.

A few months after announcing my move to the Chicago Sky, I sat on the WNBA championship podium again donning a jersey soaked with a mixture of champagne and sweat. We'd just won the first WNBA championship in franchise history—my second—and the moment truly felt like a perfect collision. My first season with the Chicago Sky, we won. Thirteen long, tumultuous, up-and-down years came to a close and gave way to the new beginning I needed. It was an incredibly difficult decision to leave a place I had called home for so long. We had a home in LA, Lailaa went to school there, and so many loved ones had surrounded us in love. During the years I spent between the WNBA and international teams, LA served as the safety net to catch us when we needed stability and comfort. In spite of all of that, and against everything I'd dreamed for my life, basketball had become the hard part. Between coaching changes and a GM I didn't and hadn't seen eye to eye with in a long while, enjoying the game became a struggle. The culture was toxic, and whether I wanted to admit it or not, I was a part of that culture and had been absorbed into that toxicity. I had heard the things being said about me: "coach killer," "spoiled superstar," "overrated." Even if it wasn't all true, I had to admit to myself that I didn't like who I had become in my years with the Sparks. It takes two to tango, so though I didn't create the culture, I was still at fault in my own way. I surrendered to the tit-for-tat dynamic. I couldn't bring my best self there, and I needed a change of scenery. I needed to see if I could be better. And I knew I couldn't be, there.

In the years since leaving the Sparks, my contributions on and off the court have been affirmed by people across the league. When you know who you are, you want to assert it and protect your reputation. I had to use all of the lessons that I learned in LA and be better in Chicago. Going back home where it all started was a tough decision, and shedding the problematic lessons I'd learned in LA took intention on my part. But, despite a rolled ankle that I twisted in shoot-around before my second game with the Sky causing me to miss seven straight games and a 16–16 record, we made it into the playoffs and stuck together. In some ways, LA taught me how to maneuver all types of different situations, and I can say I am extremely proud of the way I handled locker-room disagreements, team chemistry, and boosting collective morale. I was better because of my experiences in LA. Sitting atop that WNBA podium, I was happy that we had won, but I was prouder of who I'd been when times were tough. I knew, then, that Pat would have been proud of my growth as a human.

Time is still telling my story, and we are writing with our actions every day. When times get hard, lean into the lessons of life. Sometimes your actions and emotions need to be checked. You make mistakes and missteps, say the wrong thing, and handle situations in a way that you are not proud of. But, the next time, be better. That to me is not yelling from the rooftops or screaming who you are. Sometimes you don't have to tell your story; time will.

TWELVE

Bouncing Back

*When you learn to keep fighting in the face of potential
failure, it gives you a larger skill set to do what you
want to do in life. It gives you vision. But you can't
acquire it if you're afraid of keeping score.*

—PAT SUMMITT

A picture doesn't tell the entire story, and I am living proof.
Early in my professional career, I was asked permission for
the MRI of my left knee to be a subject in a medical school
class for aspiring orthopedic students. The class topic aimed to prove
that images don't always tell the full story of a patient's health or
abilities. Two sets of anonymized X-rays and MRIs were shown
to medical students in a lecture. Each of these students were told
that one set of X-rays was of a sixty-five-year-old and that the other
belonged to a professional basketball player. The students were then
asked to assess the images and make an informed guess which knees
belonged to whom. Nearly every participant incorrectly guessed that
the sixty-five-year-old was the athlete, citing that my knee had grade
four osteoarthritis and was too banged up to compete at such a high
level. Nearly every student recommended an immediate knee replace-
ment. Little did they know I would go on to have a sixteen-year professional career and win a few WNBA championships and MVPs
on that knee, which has been bone-on-bone since I was nineteen

years old. When I was told that a majority of students were in disbelief that my knee was the professional athlete's, I couldn't help but chuckle—I guess that's why they say doctors are still "practicing."

From a young age, I could tolerate pain and push through injuries to play like it was nothing. I broke my right foot in the fifth grade and played five soccer games straight before noticing the pain wasn't going away and getting an X-ray. Right ankle broken at the growth plate, six weeks in a cast. Then the summer before my senior year of high school, as the number one recruit in the country, I was playing summer basketball in a packed gymnasium full of recruiters and coaches when I tore my ACL, MCL, PCL, cartilage, and meniscus. Of course, I didn't know that at the moment. Early in the game, my dad, who was also my coach, called a time-out. Throughout the entire span of the thirty-second time-out, I was challenged, yelled at, and told by my dad that if I didn't offensive rebound, I would be sitting next to him on the bench. I was pissed and ready to show Dad and everyone in the gym what the best player in the country was capable of. One of my teammates got fouled early in the quarter and we lined up for the foul shot. The second shot went up and I backed up for a running start across the lane to try to clean up the miss. Remembering my assignment coming out of the time-out, I jumped as high as I possibly could to snag the rebound.

An opponent, preparing for a box out and a dirty play, bumped me on my way down with the ball. As soon as my left foot planted, my body was unable to absorb the contact and I simultaneously felt and heard my knee snap and bones grind. After, the best way to describe it is my knee felt like a noodle. The pain didn't come gradually—it was a rush all at once. As I screamed and soldier-crawled all over the court, tears ran down my cheeks and my body jolted with each sob. I looked all over the gym and saw concern across everyone's faces, as people covered their mouths and shook their heads. My teammates and coaches carried me off the court and took me to the training room as the swelling and stiffness increased and the pain intensified.

Emotionally, I couldn't keep it together. As the trainer performed the dreaded ACL test, I felt my knee shift as his hands went up and down on my knee. I knew. I knew it was bad and there was very little hope before the words we feared came out of his mouth: "I think that your ACL is torn, but we need an MRI to see the extent of the damage."

I couldn't imagine time away from basketball, and as I left the gym and climbed into the car with crutches, wearing the jersey still soaked with cold sweat and tears, I wondered how long it would be before I would step back between those lines again. An MRI revealed that I did in fact tear my ACL, but it was much worse than any of us could have imagined. I also had torn my MCL, PCL, articular cartilage, medial meniscus, and had a severe bone bruise.

I went into surgery July 29, 2003—nearly two weeks post-injury—to repair all the torn ligaments, meniscus, and cartilage. The surgeons had to go into my bone and drill to fixate the cadaver Achilles tendon that would serve as my new ACL. (When I found out that a donor cadaver Achilles tendon would be repairing my ACL, I vowed that my knee would not become my Achilles' heel—no pun intended.) The anesthesia wore off post-surgery, and I gritted my teeth trying to tolerate the pain. The doctor said he wouldn't allow me to do my rehab exercises as long as I was on pain medicine, so as soon as the meds wore off from surgery, I refused to take anything else for the pain, as I feared it would delay my recovery. I had waited long enough to start the recovery process and I was ready now.

In a hospital gown, crutches, and a humongous brace, I took my first step. After a couple hours, the hospital wanted to get me up to walk around and try to bear some weight on my surgically repaired knee. The pain and discomfort that I felt in that first step reaffirmed what I already knew: This journey back to the court was going to be a long and difficult process. Pushing through the discomfort was the easy part, and so were the long hours that awaited me in physical therapy. Being patient was the tough part! Goals helped distract from the journey that laid ahead. I set short-term goals for my knee and attacked them in rehab. Physical therapy became my new obsession.

When I left the hospital to head home to begin my recovery, the doctors wanted my knee bent to ninety degrees by the following post-op appointment that next week. I had it bent that night. I would lie on the kitchen table on my stomach to allow gravity to straighten my stiffened knee to full extension. I woke up at all hours of the night to ice to keep the swelling down, and I tried to keep my knee elevated and stay off it to speed up the healing process.

I adjusted my entire life to revolve around my recovery. I left school every day at 12:30 p.m. and went to physical therapy from 1:00 to 4:00 p.m. In the evenings, I completed homework for my high school teachers and for my trainers. Little by little, I improved. My muscles got stronger, my pain subsided, and my belief in my ability to fully return to the court grew stronger.

The most mundane and basic skills that I used to perform without thinking, like walking without crutches, step-ups, lunges, skips, etc., became milestones and reasons to celebrate the progress of my rehabilitation. I could barely sleep the night before I was to run again. I was so excited to jog and actually perspire and be out of breath. But it was slow, and I wanted to go faster. I wanted more. My physical therapist told me I had to take my time and that we could do more tomorrow. But I could also do more today, so why shouldn't we? This is a lesson I would be learning over and over. Sometimes, just because you can doesn't mean you should!

I wasn't always fearless and confident. Self-doubt would creep in especially at night, when I was alone with my thoughts and pain. I would stay up, wondering if I would ever play the same way. If this was all worth it. What if I did all this and still couldn't play basketball? Not just in body but in mind. My injury took a toll on my mental approach to the game. I watched basketball now, and most plays in transition when there was contact, I'd grimace. I was always thinking of ways people could get hurt. There was my basketball career pre-injuries, where I played free, with reckless abandon. Then, there was the after, where I could already tell the game would never be the same. Even in my prime, I was always hesitant to go up high in the air for a ball in a crowd on the court, cautiously surveying the landing space. I was afraid of certain plays, contact, and physicality. Nonetheless, with all fears aside, I wanted to return to the hardwood as soon as possible.

I constantly looked for ways to silence my own doubt. Twelve weeks after that surgery, I went to a gym completely alone to prove to myself that I could dunk again. If I couldn't, I didn't want an audience. I took a running start and slammed one home; not the best dunk, but I got it down. It wasn't the smartest decision I've ever made, given it wasn't the explosion of dunking that the doctors were worried about; it was my ability to control the landing that was shaky. But, I proved I could do what I needed mentally to silence the doubt at least a little bit. If I'd hurt myself in that gym, it would have started my rehab from the beginning. My stubbornness is truly both my gift and my curse.

If it were up to me I would have returned way sooner. I wanted to play so badly, and I hated sitting out games during my final year of high school with so much on the line. We were defending state champions, and I wanted to go back-to-back as much as I wanted to breathe air. I struggled mentally waiting for my family, coaches, and doctors to give me the okay to play competitively again. I nudged them along a bit faster than they would have liked. Right before Christmas break, I got the okay to begin full-contact practice. In my mind, there was no difference between practice and games. Doc had given me an inch, and I took a yard. My brother Marcus and I would spend the next week working out and playing one-on-one in my high school, sometimes till midnight. Finally, a couple days later on the 27th of December, five months nearly to the day after that surgery, I played in my senior-year Christmas tournament, and all the work that went in was finally worth it. The same tournament I'd first dunked my sophomore year and landed in the spotlight just two years prior was the same tournament I returned from my ACL injury my senior year. Donning a huge brace and lots of rust, I stepped on the court again with tears in my eyes. I had done it. I passed the test, and I was so glad to be back playing the game that I absolutely loved.

Our team became state champions that year for the second year in a row. The process of getting back to myself wasn't easy by any means, but I appreciated the game that much more being back on the court and repeating as state champs. After back-to-back state champions, I participated in the McDonald's dunk contest nine months post-operation, and I won. The obstacles made winning that much sweeter. I had busted my ass to get back on the court with my teammates. We finished the season ranked seventh in the country. On a recovering knee, I still won Nasimith Player of the year, Gatorade Athlete of the year, *USA Today* All-American, but even with all that, nothing was sweeter than hoisting back-to-back state championships. Winning superseded all the individual stuff. In my mind, you can debate awards, but championships are undeniable.

From there, college was only supposed to be a continuation of everything I'd just achieved. Having spent the summer playing for the U-18 USA team, I didn't attend summer school to acclimate to college alongside my teammates. That summer we won gold at the U-18 FIBA Americas championships. My knee had given me some problems with swelling and soreness. Since it was less than a year after surgery, I assumed it was par for the course.

But from the moment I arrived on campus, Pat Summitt took one look at me and shook her head. "We don't play on swollen knees." Our trainer, Jenny Moshak, had informed her of the stiffness and the need to get it checked out. I dismissed the suggestion and was overruled by Pat and Jenny, who banished me from all workouts. Watching my teammates work out while I sat on the sideline doing rehab was absolute torture. After a couple of days, Jenny decided the next course of action was to take a look at my knee on the inside, and she ordered an MRI. I was nervous, but I still believed it was just irritation from surgery recovery. We quickly got the results and the images showed severe meniscus damage. They wanted to do another surgery, and there were two possible paths this revelation could take for me and my basketball career, but the doctors said they wouldn't know the full severity until they could see for themselves up close. If what they saw after performing a minor arthroscopic surgery on my knee wasn't too bad, then they could likely fix things with a small trim and six to eight weeks of recovery. If things looked bleak, I could be recovering for up to three months. I didn't want to even entertain that alternative, so I hoped for the best.

I opened my eyes in the recovery room, and Pat, Holly (our assistant coach), and my parents were all standing around me. They said I was still a little bit out of it, and I immediately exclaimed to them, "We won!" Pat and Holly were intrigued. What exactly did we win? Still groggy I said, "The game." Even under anesthesia and on pain meds, I was dreaming about basketball. As I came to and looked around, I could tell by their faces that they were holding something back. I kept asking what the diagnosis was and did the doctor fix me up? I was met with silence. Finally I zoomed in on my dad. I asked him directly and with a sense of urgency what was going on. They had delayed enough, and finally my mom and Pat went to go retrieve the doctors. "She has a hole in her knee," Dr. Youmans said. The last thing I heard before my heart dropped and everything grew still was "She needs a femoral condyle resurfacing with a cadaver graft. The swelling and discomfort was occurring as a result of a hole where the cartilage that cushioned her knee used to be." Essentially, I needed a cartilage transplant. I would be non-weight bearing on crutches after surgery for twelve weeks and it was estimated I would be out six to twelve months, likely longer. My body went completely numb. My freshman-year season, just like that, was gone.

There are few words to describe that day. *Upset* doesn't get close. *Inconsolable* feels more apt. Basketball was my first love and my only dream at the time. Hindsight tells me that I am so much more than any one sport and that one setback didn't mean it was all over. But, at the moment, no one could confirm that I would be able to return to the court, let alone at the level I'd played before. My patience was thin, and my resilience was being tested, again. I had just cleared obstacles and hurdles months before, and now, I looked into the months ahead and I saw hurdle after hurdle. This was my second major knee surgery in a little more than a year, and the wear and tear was getting to me. After doing everything in my control to return to the court, I'd still been knocked back and lost out on valuable time with the sport I love. Had I not earned better luck? Why me? It was terrifying to not have control. Knowing that if the doctors couldn't fix my knee, there was no amount of work that could make it right. I was staring down the barrel of a future that once looked so promising and now was filled with doubt, again.

I couldn't understand what I'd done to deserve such a gut-wrenching start to my college career, especially after how far I thought I'd come. That pain was supposed to be behind me, yet here I was facing yet another surgery and rehab period. After overcoming the devastating injury and passing the "test" with my resilience and my love for the game, I thought I had checked off the box in my head of "lessons." I had learned a great deal about myself throughout my injury and I somehow believed that because I had overcome the struggles, the road that lay ahead would be prosperous and forgiving. Unfortunately, I learned that's not at all how life works.

The next few weeks were consumed by anxiety and stiffness. While I couldn't move my knee, my mind wouldn't stop spinning. A small part of me held out hope. In my head, those doctors were diagnosing a regular person with average work ethic. I wasn't average, and I thought I could overcome their estimations with my own discipline. But what I clearly hadn't learned from previous injuries is that healing takes time, and sometimes you can't rush biology. What would it mean for me to redshirt and take an entire year off? My entire future felt like it was floating in zero gravity.

One might think my previous injuries softened the blow of this one, but they didn't. Those injuries slowed down my life in Naperville, but college was supposed to be my entrance to the real world. I'd announced my college commitment on ESPN, and millions of people around the country were waiting to see what I'd do as a Lady Vol. Another procedure wasn't on my bingo card at all. But there I was not even a full year later, and I was back again. Back in a hospital bracelet staring down the barrel of another grueling rehabilitation journey. The stages of grief were in full effect, denial, anger, resentment, etc. . . . How did I deserve this? Why me . . . AGAIN? Did I not love basketball enough?

Maybe I'm being punished for something I did or didn't do, I thought to myself. I had to have done something to deserve this. Maybe it was that time I snuck and used my brother's crutches. You know they say crutches are really bad luck. I was searching for an explanation as to what I did to deserve this. I watched all the other all-Americans unscathed and working out, while I was just trying to walk, jog, and be on the court again. All the time I spent in rehab was time away from working on my game. You have to understand. I once left prom early for a basketball tournament. Everything revolved around this orange ball.

I think my father sensed the defeat in me. I was his daughter, after all, and he'd always known me better than most. My parents had traveled to Knoxville for my surgery, trying in every way to keep my spirits up. This time was different. I couldn't get myself together. I'd lost the emotional battle and every inch of my body was exhausted from trying to be resilient. My emotions consumed me in a way I'd never seen or felt before. My dad stood me up and brought me to a mirror in the hotel they were staying at. I didn't want to look back at my reflection. I didn't love—or even recognize—the woman staring back at me. Truthfully, I felt sorry for myself. I pitied myself. But he held me there until I really looked into the mirror and met my own eyes.

"You don't just show who you are when things are going great or normal or easy," he said to me. "You don't show who you are when you're cruising and things are going as planned and as anticipated. Show me who you are through this process," he commanded. I wasn't in the mood for a pep talk, but I needed one. "The only person that you have to answer to and who will be with you, truly, through this whole process is you," he said. "So you have to figure out what mentality you're going to have in this."

The tears started flowing. I realized what bothered me the most wasn't whether I would play again or even at the level I was before, but how completely unfair it all felt. Why would I have to grind again, build a muscle I had just rebuilt, be patient . . . again? I couldn't get over the feeling of anger at my circumstance. I know they say that you have to play the hand you're dealt, but I called a misdeal. I didn't deserve this. I broke down in the mirror, and I refused to look at myself. I couldn't lie to me, and by looking I was playing the hand I was dealt. I was looking my future in the eye and facing it. I didn't want this. I refused to believe that I would have to spend yet another year fighting to just play the game I loved.

I remember finally looking at myself in the mirror—at my tear-stained cheeks, my swollen eyes, my bandaged knee—and I realized why I was so upset. I felt sorry for myself. I didn't doubt myself. I knew I could do this again; I just didn't want to. Why did I need to constantly come back? How could I get ahead if I was always playing catch-up? The why shook me to my core, and I almost succumbed to that devastation. But Dad was right. I couldn't feel sorry for myself. That was not going to get me any further than I was in that instant. I couldn't give up on me before I even had the chance. I damn sure couldn't get there by questioning why every step of the way. I said I loved basketball, well, I had to prove it, again.

It wasn't quite the light-switch flip the movies make it seem, but that mindset shift really was the difference maker for me. Any athlete will tell you that conquering the mind is harder than the physical expectations of the job. It takes true discipline to not give up when things become challenging. But having to rehabilitate my knee a second time cemented my resiliency. I don't like excuses. I don't like optics. My athleticism is a reflection of the grind, and 2004–2005 was the year I became obsessed with self-improvement and self-commitment. How could I expect anyone to do more for me than I was willing to do for myself?

During this time, the loneliness and self-defeat I felt because of my injuries deeply shaped my relationships with everyone around me including teammates, friends, and family. I was not my best self and I was taking it out on anyone and everyone who was around me. It's easy to feel as though no one understands what you're up against when you're watching from the sideline. I was full of pent-up energy that I could only get out through rehab while everyone around me continued their lives unimpeded. I became guarded and stand-offish, pulling away from people even more. My sadness was the direct result of not being able to play basketball so the only good use of my energy was on getting back to where I belonged.

Even when that self-imposed exile wasn't stemming from resentment, I simply didn't have the time to focus on anything or anyone who wasn't getting my knee and me back on the court. One minute spent at a social outing or hanging out with teammates was sixty seconds that I could have been using to heal better. My tunnel vision and competitive streak were shifted into high gear during this time. I'd walk into a physical therapy appointment where my trainer would tell me they wanted me to do 100 straight leg raises at home, I would do 200. When they assigned me homework and told me to work on exercises at home for thirty minutes, I put in two hours. If they needed me to stretch as far as I could, I nearly snapped myself in half making sure I at least grazed my toes. Whether it was a cold plunge, intense workout, or diet change, every task was an opportunity that I went at relentlessly. I never ignored doctor's orders, but I didn't leave any idle time for myself, either. *This was what I had to do to get back*, I said to myself. I wasn't about to blow my chances by not taking myself and my healing seriously. I coped with my growing restlessness by working my ass off. There was no excuse or distraction important enough to get in the way of that. My freshman year of college instead of partying or going to football games I was rehabbing, getting in extra workouts, and mostly keeping to myself. In doing so, though, I lost my sparkle, joy, and sense of humor.

All I knew, then, was that I never wanted to be back in that mental or physical space of vulnerability when my dad held me in front of that mirror. The scary realization that I had no control over what happened to me, only how I reacted. I looked at myself that day thinking that if I did everything right this time, there wouldn't need to be a next. But just like I was wrong about that back in 2003, I was wrong again in 2004. My own reflection and my father's voice turned out to be fixtures in my recovery journey over the next several decades.

The Only Way Out Is Through

What made injuries particularly challenging for me was how dependent they made me. An injury that took a fraction of a second to occur took thousands of hours to repair and would sometimes linger for years after. If I messed up in practice, I could train harder to get it right the next time. If I didn't give my all or was outperformed during a game, I could watch tapes and be coached on what to do differently. But when a freak accident caused my body to shut down, I had to let doctors and medical professionals take the lead, riding the bench until I had permission to get back out there. I wasn't in control, and it was hard to deal with that.

There were some people who refused to be pushed away. They knew I was struggling and were there in whatever way I needed and would allow them to be. My mom was my foundation from start to

finish in my rehabilitation process. Some nights she could hear me in
bed sobbing in the hotel we stayed in for two weeks after my surgery.
I still can feel her climb into bed with me and just rub my shoulder
and wipe my tears. There were no words that she could find to ease
my pain, but in silence we would lie there until both of us drifted off
to sleep. My mom helped me take my first shower, go to the doctor,
attend classes, and spoiled me with my favorite foods to cheer me
up. My harsh exterior and need to pretend everything was fine could
only be penetrated by my mom's love and care. I'm grateful to the
many doctors and trainers who gave me the extra TLC and time I
needed on days I struggled to comprehend why. I am so grateful for
the friends who kept coming back to check on me after I contin-
uously put up a shield. Stephanie Elliot was a student trainer who
made it her mission to do whatever she could to ease the process and
would oftentimes pray over me and my knee! Bennett and Canaan
were our team managers who would spend Friday nights in our dorm
watching movies when I was on crutches and couldn't go anywhere.
I'm glad not everyone I turned away listened to me, because I needed
others more than I even realized.

There's certainly a helplessness to being physically incapacitated
as an athlete. Sitting on the sideline watching your teammates run
drills is lonely and disheartening. Coach knew how desperately I
wanted it. I'd sit in her office every week unpacking the culture shock
of being in a new environment, and how my one outlet and source of
solace had been snatched from me. Not only that, but it left me hobbling around a campus I was supposed to be running circles through.
Nothing seemed to be going my way, but Pat couldn't let me on the
court simply because I wanted it. I didn't understand it then, but she
was saving me for better and brighter days. When you're young, that
can feel forever away, but Pat knew that once I was let off the leash
there would be no stopping me. The wait, then, was worth it to be
truly ready.

I viscerally remember a time when I was hobbling to class on my crutches in the rain. Coach had a 100 percent attendance policy so I couldn't miss the lecture. I might have had an easier time if my stubborn side hadn't insisted on crutching instead of taking the designated bus. But, as a freshman, pulling up in a short van that beeped when it backed up wasn't going to get me many cool points. As I crutched in the rain toward the humanities building, my crutch slipped, and before I knew it all I saw was sky.

There I lay in the middle of the quad flat on my back as the raindrops pelted me in the face and then mixed with tears running down my flushed cheeks. I let out a primal scream that no one was around to hear. I finally let go, my shoulders shook, and my emotions took over. I slammed my hands in the puddles and splashed water all over my communications book and backpack. No one was there to help me up. I lay there reflecting on how my college experience was starting off much differently than I'd imagined. I yearned to experience the same excitement, joy, and nerves as every other freshman on campus as they adjusted to college life. My teammates would complain of balancing workouts, school, and social life. I would watch as they ran sprints and lifted weights, jealous of their shared exhaustions. Everyone was moving forward, and I literally and figuratively lay there stuck.

Water pelted my face as I lay there thinking, *Could this really get any worse?* All I wanted to do was scream, yell, or break something. Every molecule in my body was angry and over everything.

When you're right in the middle of a negative or challenging situation, it's nearly impossible to see your way out. Everyone stresses that when you come out of it you will be better and stronger. Toxically positive people always told me to find a silver lining or see the lesson. But sometimes the first step—even before acceptance—is to be unapologetic about the fact that the situation sucks. A few months prior I was dunking on live television, and here I was on my back in the pouring rain. Alone. That's when I realized, you won't always have motivational words or a cheering crowd. But on both of those days I was still Candace Parker, and that had to be enough. I had to be enough. I needed to adjust my mindset. *When this is over*, I said to myself while still lying in the rain with a puddle forming around me, *I'm going to remember this moment*. It humbled me going forward. Then I sat up, grabbed my crutches, and stood myself up and went to class.

All I had was myself and time. My discipline paid off, and by three months out from surgery, I was trying to practice with the team. We were mid-season and had a couple minor hiccups on our record, but it was clear we could compete for a national championship. I headlined the number one recruiting class in the country, and I wanted to do what I came there to do, compete for a national championship. After rehabbing almost my entire freshman year, all I wanted was to play, but my knee kept swelling up, and Pat had her thing about playing on swollen knees. The swelling up extended my rehabilitation. I finally agreed to redshirt and give up the hope to make a miraculous return to the court that season.

That next season, I went back for everything I felt I'd lost out on. Nearly a year away had allowed my hard work to finally bear fruit. I had a pretty nasty eight- or nine-inch scar reminding me of what I'd come through, but I didn't need the visual indication. You could sense the hunger on me before I even left the locker room. You could also see the work and feel the intensity in my preparation that summer when I finally got cleared to resume normal basketball activities. I put on muscle, got in the best shape of my life, dedicated myself to getting up at 6:00 a.m. and working out before class, and it felt so good to feel the progress and not just be working to get back to even. More than that, I'd gotten my mind right and learned to stop running from the people around me. Coach was a huge part of my not completely surrendering to the isolation and pain. She always told me the better days would come, and here they were. I'll never forget the smell of the gym my first day back or the feeling of running out of the tunnel for Midnight Madness after an entire year of antici- pation. The joy I had in that moment was indescribable; the perfect contrast to the time months before lying on my back in the pouring rain. I used to dream in my darkest days of simply playing basketball. As the Meek Mill rap goes, *I had to grind like that to shine like this.* I had come so far from standing in front of that mirror with my dad, lying on the pavement in the rain, and watching from the sideline as my teammates played at the Final Four. The work is always hard— excruciating even. But it was worth it in the end. Throughout the process, I found out who I was and that a person's morals, values, and belief in themselves can't change, whether I'm grinding or shining.

My opening act as a Lady Vol was a March Madness dunk off. Just over a year out of surgery and I was back slamming it down with ease. My adrenaline from the night kept me up lying awake in bed. I was grateful for this new opportunity and the challenges that laid behind, but also in front of me. A year of physical and personal tur- moil had given me the chance to surpass even my own expectations. There were so many moments that felt futile and where I wanted desperately to give up, since it seemed the world had forgotten about and given up on me. That wasn't me, though. I needed to feel like myself again and there was no better night than that one to remind me who I am.

It's amazing how the body follows the mind. My focus in every area and detail of life pushed me to be disciplined in my preparation that first full healthy offseason I'd had in almost three summers. (I even hit the game winner in the SEC tournament championship game against LSU!) Everything I faced, I was prepared for because I was dedicated to the process and putting the work in. The hardest thing to do is to trust the path you are on when there are obstacles.

Dunking has never been something I've wanted to be defined by. Winning the McDonald's All American contest gifted me with a new moniker that I didn't always want: "the girl who can dunk." I worked hard on my skill set and prided myself on my versatility, I didn't want to be pigeonholed as just a "dunker." For a while, there were so many moments when I had the breakaway but would opt for a layup because it was "just two points" right? I didn't want to be exclusively known for dunking when there was so much more to my game. But after an entire year away, I needed everyone to see what they'd been missing. In my first ever NCAA game in Norfolk, Virginia, against Army, I dunked twice. I say it casually because it was something at that point in my career I could do with ease. Little did I know that, up until that point, no woman had dunked in the NCAA tournament.

After the first dunk, the arena erupted. I found out later that ESPN interrupted live broadcasts, and my name immediately appeared on the sports scroll. Replays of the dunk and the aftermath of me popping the front of my jersey with Tennessee plastered across it. My facial expression was cocky as I ran down the court. "I know you see me!" Just to be sure no one could downplay my post-surgery return, I dunked again later in the game. With my tongue sticking out, I jogged across the court feeling like all the pain and training and waiting was worth it for that moment right there. After the game, the crowd lined up to share their congrats and ask for autographs. I humbly smiled, shook hands, and took pictures.

On the way out after the game, I made a mental note of the feeling I had. I often do that in life—I think pictures are great, but I bottle up the feelings and emotions from the mental note to reflect back on later. I savor and cement these memories in order to acknowledge the progress, the emotions, the hindsight. I couldn't help but think back to that empty gym where I attempted that dunk just three months postsurgery. I was scared I would never do exactly what I was doing over and over again. That little dunk gave me hope that this was possible. That's all my mind needed for my body to follow and do the work. It felt good to realize that all the rehab and physical therapy was worth it.

The dunk was personally significant for me because I proved what my body could do and how resilient it was. I don't think I could have imagined how much that March day in 2006 meant to so many others. Some saw a girl dunking. People will wave you off as a fluke unless you make your presence known. You can mess around and accidentally do something once, and people can explain it away. But when you do something twice, they know it's not by accident. Sports journalists were going crazy over my performance, and dozens of little girls and their families were lining up outside to meet me. To this day, I constantly meet people who recount that day as the first day they fell in love with women's basketball. I beam with pride, reflecting back on the feelings I mentally packaged up decades earlier for moments like this. The hard way made it *that* much sweeter, and as a result these full-circle moments were a constant reminder to submit to *your* path.

That 2005–2006 basketball season was a glorious one for me and helped restore my faith in myself. Even with my discipline and focus, a small part of me always wondered if the swelling would ever stop and if my career was going to start and end in Illinois. That the name Candace Parker would be synonymous with potential and what ifs. With Pat and the Lady Vols, I was proving that I had a lot more basketball left in me. We came up short that year, losing in the elite eight against North Carolina. The image of Ivory Latta flexing right in front of our bench up to a Lebron James who was in a sky box in Cleveland at Quicken Loans Arena played on repeat in my mind going into that offseason. The taste of defeat always has a way of motivating the work necessary to try and accomplish your dreams the next year. So that's what I did. I put my head down, excuses to the side, and I worked. During our next season, after being the only college player named to the 2006 USA Basketball World Championship FIBA team, I began my redshirt sophomore season. I learned a great deal from playing with the professional players while away at USA camp. I started paying attention to not just skills on the court, but the mindset it takes to be great and win at the highest levels. The discipline and energy required to be great.

After returning to Tennessee with the experience of playing alongside pros before the season, I was ready. This is what I came to Tennessee to do. Pat joked that I gave her a run for her money when she recruited me but I told her that, together, we were going to win and bring that trophy home to Knoxville. Tennessee women's basketball hadn't brought a championship home since 1998 but our time was coming and I was making sure of it. One of the very reasons I considered going to the University of Tennessee was to be a big fish in a big pond. I wanted to be a big part in the resurgence of the program back to a powerhouse that won championships. I dreamt of hanging banners first and foremost and my name being mentioned in the same breath as the other legends of the university, like Peyton Manning, Chamique Holdsclaw, Bernard King, and of course Pat Summitt. I wanted to win in a major way and put my university on the map, so that you could never talk about Tennessee without bringing up Candace Parker.

In 2007, we did just that. Immediately after winning the national championship against Rutgers, Pat was doing an interview with Holly Rowe. I ran by Pat and kissed her on the cheek in the middle of the live interview. Coach had pulled out of me what I didn't know was possible, comforted me in my darkest moments, and loved me through it all. After all we'd endured together, we were ON TOP with the natty! Just as I'd promised her when I committed. As Tennessee's fight song, "Rocky Top," played and the confetti fell, I knew I was crazy because I was already thinking, "I can't wait to do this again next year." Always thinking about the next goal.

In 2008, we went back to do it again. Along the way, I dunked five more times—including my personal favorite against the University of Connecticut. Considering the historic rivalry between Tennessee and Connecticut, alongside head coach Geno Auriemma's beef with Pat, I knew I had to get at least one in. Live on CBS's Saturday broadcast, Gus Johnson saw me barreling toward the basket and said,

"Parker again," before yelling, "Watch out!" I put it down on a break-away that came from an assist from my teammate Sidney Spencer. You could hear the rim snap as I flushed it down. Analyst and UConn alum Rebecca Lobo was silent, and Geno literally took a seat in the moments after the dunk. Tapping my heart, I ran up the court and pointed at my mom in the stands. Biggest stage, biggest rival, biggest moment. That night, I went home and watched the highlights on SportsCenter, and a sly smile came across my face. I wasn't zoomed in on the dunk but instead the tiny, microsecond celebration from Pat. She knew how big this moment was, not only for us or me individually, but for women's basketball in general.

They say women can't dunk, and when we do, they find a new way to deem us not good enough. They'd tell me I wasn't really great if I couldn't dunk from the free throw line, or with two hands, or in the half court, or if afterward I didn't hang on the rim. Each time I did something, they moved the goalpost. That was okay with me. I liked the challenge, and being patient with my body had worked out pretty well for me, even if I was resistant to taking the time. I remember dreaming and longing to play free and healthy and without anxiety. It seemed as though every time I would take a giant leap forward and get into a groove, something would happen! An ankle, a knee, a finger, or something would start bothering me. Anytime I had any type of flow, an injury loomed.

In 2008, during my final year at Tennessee, I was preparing to go pro. I had one more season of eligibility but wanted to focus on the Olympics and transitioning into the WNBA. I had accomplished what I came to Tennessee to accomplish: national champion (with an opportunity to do it twice), national player of the year, ESPY winner, and Honda Sport Award winner. You name it, and in my two years playing, we did it. Going back in 2008 after having success in 2007 was difficult for our team. The Pat Riley "disease of more" had taken over, and each of us wasn't entirely focused on our goals that season. We were a veteran group, and most of us had our sights set on the

WNBA. After having been starving and focused the year before, the 2008 season was filled with learning lessons, bumps, disagreements, and balancing personalities and expectations.

That October, I tuned in closely to the WNBA draft lottery, and I can remember rooting for the Ping-Pong balls to land on the Los Angeles Sparks to win the 2008 number one pick. Lisa Leslie, the legend, had missed the previous year with the birth of her daughter. As a result, the Sparks had been the worst team in the league in 2007 and secured the spot I knew would be mine.

It's hard to play regular-season games and value the importance of those games after playing in the postseason and winning a national championship. I tried to reset and go back to that girl who would have done anything her freshman year to step on the court. That mindset had shifted to what was to come in the future. All I did was count the days until the postseason. The SEC and NCAA tournaments just did something to my soul. It brought out my best. It was this feeling I would get before tip-off that only happened when everything was on the line and it was win or go home. The lights were on, and finally, March rolled around. We had a hiccup that tarnished our perfect regular season record in SEC play. LSU took home the regular season trophy and it was our turn to pay them back. We defeated them in the SEC tournament game and for the second time in three years, we were SEC tournament champs. A stark contrast from 2007, where we were regular season champions and LSU stunned us in the semi-finals! That break before the NCAA tournament can prove to be more dreaded than preseason. This time around, we thought since we won, things would be much different. We were WRONG!

It was clear from the first drill that first practice back that Pat intended to kill us in practice! The week leading up to the NCAA tournament usually fell during our spring break, which made the coaches very happy, but as a player that meant two-a-days, running, three-hour practices, and long film sessions. Pat knew how to light our fires, and she understood the importance of celebrating wins, but avoiding a hangover and the the tendency to relax after winning. She didn't want us to let up or think that, by any means, the NCAA tournament would be easy!

My senior year, the coaches in the league voted LSU center Sylvia Fowles as SEC Player of the Year. Normally, individual awards didn't matter to me, but I didn't like it when someone was considered better than me, especially since Sylvia and I had competed against each other since we were fourteen years old. I took that as a challenge. One practice, there was a drill we were doing, and I didn't go to the offensive boards. (Offensive rebounding was a thing with all of my coaches, apparently!) Coach Summitt muttered under her breath and just loud enough for me to hear, "Big Syl would have made that play." I knew what she was doing. I knew her intention, but she knew that even if I knew she was trying to push my buttons, it worked. The way to motivate me was a simple formula: Tell me I couldn't do something or someone else did it better. After that week, I was more focused and determined than ever to lead this team to back-to-back national championships. Coach Summitt had my entire attention, and I felt sorry for our opponents after that one week of preparation for the selection show and NCAA tournament.

We coasted through the first three matchups and handled our opponents pretty easily. In our Elite Eight NCAA tournament game against Texas A&M in Oklahoma City, I came out on a mission and wasted no time letting everyone know who the best player in the country and future number one pick was. I'd already scored sixteen straight points and finished that mini run with an unguardable fadeaway baseline turnaround over my right shoulder. I ran down the court, knowing there was no one in that game, no one in that arena, shit, no one in the country who could stop me. I was feeling it. There was a sense of ease in my game. I was playing it at my pace and dominating on both ends of the floor.

On the defensive end, I was in help, and the Texas A&M guard drove behind me and toward the middle. Utilizing my nearly seven-foot wingspan, I reached down at an angle behind me and grabbed the ball as she was picking it up to go into her move. I felt a sting and a pop, but I got the steal, and I started to dribble down the court on a breakaway with just me and the basket. The pain didn't subside and actually intensified as I bobbed up and down attempting to run. My arm was dangling beside me with my shoulder hanging out of its socket. I couldn't continue. I dribbled toward the sideline and picked up my dribble and slumped over. The ref blew the whistle for an injury time-out. I couldn't believe this was happening now. After righting the ship, all those long practices, the week of refocus and buy-in and preparation. I was angrier at the timing than the pain of the dislocated shoulder. *Why now?* I thought as I was helped to the locker room. I went to the locker room to be looked at, but it didn't take an expert to see that my shoulder was dislocated. As they attempted to pop my shoulder back in its socket, I kept an eye on the scoreboard from the training room table in the locker room. All I kept thinking was this was one of the biggest games in my career . . . I have to get back out there!

Our trainer, Jenny, and our team doctor helped pop my shoulder back into the socket. Immediately, my mind turned to getting back out there. They agreed to let me return after I completed a number of exercises. But when I went out to play again, shortly before halftime, I reached for the ball and immediately felt my shoulder pop back out of the joint. I could feel my arm slump heavily and flagged down my coaches to be subbed out of the game. Despite the pain, I was disgusted to be back in the locker room and knew that returning to the game was going to be harder to convince them to let me do. The medical professionals looking at me wanted to pull me from the rest of the game, which I adamantly refused. I couldn't go out like this. I wouldn't. Anyone who knows Pat Summitt knows she never does anything she doesn't want to do. I'd like to believe my stubbornness was what convinced her to let me play, but I think she knew how much completing the season meant to me because it meant just as much to her. She knew there was no way I was riding the bench during one of our last times as coach and player. She knew that if she were in my position, she would be begging to do the same. It just so happened, one of my teammates had been nursing a shoulder injury and had worn a brace in practice from time to time. That brace was in her bag under the bus. The managers dug through all the bags to find the prized treasure. They agreed I could return to the game if I wore a brace, but if it dislocated again, I was done. So I went back in with a brace holding my shoulder together and played as if nothing had gone wrong.

I headed back in with my shoulder in place and we managed to squeeze out the win! We were headed back to the Final Four. In the postgame press conference, all I could reflect on was the fear of this being our last ever game together. It reaffirmed the gratitude that I had in putting on a Lady Vols jersey and playing alongside my teammates. These injuries served as a constant reminder that the game could be taken away from me in the blink of an eye.

After returning to Knoxville the next morning, sporting a sore shoulder and the net we cut down from the night before tied to the back of my regional-championship hat, I went into UT Medical and got an MRI. For some reason, despite the bad news I always received post–radiology readings on all my past injuries, I kind of enjoyed the obnoxious buzz and hum of the MRI machine. It was oddly calming. Before I could even get my stuff together and my clothes on, my trainer had already called. With how quickly the results had been read, this couldn't be great news, I thought. I had a left labrum tear. I was quiet. After all the surgeries I'd endured, I was damn near an orthopedic surgeon when it came to my knees, but my shoulder was a different story and I didn't quite understand what that meant. By the sound of Jenny's voice on the other end of the phone, it didn't sound great. What could a shoulder recovery be? Six weeks? Maybe three months on the upper end. But I had proved I could play the night before, so playing in the Final Four was a nonnegotiable.

That entire beginning of the week leading up to the Final Four was filled with hours of rehab. After seeing the doctor, understanding the risks, and doing a whole lot of convincing, I was determined eligible to play. However, because the injury I sustained was a complete dislocation (twice), I had a 90 percent chance of my shoulder popping out again. These types of labral tears usually require surgery and then recovery. Get this because my mouth nearly hit the floor. *Six months!* My head was racing. Yet again I was at a critical life juncture—just before my last NCAA championship and the subsequent WNBA draft. This was not the time to be falling apart!

With all that was going on with the preparation and rehab for the semifinals in Tampa that Sunday and the WNBA draft directly following the championship game, I had a lot on my mind. My shoulder was pushed to an afterthought, and I told myself we would figure that all out in the near future. I rested a lot to be able to play in the Final Four. (I needed it.) But even in my bed, my shoulder ached at night. We arrived in Tampa to take on LSU in the semifinals that Sunday in a rematch from the SEC tournament. Immediately after arriving at the hotel and walking through the celebration by the band, cheerleaders, and fans in the lobby, I dropped my bags and immediately went to rehab. Every hour I could, I spent strengthening, icing, and treating my shoulder.

That night I couldn't wait to go to sleep. I was absolutely exhausted. It was the last couple days I would be a collegiate athlete and don the Tennessee orange that made me so proud. I had settled into a great groove at rehab and I started to feel confident in my ability to play through the pain of my shoulder. As I relaxed and drifted into sleep on my side with my left arm up above my head, I woke up to a pop. The heaviness of my shoulder was almost immediate, and I was jolted out of my sleep. *It was happening again.* My roommate, freshman Vicki Baugh, was still asleep. I whispered her name to try to calmly get her attention. I needed help. It was happening again. My shoulder popped out and dislocated in my sleep. I was in unbearable pain as the heaviness of my arm weighed down on my joint and shoulder socket. For some reason, anytime my shoulder would dislocate I would think of Mel Gibson in *Lethal Weapon 4*, when he was fighting the bad guy by the water and painfully tried to ram his shoulder into the wall to get it back into place. No chance. I would try a different method. I couldn't move, and I needed someone to help me, but all I could think of was *The medical staff won't let me play.* I convinced myself I could get it back into place myself. I tried at first to move my fingers, but even that was excruciating. I made the mistake of telling my overprotective freshman bestie/roommate that my shoulder was out and I needed her help. Before I knew it, she took off down the hall banging on every door in the hotel corridor, attempting to find our trainer and team doctor. Finally, after around ten minutes, she tracked down the training staff. We to this day joke with Vicki that she could have just used the telephone in our room or perhaps a cell phone, but she chose a more dramatic route. I refused to go to the hospital. In my head I always was weighing the likelihood that I would be allowed to play after a trip to the ER. After about an hour of different attempts and maneuvers and extreme agonizing *pain*, Dr. Morgan successfully popped my shoulder back into its socket.

Immediately, I tried to play it off and act as if nothing major had happened. After getting my shoulder back in, everyone in the room was uncomfortably silent but I knew what they were thinking. *Can she play?* I decided to pull the elephant up from under the carpet. "Can I play?" I asked aloud. I thought about asking them not to tell Pat, but I knew that was never even an option. I'd miss practice that day to go see another doctor and get another MRI. The reading showed slightly more damage. I begged everyone to keep the diagnosis private. Please do not let this get out to the public, my opponents, or even my teammates. We had to face off versus LSU in the next twenty-four hours, and I didn't want our team to focus on anything but executing the game plan to beat the Tigers.

During the game I donned an oversize long-sleeve white compression shirt to hide my huge shoulder brace and whipped down the court dribbling full speed. The seconds ticked off the clock in the last moments of the game. LSU was up by one, and this possession was to decide our fate. Despite a 6–26 from the field that night, my team put the ball in my hands and trusted my decision-making. There's a sense of pride when you are counted on, especially on an off night. I penetrated full speed to the basket; with my eyes on the rim, I was going to lay it up. Sylvia Fowles's 6'6" frame shifted over to help. I have always prided myself on and had been taught to generate the best look, even if it means you aren't the one taking the shot. At the last second, I whipped the ball across my body with my right hand to my teammate Nicky Anosike for a layup on the left side. For what seemed like minutes, the ball hung in the air and on the rim. I landed and turned around, the ball falling off the rim and out of the hoop. It didn't go in. My heart dropped. Out of nowhere, my teammate Alexis Hornbuckle soared and tipped in the winning bucket and her only basket of the night to put us up 47–46 with barely any time on the clock! The name of the game in March Madness is survive and advance. Two nights later, I suited up for my last game as a Lady Vol, with the chance to win another championship.

We went on to defeat Stanford two days later and avenge an earlier loss to them that season. The Lady Vols were back-to-back national champions. No one truly understood what it took for me to stand on that ladder that night and cut down the Final Four championship nets, and they didn't need to. I was so proud that, despite it all, we had prevailed. Despite my injury, I played. That despite not being at my best, I had given my all. At twenty-one years old, I took a sip of a shot with my teammates and toasted to our success. These years flew by, but boy, the days were long, the practices were intense, and obstacles tried to derail our goals and purpose. Yet here we were, celebrating. It had all been worth it. Back-to-back champs!

But it was bittersweet. I didn't want to leave Tennessee, but I knew I was ready to move on to the next level, equipped with all the lessons this journey in college had taught me. I was closing the door on a chapter that had not only taught me who I truly was, but had defined ME. Hanging banners, everyone tells you that you are great and aims to emulate your success. But not many want to go through what it takes to get there. It required getting up in the rain, doing extra reps, putting in the work even when no one will know, grinding in silence, and most importantly, looking at yourself in the mirror when you are unsure what the journey holds ahead and trusting you are built for whatever is in store. I was proud of *me*!

THIRTEEN

Don't Let Up

I don't want any other woman to feel like she has to choose
between her profession and motherhood, and definitely
not to have to hide bringing a new life into this world.

— ALLYSON FELIX

On April 8, we won the NCAA championship in Tampa, Florida, and fifteen hours later, I was just miles away attending the WNBA draft. Donna Orender, the president of the WNBA, announced, "With the first pick in the 2008 WNBA draft, the Los Angeles Sparks select: Candace Parker." Dreams do come true. Even when your hair still smells of sweat and champagne. I looked down at my tailored white dream suit and mini heels. I was standing in my childhood's biggest aspirations.

It's a quick turnaround, to say the least, in the WNBA. Training camp was to start later in April, and there were so many things to accomplish between now and then. I had to sign with an agent, pick a shoe company, figure out other endorsements, close out my classes at Tennessee to ensure that I completed them to graduate, and . . . deal with my looming shoulder situation. That night after the draft, I flew out to Los Angeles to meet my new organization. The next day, after completing my physical evaluations for the Sparks, I was told by another set of doctors that I needed shoulder surgery to repair the repeated shoulder dislocations and torn labrum that had gone ignored. As soon as I landed in LA, I set my sights on bringing a title to the city. But I wanted the title *that* season. How incredible would it be to complete a triple crown? We won the national championship; I wanted a gold medal in the Beijing Summer Olympics and a WNBA championship in the same calendar year. I wanted to prove that, despite being a rookie, I was one of the best players in the league. As with Tennessee and my thirst for the NCAA championship, it was time to deliver on all the hopes and dreams I had for myself and those around me. It was no surprise that I elected to opt out of the surgery so that I could play.

I was in a true season of abundance. I learned not to take things for granted and to remain where both feet are planted, but it was really difficult in this season of life. After all the injuries, surgeries, and physical therapy sessions I'd endured, I fought to keep from looking ahead. But this time, the irony was that I had to fight the urge to look back, and a part of me missed college. This was a feat I had literally always dreamed of. The chance to be playing at this level was everything I wanted and more. I didn't have adequate time to process and close one chapter and then advance to the next. This part of my life just kind of ran together in a blur. An embarrassment of riches is a pretty accurate description for what the spring and summer of 2008 felt like, and yet I didn't have time to truly revel in it. There literally wasn't enough time in the day.

I finished up classes while practicing with my new teammates, some of whom were ten to fifteen years my senior. I was caught between two worlds: partly still in college-student mode while building my future professional life on the side. While my friends back in Tennessee and Illinois were being young and carefree, I was in business meetings picking a financial adviser, looking for a house, moving out of my apartment in Tennessee, and traveling back to actually walk at my graduation—all within a few weeks. It's a strange and isolating experience to get everything you've ever imagined and realize it doesn't feel at all like what you thought. I couldn't shake the overwhelming feelings of weariness and exhaustion. I regret not being able to really lean into and experience everything individually but for most of this season, I recall being antsy for the special moments to come to an end. I wanted the memory but it took a lot out of me to be present and energetic for everyone and everything. These are milestones and big moments if just one happened in a year, let alone all happening within a month of one another. It all felt clumped together and rushed, a national championship without a parade, WNBA draft without a party to celebrate, graduation and immediately boarding a flight back to make practice, and being thrust into adult life without the time to really take my time and make decisions I was absolutely sure about. Every time someone would remind me that 2008 had been quite the year, I shyly smiled and nodded, feeling the guilt that I truly wasn't appreciating it the way I should.

By the time I returned from walking across my graduation stage, I was set to debut at my first WNBA game. The last couple weeks had been a whirlwind. There was the adjustment and changes of professional life and the physical exhaustion of training camp in which we had twenty-one straight days of two-a-days (Michael Cooper was a Pat Riley disciple and the way we practiced you could surely tell). Our Sparks team was full of veterans who had been in the league for quite some time. Two veterans who took me under their wing were Delisha Milton Jones and Lisa Leslie. From day one in training camp, Coach Michael Cooper set the bar and expectations high. In one of his first interviews after I was drafted, Coop, as we called him, said that by drafting me to the Sparks it was like the Lakers drafting Kareem Abdul-Jabbar, Magic Johnson, and James Worthy all rolled in one. Coop was the first coach since my dad who took the reins off and put the ball in my hand and let me play. Sometimes I was asked to play point guard, sometimes I guarded shooting guards, and he would put me in position to make plays and score in the mid-post.

(*above*) Basketball is in my blood.

(*right*) Been about it, and I'm still about it! Baby hair Candace. My mom always had me looking fresh!

(*above*) My brothers, even from a young age, have always been my heroes. Marcus is on the far left and Anthony is holding me.

(*left*) The Parkers (from left) Anthony, Mom, me, Dad, and Marcus. These are the people who made me who I am. Through ups and downs I know that no matter what I can lean on my family.

Seeing Anthony get drafted into the NBA was a pivotal moment in all of our lives. I wanted to be just like him.

his is the dollar bill my grandfather gifted me when I was born, and I keep it in my office on my desk to is day as a reminder of legacy.

The first time I met Pat Summitt, I was thirteen years old, and my mom snapped this picture. I was 6'1" and maybe 150 pounds soakin' wet! Pat looked at me and in a Southern drawl said, "We're gonna have to take you home and fatten you up!"

Pictured here in 2000 at the AAU Nationals in Orlando, Florida. I loved being coached by my dad, and w shared so many beautiful basketball moments together.

Here I am on signing day, between my two parents. We all knew Tennessee was the best fit for me; it just took me some time to officially commit. Looking back, this was one of the best decisions of my life.

At the 2008 ESPYs with my brothers, Marcus and Anthony, as well as my then-fiancé Shelden. That night, I won Best Female College Athlete *and* Best Female Athlete (overall).

Pregnant with Lailaa and enjoying a much-needed vacation in Mexico.

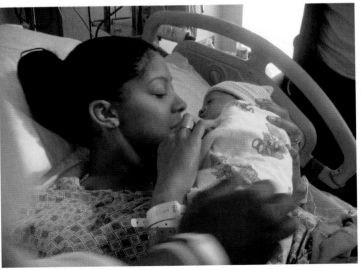

When Lailaa was born, the world stopped, and my purpose was refined. She is the first to make me a mommy! Suddenly, everything else came in second, including basketball.

Mom first, baller immediately after. Just two weeks to the day I delivered my precious baby girl, I was back working out. Fifty-three days after Lailaa was born, I played in my first game.

Lailaa and I visited Pat and the Tennessee Lady Vols on a road trip in Austin, Texas. During practice, Pat carried Lailaa around, played with her, and even took her to play the drums! This remains one of my favorite pictures of Pat. She remains a role model for me in how to balance a career and motherhood.

CANDACE PARKER BASKETBALL COURT

IN RECOGNITION OF NAPERVILLE'S VERY OWN CANDACE PARKER, THE NAPERVILLE PARK DISTRICT IS PROUD TO DEDICATE THIS BASKETBALL COURT AT SPRING-FIELD PARK IN HER HONOR. THIS IS THE PLACE WHERE, FOR MANY YEARS, PARKER PRACTICED AND HONED HER CRAFT UNDER THE GUIDANCE OF HER FATHER.

PARKER'S DESIRE FOR EXCELLENCE LED HER TO A SUCCESSFUL BASKETBALL CAREER AT NAPERVILLE CENTRAL HIGH SCHOOL WHERE SHE RECEIVED NUMEROUS NATIONAL HONORS. HER CONTRIBUTIONS TO THE REDHAWKS DROVE THE TEAM TO STATE CHAMPIONSHIP TITLES IN 2003 AND 2004.

AT THE UNIVERSITY OF TENNESSEE, PARKER ASSISTED HER TEAM IN WINNING BACK-TO-BACK NCAA CHAMPIONSHIPS IN 2007 AND 2008, AND SHE LED IN SCORING AND REBOUNDS DURING HER FINAL SEASON.

IN 2008, PARKER HELPED CLINCH THE GOLD MEDAL FOR THE U.S. WOMEN'S BASKETBALL TEAM DURING THE OLYMPIC SUMMER GAMES IN BEIJING, CHINA.

PARKER WAS SELECTED BY THE LOS ANGELES SPARKS IN THE FIRST ROUND OF THE WNBA DRAFT IN APRIL 2008, AND EARNED THE WNBA ROOKIE OF THE YEAR AND MOST VALUABLE PLAYER AWARDS, MAKING HER THE FIRST WOMAN TO RECEIVE BOTH HONORS.

DEDICATED JULY 30, 2009.   Naperville Park District

The same court I learned to play on now bears my name and story.

Naperville has always been home, and the courts there made me who I am. To have a court renamed after me was full circle, and baby Lailaa was there for it all.

I'm *so* grateful to my mom—who my kids call "Honey"—for joining me abroad and allowing me to be a mother and a baller. I couldn't have done it without her love and support.

I worked for *yearsss* toward this win, and it was so sweet to share it with my baby girl Lai. (Jerritt Clark/ Getty Images Entertainment via Getty Images)

Anya and I exploring the rich history of Moscow in front of Saint Basil's Cathedral on Red Square.

Kahleah Copper is my little sis, and it was an honor playing—and winning!—alongside her and the rest o the 2021 Chicago Sky team. (Jeff Haynes/National Basketball Association via Getty Images)

(*left*) Marrying Anya was one of the best days of my life. As we danced together in Mexico, I relished in the fact that this was only the beginning.

(*below*) One of my favorite traditions is Anya cooking the most delicious Russian dishes for New Year's Eve at home. Here she is standing in front of Оливье (*olivye*, potato salad), Борщ (borscht, classic beet soup), Кулебяка (*kulebyaka*, an elaborate and enormous pie stuffed with salmon, rice, and pickled chard), and Селедка под шубой (herring under a fur coat) as I give the chef a kiss!

Posted up with my Olympic gold medals and championship rings.

When things get tough in life, in the words of my dear Coach Summitt: Left foot. Right foot. Breathe. Repeat. When she told me this, I decided to have it tattooed on my arm shortly after her passing in 2016.

Broadcasting is a passion of mine. As a hoop head, being able to talk and debate the game of basketball with my coworkers and friends at TNT—Ernie Johnson, Shaq, and Kenny Smith—has been a dream come true.

Holding Airr Larry Petrakov Parker—
"Goose"—just after he was born. It was
love at first sight!

When Hartt was born, he truly
became the heart of our family. He is
the perfect addition, and immediately
we couldn't imagine life before him!

Injuries have never stopped me from mom-ing. Here I am cuddling Airr, who we lovingly call Goose, while laid up with the pups and elevating my leg after my first navicular fracture and ankle reconstruction surgery.

Tennessee all day baby! Hartt and I cheering on the Vols. I like to say that I bleed orange!

Family is everything to me! Here we are, our first time trick-or-treating during Halloween as a family of five. We were the Tune Squad from *Space Jam*!

I've worn many casts during my career, but this one was my career-ending injury. It was painful to say goodbye to basketball, my first love, but it also gave me more time with my ultimate love: my family. Here I am reading to Lailaa, Airr, and Hartt. Little did they know they softened the blow of retirement.

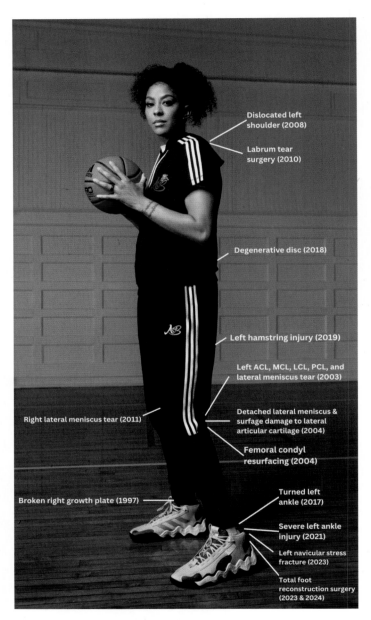

Dislocated left shoulder (2008)

Labrum tear surgery (2010)

Degenerative disc (2018)

Left hamstring injury (2019)

Left ACL, MCL, LCL, PCL, and lateral meniscus tear (2003)

Right lateral meniscus tear (2011)

Detached lateral meniscus & surfage damage to lateral articular cartilage (2004)

Femoral condyl resurfacing (2004)

Turned left ankle (2017)

Broken right growth plate (1997)

Severe left ankle injury (2021)

Left navicular stress fracture (2023)

Total foot reconstruction surgery (2023 & 2024)

Better the hard way. (Atiba Jefferson)

I was in heaven with all the freedom, but more so the responsibilities he trusted me with from day one. But, it wasn't given, it was earned. Day two in training camp he put me on the second team. On the white team, I skeptically turned my jersey over and joined the team on the other end of the court. Immediately, Coop blew the whistle to scrimmage. I called my own number on the first play down, driving to the hole to score, when *boom*, Delisha, "D-Nasty" as I came to learn, came across helpside and blocked the ball, but not without going through my head, shoulders, chest, and every part of my upper body. I waited, but the whistle never came. No foul? I cussed, pumped my fist, shook it off, and ran down the court. A couple plays later, I was laid out by a vicious screen by Lisa Leslie. By the third time, I knew what this was. This was to teach me a lesson. Coop smiled behind his whistle, only blowing it for the black team and laughing the more frustrated I got. I ended that scrimmage pissed off. This was their plan, to toughen me up, show me there was a pecking order, and expect me to just roll over and take it. Shortly after the practice ended, I entered Coop's office pissed off. How dare they think they can play unfair? He shook his head, agreeing with everything I was frustrated about. Then he interrupted me and said, "Silk, I think you can get MVP your first year in the league." Silk is the nickname he gave me and to go along with Lisa Leslie's "Smooth." I barked back at Coop, "Fuck MVP, I want to win Finals MVP." That would mean we would win the championship. The goals were set.

I was ready when the season was finally set to begin. Battle-tested by some of the best to ever play the game. A lot of rookies have to wait to be initiated by the physicality of opposing teams, my teammates did this to me every damn day in practice. If you didn't hate losing, you would learn to playing for Coop. Every drill was a competition that had a winner and a loser. Losers ran . . . a lot! Stubborn, I refused to give in and quit. Some days were harder than others, but I loved the challenge. The first game, I was ready. Excited to finally don the Sparks jersey in a real game, we were up against the defending champions from 2007, the Phoenix Mercury. I grew up watching Cappie Poindexter and Diana Taurasi, I remember watching them in the finals the previous year, dreaming of being able to compete against the very best. Envisioning how I would guard a pick and roll and how I can exploit their defense. When my name was called to run out in my first ever professional game, I told myself how proud I was to be even playing today. Sometimes when expectations are high, we don't celebrate the progress, on this day I did. With a black shoulder brace on my left shoulder protecting a torn labrum and a scar to remind me of the three knee surgeries I already had, I ran out to begin my professional journey. Just a little over a month since we cut down the nets in Tampa, Florida, for the National Championship, my first WNBA game tipped. That first game was high scoring and probably one of the most complete games I have put together in my career thus far. We got the W on the Mercury's home court and I dropped 34 points, 16 rebounds, and 9 assists. (Although by today's tracking of assists, I definitely had more than 10!) The greatest debut by a rookie to date in the history of the WNBA. I was grateful for training camp, the preparation Coach Coop put me through, and I was proud of myself for fighting through the discomfort of knowing things weren't fair, they weren't meant to be fair, but sticking with it . . . that prepared me to shine when the big lights were on and it was game time.

My rookie year was filled with big moments and memorable games. In June, I joined Lisa Leslie and made history as only the second WNBA player to dunk in a game—and I did it again the very next game. My presence in the league was felt, and I was just getting started. By July exhaustion had set in. I was deep into the season and enjoying a glamorous night at the ESPYs to accept another set of awards. Standing on the red carpet with my hair and makeup perfectly manicured to match my silky golden dress, I felt beautiful. My teenage crush, David Beckham, called out my name as Best Female Athlete of the year.

Late July, we faced up against the Detroit Shock (now the Dallas Wings) and the game was intense from the beginning, as if the energy from the original NBA Malice at the Palace brawl lingered in the air. Only this time, instead of the Indiana Pacers as the opponent, it was the Sparks. Our coaches had history. Bill Laimbeer was a part of the "Bad Boys" of the Detroit Pistons who were known for their physicality against opponents and especially a certain 6'6" shooting guard who played for the Chicago Bulls by the name of Michael Jordan. Michael Cooper didn't mince words in our preparation for the Detroit Shock game in shootaround. Already I could tell Coop and Bill did not like each other, and it wasn't for show! The game remained fairly close with us keeping a healthy ten point lead through most of the first three quarters. When the fourth quarter came around, the physicality and aggressiveness grew and, despite some obvious fouls on both sides, the referees swallowed their whistles.

With ten seconds left in the game and our lead dwindling down, Cheryl Ford missed a free throw and I jumped up for the defensive rebound ... as did every other player under the basket. I wrestled for the ball and came out of the pile with it before Ford snatched the ball. I can lose control on principle and I took exception to her childish behavior. Lisa Leslie tried to keep me calm and remind me not to let them get under my skin, but I was pissed! I yelled at the referees to get the game under control. A few plays later, my teammate Marie Ferdinand-Harris was at the free throw line. As we lined up for a game that looked to be pretty much in the bag for us, I looked across at DeLisha Milton-Jones and she mouthed to me, "Bend your knees." I knew what that meant. Plenette Pierson had an intense look on her face and was down in a stance, ready to box out. Marie dribbled her free throw routine, and just as it left her hand I thankfully anticipated the hard box out that ensued. Using my arms, I threw her off balance and she stumbled momentarily. She was mad and jumped up quickly to her feet, taking exception to the last play. I backpedaled downcourt, and Pierson ran up on me going chest to chest. I started to lose my balance, and as I fell, sensing an extreme disadvantage if she remained on her feet, I "helped" her down to the ground with me. Just kidding, I wrapped my arms around her hips and wrestled her to the floor, ensuring I landed on top of her. A brawl ensued! Coaches and players all jumped in to join the action. Punches were thrown, tempers flared, and by the end there were numerous suspensions, ejections, and fines handed out from the league office. We got into the locker room after the game and the police escorted us quickly to the bus with no shower. We headed straight to the hotel with a W in hand! Pretty soon I see a shadow appear over my seat. Coop stuck his hand out and said, "Silk, they tried to punk you and the entire league now knows you don't play that. I'm proud of you!" All those days in practice on the white team sure weren't for nothing!

My Light at the End of the Tunnel

Traveling back from the Beijing Olympics with my gold medal around my neck, I recall feeling more tired than I'd ever felt in my life. It had been a grueling year jumping from the USA basketball qualifier at the end of 2007 straight into my final NCAA season and collegiate championship straight to the WNBA draft the next day. The moment I signed on with the Sparks, the whirlwind continued from the regular season to the Olympics. The WNBA takes an Olympic break for roughly a month and play pauses while the many Olympians from all countries in the WNBA compete for the gold. A few days later, I was back in a Sparks jersey suiting up for our last couple weeks of the regular season before we headed into playoffs. I was exhausted and struggled to acclimate to the time change. I swatted the fatigue away, assuming that it must have been my grueling schedule and subsequent jet lag catching up with me.

The days passed, the regular season came and went. I got through the playoffs, but I still didn't feel like myself weeks after returning from the Olympics. Just days after our heartbreaking loss to the San Antonio Silver Stars, I found myself back in San Antonio to accept the Rookie of the Year and Most Valuable Player trophies in a press conference. Again, I was grateful but exhausted, and couldn't wait for the much-needed break that was to follow these next couple of days. I had a roller coaster of emotions that switched from the high of accepting historic regular season awards to the low of the heartbreak of watching teams play in WNBA Finals I felt should have been us. After the game, I headed back to the hotel to get some rest. I turned on ESPN and watched as SportsCenter flashed my face and played highlights all across the screen. I watched as I did my patented in and out dribble and finished with the left hand. Then, a split screen appeared noting the only other player in professional play who achieved the feat of being named Rookie of the Year and MVP in the same year: the great Wilt Chamberlain!

As I packed for my early morning flight back to Los Angeles the next day, I suddenly got sick to my stomach and ran to throw up. Confused at first, wondering what could have made me sick, a quiet thought tiptoed into my mind and planted itself there: *You're pregnant.* It couldn't be. I had had my cycle like clockwork since returning from the Olympics. But it wasn't *impossible.* Shelden had recently relocated to Sacramento as he'd signed a deal to play for the NBA's Sacramento Kings after spending nearly the entire summer with me wherever I was at the time. He accompanied me on WNBA trips and to Beijing, and we'd recently decided to make LA home and purchased a house together. We were still in our honeymoon phase after being engaged eighteen months prior. It was now October, and it was time for a much-needed break back in Los Angeles. After a couple of days of rest, I realized I was still absolutely exhausted and could barely keep my eyes open. Something was off. *Maybe . . . naw, it couldn't be.* I needed to know for sure. As the last draft's number one draft pick and the well-known rookie on the block, I was way too recognizable to stroll into a Los Angeles Walgreens and pick up a pregnancy test myself. I wasn't trying to have people in my business or cause a frenzy before I actually knew what was up. My best friend from Tennessee, Justine, purchased a pregnancy test and FedExed it to me overnight. Being young, I leaned on my friend and decided to keep this between her and me until I knew the results.

As I waited for the test to arrive I mulled over the possibilities, and different scenarios ran rampant in my head. I've always wanted to be a mother, so I couldn't not be happy if the test was positive. I realized that though this would be good news for me, I'd have some explaining to do. People look at me and think my success has come with freedom, but with great opportunity comes great expectations. If I was pregnant, this would significantly impact my basketball career and possibly my potential future earnings, whether I wanted to admit it or not.

I had just signed a multimillion-dollar contract with Adidas, Gatorade, and an overseas team, UMMC Ekaterinburg in Russia to play during the WNBA offseason The deal was historic for women's basketball globally and had brought a lot of anticipation as to what that investment would yield. Initially, I had no clue what having a baby would mean for that. Would they delay the contract until the following season? I'm no lawyer, but I imagined I'd be lucky if they waited for me at all instead of nullifying our agreement and securing new talent.

When I finished peeing on the stick, I sat down on the floor in my closet and waited for what seemed like an eternity. After a few minutes, I got up to go take a look. I didn't rush the short walk from the closet to the bathroom. Whether I liked it or not, this was a fork in the road no matter how I looked at it. Right before I looked, I remember thinking, *I will be disappointed if I'm not.* I saw two pink lines, clear as day. My heart nearly beat out of my chest and my breathing intensified. I was pregnant! This moment I had dreamed of for years was happening. I chuckled and shook my head, stunned. *I'm going to be a mom!* A lump formed in my throat. *Would anyone be happy for me?* I was worried that sponsors, team representatives, and fans would be disappointed. *Disappointed* in one of life's greatest moments. Again, I sat all alone as a mixture of happy tears and fearful tears dripped down my cheeks. I was in disbelief.

Some people that I told suggested I continue to play and terminate my pregnancy. There was always time to have children later, but right now, I had to choose the business and capitalize on my momentum. I have always believed in a woman's right to make the decisions about her body and life that were best for her as an individual. But I had always dreamed of becoming a mother. I played house and with dolls until I was almost a teenager, I had named all four of my children before I even began dating, I babysat any off time I had, and I was obsessed at being an aunt! I never imagined living in this moment and having reservations and fear. This was the first time in my life I wouldn't be choosing basketball.

My pregnancy revelation was a stark contrast to how I had lived my life up until that moment. Basketball became secondary in a blink of an eye. There was no other option for me, and though I wouldn't fault any woman in my same position who chose differently, I had to follow my own heart. It's frustrating that no matter what choice we make, we are being told to delay, hold off, pause, and sacrifice when men are encouraged to have it all with no downside.

Even though we hadn't planned to get pregnant right after my rookie year and Olympic run, I was ecstatic. I immediately felt protective of the little bean growing inside me. As I told more people, that mama-bear energy only grew; not everyone was as thrilled as Shelden and I were. I wanted people to share in our joy. To congratulate me on having it all. To see that playing basketball and growing a family didn't have to be at odds with each other. All that most people saw were rosters, ROIs, and their own resentment. Even though I continued training, practicing, and playing up until two days before I delivered, the speculation centered around what would come next. I knew I had a lot more basketball in me and had played with some of the best ballers and found that being a mom hadn't stopped them at all. I won Olympic gold with Lisa Leslie and Tina Thompson, both mothers, so I knew how capable and resilient a woman's body can be. If I could win Rookie of the Year and MVP in the same season on a torn labrum and in my first trimester of pregnancy, then I could do anything.

After finding out my due date, I circled on the calendar when I wanted to come back to the court. While my unborn daughter remained the priority, basketball still was in a way what it had always been in my life. With my target in my line of sight, I reverse engineered the recovery schedule and workout regimen that would have me ready in time. I treated pregnancy as if it was an injury. I set goals and daily tasks, and I planted seeds with the organization and my doctors of my plans to return. I talked everything over with my obstetrician, who agreed that it was best to induce labor at thirty-nine weeks, about one week before my due date, to reduce issues in delivery. (I wasn't opposed to delivering a week early, as it gave me one extra week to return to the court.) Scheduling birth was an added benefit, giving me six to eight weeks between giving birth and my planned first game back.

A few months before my due date, an ESPN magazine was released with my pregnant belly front and center. "How Big Can Candace Parker Get?" the headline asked. The entire shoot was such an affirming experience and gave me back something the media, league executives, and even fans had tried to take away: my joy. People were so focused on whether pregnancy would thwart my career, and it robbed me of a lot of the happiness I felt about bringing my daughter into the world. Hiding something that I viewed as my greatest achievement in life was extremely difficult. I overcame the scrutiny that came from the audacity I had in daring to journey into motherhood, but now came the hard part! I had so much to prove and so many stereotypes to dispel in a league by and for women. I couldn't understand why the WNBA wasn't better at holding players as full human beings with personal and professional lives.

I struggled deeply with people only seeing one side of who we are as athletes. Most of the public discusses and debates our lives as though we are robots designed to perform, put up numbers, and help our organizations win. Nothing else. Life has always been bigger than that for me. My brother had two children while playing basketball. I always envisioned my children being a part of my career and at my games. Now that I was actually making that dream a reality, it was a lot less blissful than I'd hoped. Most days, I was mentally drained and exhausted from defending a pregnancy and child that I wanted more than anything.

So many women are forced to make difficult choices; we worry about the timing of our pregnancies and hide our bellies in embarrassment. We are expected to justify and reaffirm that pregnancy will not stop us from doing our jobs and advancing our careers. I should have been able to focus on prenatal pills, stocking a nursery, and other to-dos that normal moms worry about. Instead, I was mapping out my comeback and carrying a burden and feeling the pressure to prove that I could get back on the court as fast as possible!

On May 13, 2009, after thirty hours of labor and two pushes, out popped my entire world. Lailaa Nicole, my reason, was here. I remember hearing that having a child is like having your heart walking around outside of your body. My connection to this beautiful little girl was immediate and profound. I immediately loved her more than life itself. And without a shadow of a doubt I knew even before she was born I would die to save her, but after she was born I knew I would live *for her*. Seeing her made me want to open every door, fight every no, and prevent the world from dimming her light. I studied every dimple, birthmark, and feature that first night together in the hospital. I looked into her eyes, and my entire soul lost track of time, goals, money, etc. As Lailaa laid on my chest, I played Lauryn Hill's "Nothing Even Matters" as we drifted off to sleep with her in my arms.

During my entire pregnancy, I'd worked out and tried to stay in the best shape I could, which really helped. At the time, my doctor in

Sacramento cleared me to work out so long as it didn't involve lifting over my head. (He also said something about not letting my heart rate go above 120, but that wasn't realistic. I was an athlete.) Overall, I kept in pretty good shape while pregnant with my daughter. I gained thirty pounds, and as a result of a delivery plan gone right, I delivered vaginally, which kept me on track for a return in six to eight weeks. Post-delivery, I chilled and did only light walking the first week and a half to two weeks. After my two-week visit with my OB I was cleared to do "some" working out. Now, the "some" was up to my interpretation. Leaving it to me had always been trouble. My "some" was a lot of people's "a lot"! I am not a dip-my-toe-into-it-and-see-how-it-goes kind of person. I'm a full-throttle, all-or-nothing, cannonball sort of person. My brothers were in town to see Lailaa for the first time, and I took it as the perfect opportunity to get my first workout in. I planned a solid lift and core work in addition to a standard basketball workout. My older brother Anthony asked me after my lift, "Are you sure you aren't doing too much? You might want to work your way back a little more before jumping into basketball." Stubborn me didn't have time to take things slow. My timeline was approaching, and I needed to stay on track.

I ran up and down the court at a snail's pace, but after completing roughly an hour of basketball drills, skills, shots, and post moves, I felt a slight pull in my back. I was afraid to let my older brother see me wince, so I played it off. When I arrived home, I could barely lift my legs out of the car. Every inch of my body was sore, and my back was tight. I finally had to admit to my brother I had overdone it and canceled the next day's workout. Looking back I was a complete idiot. How did I think after all the changes my body endured—creating human life, the weight gain, the opening of my hips for birth—I could just jump back into playing basketball like it was nothing? After some soul-searching, a smarter new approach, and some rest and recovery I gradually went back to regular workouts. My pregnancy workout routine paid off because, even though I was definitely slower than before, getting back on the court felt like remembering to ride a bike in some ways. I missed the first few games of the season as I trained, but on July 6, 2009—nearly eight weeks to the day after giving birth—I returned to the court to play for the Los Angeles Sparks. Before the game, I meticulously scheduled Lailaa's and my napping and feeding schedule so that she had enough milk during the first half. I'd been exclusively breastfeeding Lailaa since she was born, and my comeback didn't stop those needs. A growing girl's gotta eat, even when it's half-time of her mommy's big reentrance.

During my first game back, it felt good to be back out there, but my performance didn't meet my expectations. The pace was definitely harder on me than I thought, but I was keeping up. I wasn't the Candace Parker of old, but I deserved a bit of grace, and I had to remind myself to take it easy.

One game, in the first couple of weeks since my return, I attacked the basket, almost like old times. I felt a bit of my step coming back and my game slowly improving. I got bumped by another player on my drive to the basket and finished the bucket. The crowd and my team-mates erupted, and I awkwardly froze. All women out there know the struggles postbaby of the dreaded sneaky sneeze that can catch you off guard. Well, mine just so happened to come in the form of a foul. This couldn't be happening. I locked eyes with Lisa Leslie and gave her the look. From mom to mom, she understood. I had peed just a bit. We laughed and laughed about that one. The joys of motherhood. As I told members of the media at the time, "There's room for basketball, there's room for Lailaa. I have, from a young age, said I wanted both. Right now I'm living my dream because I have the best of both worlds." Yes, it's challenging. Yes, at times I don't have it all together, but I'm proud of myself. My stats and my play early on weren't up to my standards, but I would come home from a hard day at practice, and instead of rehab, breaking down film at all hours of the night, and extra shots, I would lie down on the floor and play with my daughter. My baby girl would make me forget about it all. Her smile forced me to live in the moment and not rush to the next day, game, or event. For the first time in forever, I had balance, and I gave myself grace. I was finally where my two feet were. I have my daughter to thank for that.

Battle Scars

After having deferred an overseas contract because of my pregnancy, I knew the logical and most lucrative answer was to head to Russia and play the season I'd committed to. But a part of me really wanted to focus on my physical health and recovery. I was a roadrunner, having played nonstop basketball since I was just a girl. My high school career led me straight into Tennessee, my offseasons were spent in between USA Basketball and Tennessee training and after graduating I had no time before I had to be in WNBA mode, and the last offseason I was expecting a child. My first true offseason, I asked myself, did I really want to go overseas? UMMC had waited for me to recover and kept my original contract, which they didn't have to do. They made it clear, they needed me. I needed them, too. The money they were offering far exceeded what I made in America and would set our family up in major ways. But could my body really hold up? I badly needed shoulder surgery that I'd avoided while I was pregnant, and I felt like every day I was delaying the inevitable.

I made the logical decision and decided to go to Russia, but my body kept score, ultimately winning in the end. That's the thing about physical health. We think we can force our bodies to work around us until the need for rehabilitation and care catches up with us and we find out the truth. Nothing can bring you to a halt quite like an overworked body. It will find a way to clear your schedule and cancel out all other noise, but only because we ignored the warning signs before. The body will have its needs met, one way or another.

I thought—or hoped—that there was no one or nothing capable of deterring me from my plans of killing it in Russia and coming back stronger than ever to the Sparks. (Hello, Can-Do!) But throughout 2010, I experienced injury after injury—mostly repeated shoulder dislocations. It was a disaster and left me dealing with excruciating pain that made me wish I had never ignored doctor's orders. Now there was no choice of opting in or out. I needed surgery desperately, or I wouldn't be playing basketball at all.

I wish 2010 was the end of my series of unfortunate events, but when the damage is done, pushed to the brink, ignored, and compounded over time, even surgery is a form of temporary relief. Pain became my new normal. In and out of doctor's offices, spending as much disposable income as possible to get relief from the pain. Trying new procedures and leaning on cutting-edge technology just to get my body to do what it is supposed to naturally. To this day, I long for a time when a random wrong step won't send my body into a downward spiral, that getting out of bed won't be a challenge, and my knees don't crack and creak with every step. Even now as I'm on the other side of playing professionally, my body will never go back to what it was before basketball.

People always say find something you love and you will never work a day in your life. I don't know if that's true, but what I will say is it makes the work joyful and satisfying. When you love something, you realize the struggle is worth it. I used to smile during conditioning as sweat dripped down my face and my chest rose and fell, out of breath and exhausted. I loved the journey. I loved the process. I loved the challenge. Basketball ignited a passion in me that made me love it during the highs and realize I loved it even more during the lows. Injuries reaffirmed my love for the game. Injuries taught me to challenge, rise, bend but not break, and overcome time and time again. I just wish I didn't have to live with the consequences of playing at all costs.

Having to live without the joy of playing basketball, but with all of the lasting effects from the game I love. Both of my knees are bone-on-bone. I can't jog without pain. I can't just get up and do regular active things like beach volleyball or football. I get injections and epidural shots annually to manage the pain and to remain mobile. I do it because it allows me to swim with An and Lailaa, hoop with Goose, and get low to the ground to play with Hartt. My family is worth it all and then some. But I sometimes ask myself, was my career worth the pain?

If I could, I would definitely change the impact this sport has had on my body, but in doing so I might change the accomplishments I achieved. The sacrifices I made allowed me to win big but come at a great cost to my family and me. I overheard my daughter at the tender age of three explaining to a friend at the park that "my mommy has bad knees." I felt guilty every time Lailaa asked me to do something active, and then the disappointed look that followed when she remembered I probably couldn't. My kids won't get to experience an agile mommy. But, if younger Candace hadn't pushed through injuries or had retired a bit earlier, it could have changed the shell I'm left with. It would have changed me.

It's a gift and a curse, a mentality that isn't easily switched off when it's for the good. I think I just needed someone to protect me from me. I have to touch the fire to know it's hot, and even then I still every once in a while need to make sure. I don't like "No, you can't." It does something to my soul. It makes me want to prove that I can even when I shouldn't. It has worked in my favor in a lot of ways but also is my detriment. I've learned to grit my teeth and endure anything, no matter how excruciating. That's the Can-Do in me. I wish I had learned all those years ago that just because you can doesn't mean you should.

When Pat Summitt told me I couldn't play on a swollen knee, I was furious at first. I'd been playing on swollen knees well enough to win a dunk contest. Now that I was here she was keeping me from playing? I was more valuable than I was giving myself credit for, and I needed to be protected from myself. If it were up to me I would have played hard and wrong for as long as I could. Who knows how much sooner my body would have given up on me and which accomplishments I never would have achieved. Pat saw Candace the person as more important than Candace the college hooper, and it's part of what makes her so special. I wish more people had intervened the way she did.

At a certain point, my life and body became entangled in a toxic merry-go-round. I'd go out onto the court and give it my all, banging up my knees, shoulders, and back in the process. The moment I stepped off the court, I was fixing myself up for the next time I'd be back. That meant deep levels of recovery. Walking the dogs during the season and going to the park with Lailaa were all tasks that I paid for later with swelling, stiffness, and more pain. I invested so much time, money, and experimental remedies in order to glue the broken pieces of my body back together only to have brief relief undone by more pain and more ailments as a result of compensating for past injuries. But there seemed to be no stopping the ride.

Playing, rehabbing, recovering, and resting became all I had time for. It was exhausting and sucked the fun out of life as a mom, wife, sister, and friend. I wanted to be able to go on vacation and participate in the full itinerary without assessing the likelihood of being injured or how much it would hurt. I wanted to play football in the sand, hike, and race my kids. Doing activities became like assessing whether you wanted to deal with a hangover the next day or not for a little fun. I wanted to walk around the farmers market all day Saturday and play beach volleyball on a Sunday. Even with the best doctors and equipment on the planet, simple tasks were never so simple for me.

I know a thing or two about feeling defeated and worn down by the need to constantly rise to the occasion. Sometimes the drive to be great is so consuming that even when you are at your best and you are excelling, it's never enough. In the book *Same as Ever*, Morgan Housel perfectly captures the difficulty in the balance of enough. You only know when enough is enough after you've gone too far. I, unfortunately, have crossed over that threshold multiple times and have since learned the balance of living in the moment and controlling the obsession to have more or to win at all costs.

Recently, while I was watching *Good Morning America*, they were celebrating the first-year Tennessee women's basketball coach, Kim Caldwell, coming back just one week post-delivery of her new baby boy. My immediate reaction was how incredible and strong women are (which is true)! Women never cease to amaze me in their ability to do it all. But in not wanting to sacrifice, attempting to prove the ability to balance both work and life, did I unintentionally contribute to the pressure to do it as fast as possible? *Just because we can do something doesn't mean we should.* I came back fifty-three days post-delivery and I used to wear it like a badge of honor. But now I have a greater perspective. The reason maternal leave exists in the first place is to limit expectations and give much-needed time for that beautiful period of life. Did I actually influence others to follow in my footsteps? I regret, looking back, the time I missed. Where for six short weeks, instead of focusing on and memorizing Lailaa's smell and her cries, and giving my body grace, I was juggling the newness of motherhood, putting my healing body through more strain working out, and fighting back tears from hormones and sleep deprivation!

I used to think it was heroic that I literally got my eleven stitches taken out from tearing when I delivered the day before my first basketball workout, still wearing my panty liner because I was still bleeding. Women often put pressure on themselves to continually dispel the notion that we can't do it all. The limitations placed on women force us to feel the need to prove that we are more. These days, as I watch friends, family, teammates, coaches, businesswomen and stay-at-home moms bring life into the world, I realize that if we all see a rapid return to what we do as strength, if we don't come back at warp speed, is it seen as weakness? The strength it takes to balance motherhood AND work is heroic in itself, whether we do it 53 days or 365 days later. There's no weakness in taking the time to enjoy moments you can't get back. Heroes shouldn't always feel like they have to wear capes.

The same is true for anyone dealing with debilitating pain or loss. Whether it's emotional or physical pain, I learned just because you can endure it, doesn't mean you should. It makes our nights sleepless and makes the abilities others take for granted elusive, no matter how hard we work. But, in some ways, injuries were also my introduction to better work-life balance. Something had to change. My recovery seasons were some of the only times I was able to really be off and home with my family. If the team was away and I was injured, then I wouldn't be expected to travel and could enjoy my loved ones so long as I was rehabbing and recovering. I didn't love being constrained in what my body could do, but I loved ambling and being in no rush to get anywhere. No alarms to set. No practices or games to clock in for.

The more I tasted and savored that freedom, the more I resented giving the best parts of me physically to the game and leaving so little left over for the moments that mattered more. During my last season in the WNBA, I was in so much pain that on my off days I had zero gas in the tank. I'd get a massage the night after the game, go to sleep, and still wake up in pain. Getting out of bed was the hardest part of my day, second only to going downstairs. Those first steps were excruciating as my joints creaked and bones cracked. As I padded across the floor to the bathroom, my body slowly warmed up, but the pain remained. Gravity seemed to drag me down the steps. I could barely walk around, but I knew I had to. I would try to resist, but I would go to the medicine cabinet and take the maximum dosage I could take of an anti-inflammatory. Sometimes, I would even get on a steroid pack for weeks at a time. Was it helping put a Band-Aid on the pain? Yes, but was it causing more possible health problems later? What about my intestinal tract, kidneys, liver, and stomach?

To make it to the next practice, let alone our next game, took a lot of rehab. Cold baths, anti-inflammatory pills, more massages . . . all just to be good enough to do it all again the next day. The times when I was feeling decent came few and far between. At one point, I was tired of feeling crappy trying to play basketball. During warm-ups,

I'd sit on the baseline before practice, staring down at the other baseline and dreading the thought of running up and down the court. I used to love it! Even in practices, I loved to compete and have fun with what I knew I could do better than anyone else. Now my body and mind were disconnected, and I wasn't the only one struggling with it. I could tell it was difficult for my teammates to understand why I was so slow. Why it took so long for me to warm up when they could get into the flow of practice within a couple minutes? Why I activated and stretched so much. Pain sucked the joy of the game from me. I had survived as long as I could . . . It was time.

That's the process of pain that few people talk about. Pain is isolating and dulling, but also clarifying. It quiets the electives and zeroes in on matters of the heart like never before. As such, pain is life's natural truth serum; all walls and masks fall down so that the pain can speak and point you to what needs to be repaired. When we're hurt and angry, we speak uninhibitedly. When we're grieving, we lose our patience and diplomacy. The pain of disappointment gives us the courage to say the previously unspoken. In the silence of my pain, I was able to hear my heart more clearly. It didn't cause me to fall out of love with basketball but rather to fall in love with who I am when I'm not on the court.

At my last home game for the Aces, I stood at the mouth of the tunnel looking out. I should have been soaking it all in, scanning the crowd, memorizing faces, and savoring the feelings. In reality, all I could think about was how I was going to run onto the court when my name was announced and whether my foot was going to fail me. By this point, my feet were burning with every step. Favoring one injured foot, I overcompensated so much that I pulled my Achilles on the other foot and had a grade-three strain. They say your brain can only process one pain at a time, so my brain was shifting from foot to knee to Achilles and back again. I never had a break, and I couldn't enjoy the moment because of how excruciating the pain was. I couldn't even enjoy the moment.

My biggest fear when staring in that mirror all those years ago was that I'd never do what I loved again. What eighteen-year-old Candace had yet to learn was that basketball may have been my first but was never destined to be my only. There is so much more I have to give and receive from the world. If I had given up then, I'd never have Lailaa or Anya or Goose or Hartt. I'd never have set records, helped changed the way the game is played, won championships, won multiple MVPs, or Olympic gold medals. I'd never have met, done, or seen many of my favorite memories. I'm grateful to have been surrounded by people who could affirm that in me and speak up for me when I was too tired to advocate for myself.

Pain is a relentless teacher whom we don't realize how much we've learned from until she's already gone. Pain clouds your mind and intensifies your feelings. I tolerated and prolonged pain because I couldn't imagine life after basketball. My entire career I always imagined the end. Walking off the floor on two feet, healthy, uninjured, not in pain. I wanted to fight for that ending that I had imagined all those years ago. But pain eventually overtook my joy. I knew this relationship with the game had come to an end.

Basketball has made me who I am, but it's not all I am. I was afraid to let go of the game. But I didn't want to play basketball this way. I mourned the loss of the way I used to play basketball, joyful, uninhibited, and pain free. That was gone and was never coming back. Once I realized that, I couldn't wait to separate from this version of basketball that I had come to dread. I was holding on to the past and in essence neglecting and abusing my present and future. I needed to listen to myself. I finally did. I retired April 28, 2024. I'm proud of myself for fighting, preserving, and knowing when enough is enough. Life is miraculous, and each day is a chance to predict the future through our actions and daily deposits. There is always something or someone to push through for. Next time, try letting that someone be future you!

FOURTEEN

Who Will We Choose to Be?

Practice? We're talking about practice.

—ALLEN IVERSON

In 1996, all the world watched as women took center stage in the Summer Olympics in Atlanta, Georgia. There I sat on the couch as a little girl, eyes glued to the TV as Dominique Dawes demonstrated her unparalleled athleticism in gymnastics on the floor exercise and Mia Hamm and her teammates captivated the world in front of a record 76,500 fans and brought excitement for soccer to the United States. But the women's basketball team I watched closer than the others, wide-eyed as Lisa Leslie dominated the Brazilian team to capture the gold and avenge their loss in Madrid in 1992 in front of 32,000 people. The historic moments of the 1996 Olympic Games were years in the making. This was the first generation of girls who were even allowed to play sports since the inception of Title IX in 1972, which stated:

No person in the United States shall, on the basis of sex, be excluded from participation in, be denied the benefits of, or be subjected to discrimination under any educational program or activity receiving Federal financial assistance.

But what was even more exciting was that an entire generation of young girls was watching the athletes be unapologetic, aggressive, fierce, and strong. And I was one of those young girls. The 1996 Olympics was a catalyst for so many things, including, in 1997, the inaugural Women's National Basketball Association season.

The WNBA served as a beacon of hope and promise all mixed in one. To all the young girls who were told to wait your turn, the WNBA provided a place to play. For sixteen years, I got to lace up my own signature shoes, act in TV shows and movies, be the first woman on the cover of *NBA2K*, star in commercials alongside my daughter, play in sold-out arenas, travel to faraway places, meet my idols, dunk on opponents and foes, hit game winners, hang banners, and work with teammates turned forever friends, all because I fell in love with this orange ball and I had a place to play—a platform to compete alongside other women who grew up loving the game like I did. I knew going into 2023 that it would be my last year in the WNBA, and the little girl in me mourned every minute of that season. It's hard to say goodbye is an understatement. The years were long, but the days were short. Seasons flew by, but I knew the time was coming to say farewell to a game that had given me more than I could ever imagine.

All of those memories, highs, wins, championships, and milestones didn't come without a price. There's an immense responsibility every WNBA player feels coming into the league, not only performing and adjusting to the professional game, but protecting, growing, and helping to advocate for an entire burgeoning association. Within only a few years, I couldn't shake the feeling that there didn't always seem to be an emphasis or proactive thinking around women's well-being despite this being a *women's* league. Women players were regularly disrespected, underpaid, and vulnerable to policies designed for us without us, but also sometimes by us. Despite the progress made, sometimes fast and at times slow, the league needed to step up its game and, plain and simple, be better!

James Baldwin has a saying about loving America so much that he insists on the right to critique America. Baldwin describes a true patriot as someone who can make this nation they cherish, one that lives up to its promise. I really resonate with that idea—especially in the context of the WNBA. Being part of this league has opened up doors I didn't even dare to dream existed. Seeing how far we've come since the late 1990s is truly mind-blowing. But we still have a long way to go, and those of us who have seen the WNBA from the inside have to be the ones to champion and fight for those changes. I believe wholeheartedly that those closest to the problems are also closest to the solutions. There has to be a willingness to listen and not just plan for the present, but anticipate and navigate what the future could be.

Ownership Matters: Learning from the Past

I remember watching *Winning Time* on HBO, a show that chronicles the rise of the Showtime Lakers dynasty, including some pivotal moments like Magic Johnson being drafted in 1979—his rookie year, family, and rise to stardom—as well as Kareem Abdul-Jabbar's dominance in a very different America and NBA landscape. Racism, violence, underinvestment in the league, and NBA playoff games being shown on tape delay were the norm. It was an interesting contrast between the rookie and veteran experiences. I saw a lot in common between the way things were then in the NBA and the way things were for us in the WNBA. In the 1980s, fans questioned whether a predominantly African American league could be successful in the midst of racism in America, the Black Panther Party, police brutality, and social division. Media, advertisers, and fans were skeptical of whether they could market the NBA; the NBA was put in a box.

The same year that Magic Johnson was drafted, in 1979, Dr. Jerry Buss bought the Lakers for $24 million. Magic Johnson was coming off of a college National Championship at Michigan State in which they defeated Indiana State and a sharp shooting scorer by the name of Larry Bird. The start of a rivalry that would be one for the ages as Bird was picked the year before in the draft to play for the championship dynasty Boston Celtics. This rivalry began in college and followed the pair to their new professional franchises. Dr. Buss wasn't the sort of cookie-cutter owner that the league had been used to. He pushed boundaries, invested heavily, innovated, and wanted to win. In addition to purchasing the Lakers, Buss also bought the Forum in order to use the arena for Lakers games, concerts, and other sporting events. He opened an exclusive club at the Forum where they served drinks and food, and it was the spot to be at postgame in LA. Dr. Buss envisioned the average Lakers game being an event. A moment. He aimed to establish an atmosphere surrounding the game that was as enticing as the players on the court. It was never *just* about the game, it was about making it an experience, an event, a place where the who's who were.

Buss's journey to revolutionize the NBA experience began by inviting celebrities and the who's who in LA to Lakers games. He invented the courtside-seat experience by extending seats that used to be reserved exclusively for media and opening them up to the stars. Buss realized intimate engagement with the players and in-game action was prime real estate. For the courtside seats that didn't go to celebrities and media, Buss charged more and ensured everyone treated it as a premium experience. The growth of the Laker Girls—women who were sexy and provided entertainment during halftime and time-outs—also became an integral part of this plan. Although most fans of the Lakers are blown away by Magic Johnson's ability to play all five positions while winning an NBA championship his rookie season, I was blown away by Buss and his investment in the team. But he wasn't done. In 1981, Buss signed Magic Johnson to a twenty-five-year $25 million contract (which is equivalent to roughly $84 million today). Continuing to raise the bar in the NBA is what set the stage for the players of today to have the stage and the value they have. There was a passion, intention, and diligence in how Buss built a winning organization both on and off the floor when many at the time insisted it was a waste of money because the NBA would never be a profitable business. As of 2024, that organization is valued at $7.1 billion. What do they say in business, "Scared money don't make money!" Passively investing in anything leads to passive returns. Ownership is valuable and crucial in everything.

For so long, the WNBA waited for its version of Buss. In 2021, he arrived. He came in the form of a white suit and an interesting haircut and was already the experienced and passionate owner of the Las Vegas Raiders. Mark Davis took the WNBA by storm. First order of business, he pried Becky Hammon away from her assistant-coaching job with the San Antonio Spurs to be the head coach of the Aces. And he did it by paying her a head-coaching record salary of $1 million. At the time, it didn't sit right with me that a head coach would make not only more than the star player but almost as much as the entire team combined. The WNBA salary cap in 2021 was $1.3 million. But as a result of a collective bargaining agreement that limited how much he could pay the players, Mark Davis was able to leverage that coaching salary, and invest in his team. He turned heads with his audacious investment and bold move in the only way he could within the rules. From head coach to president to the staff, everything Davis did was deliberate, intentional, and with the players' best interests at heart.

Player development was at the forefront, and assistant coaches were hired with the goal of retaining the players they drafted and making them better. Team housing was phenomenal. The players had a state-of-the-art facility equipped with its own weight room, recovery-training room, chefs, basketball courts, offices, film room, etc. You name it, they had it. On top of that, Vegas home games became a true spectacle to see. The in-game entertainment and story-telling through photography, videography, social media, and arena visuals were captivating. There was no stone unturned and no expense spared in player and fan experiences. The Aces were deliberate in connecting the team to the community, hosting numerous events and participating in charities to establish a connection between the team and its fans. Support flowed both ways. Ever since then, under Davis's leadership, home games have all been sellouts, and the Aces won back-to-back championships in 2022 and 2023. As Pat Summitt always said, you win with people and passion. Success starts at the top and trickles down because the leaders set the tone; as Theodore Roosevelt noted: "No one cares how much you know until they know how much you care."

Two seasons against the New York Liberty distinctly stand out in my mind. Though I played against the franchise for nearly two decades, what I remember are the two seasons where we fought the New York City traffic and drove nearly thirty miles north of where the Liberty played at Madison Square Garden for the past nearly twenty-one years. They went from playing center stage at Madison Square Garden to White Plains and the Westchester County Center. Opponents used to circle the Liberty game on the schedule for an opportunity to play in the Mecca that was Madison Square Garden. Now, we dreaded it. It was *awful.* From a player standpoint, the facilities were old, the locker rooms were outdated, and it was a pain to commute to. From a fan standpoint, the Liberty went from once being a staple-of-the-league franchise to averaging a little more than twenty-two hundred people. What fan would enjoy a small arena that was old and stuffy and lacked entertainment? Just off of the venue, the Liberty screamed undervalued and underinvested in. As a result, attendance dropped, and they had an inability to attract free agents to one of the best markets in America. In 2018, New York went 7–27, and as a result of their continued rocky performances, they earned the number one draft pick in 2020. At the end of 2019,

Clara Wu Tsai and her husband, Joseph Tsai, purchased the Liberty in a fire sale by James Dolan. Their first course of action was to relocate the team. As a result of also owning the Brooklyn Nets and the Barclays Center, the Tsais decided to move the Liberty back to New York City. They invested in the team, cared about the fan experience, and in turn gradually began to land free agents and fans slowly came back to watch. After a few years, the New York Liberty brought home the 2024 WNBA championship in front of 18,090 screaming fans in Barclays Center. Change comes from the top!

I get it; there was a long time when it was difficult to even sell a WNBA team. Historically, WNBA teams were tied to NBA teams directly through ownership, and that model was intended to provide practice facilities, elevated player experiences, and financial resources for hiring and scaling the league. Years later, in 2001, the NBA launched a new NBA D-League, or developmental league. This league was aimed at the next tier of potential NBA talents, giving them a place to play and grow their game to eventually be able to develop into a contributor for an NBA franchise. As more owners doubled down and invested in the D-League (the now G League), the WNBA took a back seat and a lot of owners elected to sell. During this period of time, a number of teams either sold to new ownership, relocated, or folded. These years would have a huge impact on the WNBA at that time as well as for years to come.

Let's be real, David Stern and a number of NBA owners made it possible for the WNBA to have a launchpad to even exist in the first place. Still to this day, a number of WNBA teams are owned by NBA owners, and as a league the WNBA is 50 percent owned by the NBA. A majority of the WNBA's biggest investors haven't looked at the WNBA as a true investment. The NBA is constantly seen as a philanthropist, and the WNBA its cause, so us "girls" should be grateful for the chance. The business plan, marketing, and target audience changed daily. The NBA was seen as the North Star in everything we wanted to be, but it seemed we weren't utilizing any of their blueprint to get there.

The WNBA took a "take what you can get approach" and few standards were set as to what new owners were expected to bring to the table. WNBA leadership left it up to individual owners to identify buyers, and this hands-off approach allowed many teams to fall to owners who simply weren't equipped. That's how dynasties like the Houston Comets get shut down within a year of an ownership change. Ultimately, the WNBA as a whole suffered because senior leadership across the league didn't understand the importance of not just ownership but their investment in the franchise as a whole. By being so reactive, WNBA leadership missed out on what is possible through foresight and preparation.

Owners like Clara Wu Tsai and Joseph Tsai, Mat Ishbia, and Mark Davis were the beginning of the change in mindset surrounding WNBA franchises. Until recently, franchises were invested in like a charity, with little hope of actual monetary return. They did it to feel good and "support" women's sports. Now, the masses are flocking to invest in women's sports in general. It takes money to make money, but it also takes foresight and vision to build a product that people will enjoy. From bringing better practice facilities to crafting innovative fan experiences, including beloved mascots to culinary and beverage activations, they have shown that it matters when building a successful franchise. Build it right and, owners like these have shown, there will be better coaches, better players, excited fans, and the championships will come. The race to the top should include a race to invest. The WNBA for so long tried to level the playing field within the league by equalizing competitive advantage with rules within its CBA. In essence, the WNBA stymied its own growth and competition within the most important part of a franchise, the owners. Ultimately, owners who want to invest in their teams will win and weed out the ones who don't.

The time in women's basketball has reached yet another fork in the road. Investors from all genres flock to invest in the WNBA like never before. However, now it is even more crucial to seek out vision, purpose, network, connection, and even more so people who understand the history of the game. I hope the WNBA learns from the past and is strategic in who they allow as owners of teams in our league. The WNBA has stood for so much for so long, and that needs to be represented from the top down. Those who can write the biggest checks often are also individuals who didn't believe girls should or *could* play basketball up until months ago. To take the league where it needs to go, you have to know where it has been.

There are so many people who have been in the "fight" on the ground ensuring that the growth of women's basketball continues and now are being pushed to the side. Understanding the rich history and value, stories, and purpose is critical. I hope the WNBA recognizes the need for ownership to represent the league that is. It should understand the foundation for which the women's game has grown and thus represent and raise up the voices and unique game of the WNBA—a predominantly Black league made up of women from all different backgrounds. I want to see more players and women in business having the ability to join groups and help be a North Star in all things women's sports. I want to see more owners who look like and represent the diversity of thought within the league. Our league has always been special, and this growth has always been possible. We just needed vision, time, network, and opportunity. That begins at the top!

Know Your Worth

At the University of Tennessee, our school and the women's basketball team in particular had massive followings, which were built over time and nurtured intentionally. Even before social media, we were on SportsCenter, ESPN, the cover of *Sports Illustrated*, local news, billboards, you name it. We flew charter, worked out in newly built practice facilities, and had access to top medical care, massages, and luxurious travel. All in all, we were supported, uplifted, and provided all of the opportunities to succeed. I had heard the rumblings from a great deal of players about the inability of the WNBA to capitalize on the foundation a lot of its stars had built throughout their college careers.

I entered the WNBA in 2008 doe-eyed, hungry, and passionate about the sport I loved. I rolled up my figurative sleeves and worked to not only try to be one of the best, but help leave the game better than I came into it. On the first day of training camp, I was surprised to realize that we were going to be practicing at a local community college. Throughout the season, we shared the Staples Center with the Lakers, Clippers, Los Angeles Kings, and countless other events and concerts that were hosted there. Some days we had access to the locker room; some days we had to empty it out so that someone else could use it. Even when I was playing with the Chicago Sky, we shared Wintrust Arena with DePaul and different events and activities, so we practiced at a recreational center and had a locker with a key that was issued by the downstairs front desk.

Our playoffs season, arguably the biggest time of the year for the WNBA, often conflicted with the start of the NBA season and the NHL playoffs. During our championship run and numerous other series, we were forced to play at alternate venues because the arena was booked. This predicament was understandable for a while, growth takes time. But the clock kept ticking and there was no push or sense of urgency from the league to work toward solving some of these problems. The struggle of television time slots, arenas being over-booked, and the WNBA always having to be the league that adjusts, put an already struggling narrative out there even more so. In 2017, for game five of the WNBA finals, the dynasty Minnesota Lynx were forced to play a do-or-die game for the WNBA championship at the University of Minnesota arena because the Target Center was booked. We don't need perfection, but we do need a league that cares enough to ensure their schedule will be prioritized and that players won't be shuffled around like cards. Venues and facilities being available for games and practices is critical to giving fans an entertaining home experience to look forward to. Every time a conflict arose with an arena or practice facility, it devalued the WNBA as a whole.

Public perception of your league matters when it comes to growth and value. Around my third year in the league, the WNBA signed a deal with Holiday Inn Express, no disrespect intended, and made it mandatory for all teams and players to stay there. There were countless times my teammates and I would be asked by fans what we were doing at that hotel. The perception around women's basketball was already that we didn't make a lot of money, and to then double down and have us stay at Holiday Inn Expresses created even more of a mountain to climb in getting others to see our product as valuable. Every man living in his mother's basement degraded and devalued our worth, but now the WNBA as a whole did it for them. This was yet another example of the WNBA undermining its own product. As they say, you never get a second chance to make a first impression. In a world that already hurls so much negativity toward women athletes, WNBA leadership needs to be extremely strategic in what partners we align ourselves with and how it positions players.

Leagues are successful on the backs of superstars and equipping them with the tools and support to succeed. The WNBA seemed to have no plan on retaining and expanding the following that its superstars had in high school and college. From Chamique Holdsclaw to Diana Taurasi and myself, to Maya Moore and Breanna Stewart, a number of us players entered the league with massive followings only to have those platforms dwindle as our years in the WNBA ticked on. A lot of the momentum that could have been capitalized on was wasted due to a lack of strategy or new ideas. Why wasn't I taken back to Tennessee for preseason games or exhibition opportunities?

Why didn't the WNBA work directly with the university to establish a relationship that continued to facilitate a connection between the university and the franchise? This wasn't a player problem, a lot of the WNBA stars had achieved tremendous success and following in college, it was a WNBA problem.

The consistent justification for underwhelming player experience and pay that was downright disrespectful was that we should feel grateful to have a league to play in to begin with, and that better pay and benefits would come with more visibility and profit. Patience was preached and as the years ticked by and there was no plan or vision put in place to prevent brands from dwindling and the following from deteriorating, patience ran out. Year after year, players put the league above themselves because playing at home in front of our family with the chance to help "grow the game" was framed as a small price to pay. Even when I was making twenty to thirty times my WNBA salary overseas, I still hopped on plane after plane prioritizing the WNBA above everything else. One season concluded and I'd start the next one less than two weeks later. We players really shouldered the weight of not losing the WNBA, so much so that few questioned whether league leadership was properly utilizing its resources and investing in player success. Start-ups know, sometimes the greatest ideas fail, not because of the idea but because of the execution.

We blindly trusted that doing without now would somehow lead to better pay and benefits when the visibility and profit increased. That meant six a.m. flights out of cities to catch the cheapest price even if it led to tired legs and physical exhaustion. Lack of practice facilities led to zero flexibility for player development and off-season work. Limited budget meant coaches turning down WNBA jobs for other opportunities. Underfunding led to being short-staffed and players missing out on health and wellness, player development, and injury prevention, and the list goes on and on. It felt like the league as a whole was preying on our genuine love for the game. At so many points across my career I've wondered why things couldn't be easier. Understanding that we need certain things to succeed, but then not equipping the players with those things did not make sense. Everything felt unnecessarily difficult as the dangling carrot was moved farther and farther away.

Money Changes Things

In 2008, at the time a record-breaking debut of 1.07 million people watched ABC, it was the most watched WNBA game since 2001. I entered the league with a splash of my own. In addition to becoming the first and only rookie to win both Rookie of the Year and Most Valuable Player in the same season, my presence in the WNBA set other records as well. The WNBA had triple the amount of sell-out games from the previous season. Along with signing partnerships with Gatorade and Adidas, I had tremendous momentum within the first few months in a Los Angeles Sparks uniform.

But there was quite the difference in 2024, when Caitlin Clark burst onto the scene and viewership increased. Something shifted when social media took over. Girls and women everywhere no longer had to wait for decision-makers to deem their stories worthy of telling. Female athletes took the reins and proved that people would be interested and follow if given the chance. Numbers didn't lie in the likes, views, and other digital insights. Initially, the WNBA still took a back seat and failed to truly capitalize on its storytelling at a fraction of the cost. Players have always been at the forefront of growth and expansion in this league. Sometimes, you have to set your own price, and one rule change did just that.

In 2021, The NCAA passed a rule that allowed college athletes to capitalize on their name, image, and likeness (NIL). College athletes everywhere, competing on the biggest stages, could now reap the financial benefits from companies and partnerships. Suddenly, the players drafted from college had a price, and the bar was set! Players like Caitlin Clark, Angel Reese, Paige Bueckers, and JuJu Watkins who have had massive followings since high school, can set the price for what they are actually worth.

NIL created space for a new intersection where talent meets visibility. Few truly understood how transformative it would be for the game of women's basketball, until Caitlin Clark exploded onto the scene at the perfect time to be catapulted from a local hero into a national superstar. After two years of captivating storytelling, exciting rivalries with LSU champion Angel Reese, smashing NCAA records, and playing in primetime games, Clark's value was undeniably set, and the impact reverberated through the league before she was even drafted. In anticipation of Clark being the number one draft pick, the Indiana Fever front office received a spike in ticket sales, and games were moved to larger arenas before her name was officially on a jersey. The visibility was aided by the University of Iowa, but also by the countless commercials, deals, partnerships, and apparel that was able to be sold with Clark as the beneficiary!

Reese similarly saw massive gains, which she capitalized on masterfully. After doing her best interpretation of John Cena's "You can't see me" move, Reese went viral and sparked a national debate about competitiveness and race. The moment was eerily similar to when Magic Johnson and Larry Bird entered the NBA, and it reminded fans—old and new—that women can be just as intense and exciting to watch as men. Reese's success didn't remain confined to the typical spaces for women athletes; she announced her intent to enter the WNBA draft with American *Vogue*. "I like to do everything big," she told *Vogue* in her interview. By the time Reese was suiting up for the Chicago Sky, her endorsements far exceeded her WNBA salary. The difference in the past versus the present with NIL was that college athletes entered the league with a set price and came already signed to massive endorsement deals and partnerships. The WNBA benefited from the stars.

The WNBA knew they couldn't fumble the opportunity before them, and they didn't. For the first time in a long time, I can see the improvement and growth in the quality of the storytelling, the investment in better practice and playing spaces, and the media partnerships to reach fans where they're at. I laugh to keep from crying because the WNBA approved charter flights the year I retired. I said I wanted to leave the game better than I found it, right? All jokes aside, the WNBA has made tremendous strides from where it started to where it's at now on the backs of its stars. The league has an opportunity to capitalize on the tremendous talent, viewership, and investments over the last few years. The WNBA needed to stop holding the WNBA back and prioritize the players and their brands far before players had to do it themselves. There's a chance now to be proactive and understand that player experience and player value raise the value of the league as a whole. I'm so proud of the past, present, and future of women's basketball because we understand our power and throughout the growing pains we have always known the capable value of the league, at times even before the league itself did.

To All the Mamas in the Place . . .

Having a child while actively playing felt like I was in an adversarial position with the executives around me. The unspoken truth was clear, you are an athlete and therefore valuable only when you can perform. It was a deeply impersonal process, and I know I'm not alone in recognizing that an overhaul is needed.

There was no paid maternity leave when I first started, a major dropped ball. You received your pay when you returned to the court. My health care during and after pregnancy was courtesy of the NBA where my then-husband was playing. My "maternity leave" was constructed on my own and, as a result, on my dime. I was fortunate to have the means and the ability to fund a regiment of trainers, masseuses, workout coaches, and physical therapists, though I know others weren't as fortunate. And the ones who weren't lottery draft picks or couldn't or didn't pay for additional care usually found themselves out of the league. I wish I could say that the WNBA was a bigger part of that joyous moment and my physical recovery, but there's no league mandate or standard for what the league and individual organizations were required to provide for players on maternity leave. Once Lailaa did arrive in all her cuddly cuteness, new logistical nightmares consumed my life. Though Lailaa was covered by her dad's access, that didn't include expenses associated with her traveling with me. When we traveled to away games, all players with fewer than five years of service were placed in shared double rooms at the hotels we stayed in. There was no privacy, which was bad enough as grown women and professional athletes. But when traveling with my daughter, I couldn't subject my teammates to her unpredictable schedule and early mornings. We also needed space for breastfeeding, handling meltdowns, naps, and downtime with my mom while I was at practice or a game. But if I wanted a room to myself, I had to cover the costs.

Who was going to watch my child while I trained? If the answer was my mom or husband, I still had to cover their travel out of pocket. If I'd had no family and needed a nanny or babysitter, I'd also be expected to pay those fees. And who was going to help me pump, freeze, and store my breast milk? Access to pump rooms and approved sanitation methods was sparse. Who was going to make sure we had dedicated spaces for both moms and children? These and other questions went largely unanswered by the people tasked with player development and holistic wellness. Most of the expenses and logistical energy associated with having a child were ones I took on myself—despite me working in an industry that profited immensely from my return to the court and my absence from said child. Thankfully endorsements and partnerships helped to lighten that load a bit, but not every player secures the lucrative brand deals needed to make the difference. I oftentimes ask myself why the WNBA as a league of women and gender-marginalized players would not be at the forefront to be advocates and examples of spear-heading the advancement of maternity leave rights and reproductive care?

With distance and more life experiences, I can empathize with the precarious position that WNBA executives are caught in. They are running a professional sports league and need athletes on the court to do it. While babies are beautiful and precious, pregnancies stretch the limited roster capacity that WNBA teams have. I get that. But those setting league-wide policy at the WNBA have to also understand that they are recruiting women to play at the height of our physical capacity for both basketball and childbearing. To ask players to put their dreams of growing their families on hold for a league that won't even offer full health care or support using fertility treatments post-basketball is wrong no matter how you spin it. Until there is more robust support for WNBA players to become parents on their terms and with full support of the WNBA, players and executives will always be opponents in this sector.

I believe in choice, which is not just a mythical creature. Choice requires accessibility, and up until 2020, many WNBA players were giving their all to a league that could cut or trade them without a moment's notice. Even at the present, the WNBA limits access to the ability to family plan to players with eight or more years of service. Until there is clear language and thought given to some of the many challenges surrounding motherhood and basketball, like player availability, maternity leave, trading a pregnant player, drafting a pregnant player, etc., there becomes more room for more to go wrong. We need language in the CBA that definitively protects mothers and is fair to franchises.

On the flip side, there is also an undeniable need to have rosters of players who are physically able to play. With limited resources it becomes even more critical to account for injuries, pregnancy, or other areas where players may be unable to contribute to the on-court effort. There are no stipulations regarding pregnant players being traded or cut. A lot of executives are hesitant to cut players after having babies for fear of breaking the rules or being sued, even when the decision is unrelated. Ambiguity hurts everyone involved.

The WNBA isn't alone in this struggle to live up to its projected values; many professional sports associations struggle to approach women athletes on the conversation of pregnancy and having children with nuance, empathy, and transparency. Olympic track star Allyson Felix said it best: "They want the athlete after they have the baby, but where is the support during the pregnancy?" Felix knew this well; when renegotiating her contract post-pregnancy, Nike offered a deal less than half what they'd given her in previous years. When Felix asked for the contract to clearly state she wouldn't be punished for postpartum performances, she was told no. "It's one example of a sports industry where the rules are still mostly made for and by men," she wrote in the *New York Times*.

Having children is not—and should not be treated as—a career ender for athletes. When I gave birth to Lailaa I didn't have a single WNBA championship yet, and there were so many records I'd yet to both break and set. "For women [pregnancy] can and should be able to be part of a thriving professional athletic career," Felix continued. "I dream of a day when we don't have to fight in order to try." Something (or someone) has to give, and it can't always be the players already risking their bodies to shatter expectations, put on a show, and keep the profit flowing. Without the players, there would be no athletic associations. It's time to start acting like it. The WNBA has an opportunity to set the standard and the bar for maternal health, family planning, and childcare. As a league made up of women, why wouldn't the WNBA be at the forefront?

Who—or What—Are We Selling?

Early in my rookie year I arrived to do an Olympic shoot. It would be one of my first photo shoots since entering the WNBA. We walked into the dressing room and saw what their idea of wardrobe would be. Immediately, I thought nothing of it, but my agent, Aaron Goodwin, told me to get my stuff and we were going to leave. At the time, I understood my desire to position myself away from the sexy, scantily clad female athlete, but I wondered why he was so furious. When we got in the car he explained to me that the first photo shoot I did as a professional would not be in that light. I am a basketball player, a damn good one, and he refused to allow me to be placed in a box. There was a time and place for that (I did in fact later in my career pose nude for the ESPN body issue), but my first big shoot would not be with so little clothes on. I took that to heart and from then on, sometimes to my own financial detriment, always aim to do everything authentic to who I am and what I represent. Men didn't have to take their clothes off to have a successful brand in sports, why should women? Sex sells. Let's admit it! Consumers love looking at it and the world loves to make women more feminine, beautiful, and judged not always on their performance but on their looks. The WNBA in fact was built on its players being portrayed as ladylike.

Sports marketing and advertisements are meant to evoke emotion and convey the deep passion we feel each time we step onto the court, field, track, or gym floor. We fall in love with athletes because they dominate their respective fields, but we grow to know who they authentically are through their media portrayal. Missing the mark on marketing and storytelling can set a player—and sport—back years, and that's exactly what happened in the WNBA. For a long time, it was clear senior executives had no idea who their players were and how to represent them or who their audience was or how to speak to them. Every other year there seemed to be a campaign trying to make the women of the WNBA sexy. (I'll never forget the shoot of Diana Taurasi in a tube top tied around her neck posed with her hands holding her hair up sexy or Alana Beard in booty shorts, Becky Hammon in a cut-off midriff, and Dawn Staley in hoop earrings and a deep-cut top). Then it was the campaign where they were marketing to fathers through nostalgia by emphasizing WNBA players as just like their daughters. Still the emphasis wasn't on how we played but on dads looking at us and thinking, *Awwwww*. Then there was marketing to all the naysayers out there via the "Expect Great" commercial. Very rarely was there a campaign authentically portraying the WNBA players and who they are and their style. The campaigns weren't created for the passionate, loyal fans who were already a part of the league. A majority of our fans were Black women and LGBTQ+ people; the WNBA ignored that community just like they took a "don't ask, don't tell" approach with their players. By not marketing to that built-in fan base—and others like them who would show up to watch great basketball—we lost out on the potential growth. The WNBA attempted to portray its league and its players as something that it wasn't to appeal to a demographic that never should have been our target audience.

Broadcasting has the potential to transform fan experiences, turning casual watchers into devoted connoisseurs. In turn, players keep getting better as new generations are entrenched in a game that requires greater skill, stamina, and consistency. At the end of the day, basketball—like other sports—is about entertainment. People are paying to watch players get out on the court and give the best show. At home, viewers watch the best in the world compete in the WNBA, and there is a need for the broadcast to have great analysts, play-by-play, and reporters of the game being produced. We are asking players to be better, well the same standard needs to be held and applied to television. The power of what the NBA has mastered is using the NBA players and matchups to create on-air personalities who are really good at telling the story. Broadcasting includes the positive AND negative!

Women's sports have not always been beloved or respected, so fans, players, and executives alike have played a protective role. Naturally, we feel a sense of ownership over this precious league we've built and nurtured. Particularly because of how sexist feedback on women athletes can be, we've erected a buffer that has covered those inside the bubble. We don't want to thwart opportunities by tearing down someone who is trying. But playing a sport requires critique and not always constant positivity about what we are seeing on the court. Every play isn't outstanding and every pass isn't the best we have ever seen. When the league was in its infancy, that made more sense, but after several decades, the WNBA is a full-grown adult, and we are actually stunting the league's growth by not engaging with the game more critically.

The transparency is part of a larger willingness to push the game beyond complacency. In turn, players give more, and fans learn better basketball IQ and to expect the highest level of basketball. The NBA facilitates shows driven mainly to spark debate and talk around the league and its players. That rigorous critique has birthed a pristine reputation that the NBA is the premier destination for fans to engage with the sport. Those fans bring admiration, trash talk, drive, and the kind of energy that invests in franchises over time and follows players' careers across teams, decades, and other life milestones. It's the enthusiasm we want to usher in more, but we can't do it with the status quo. The WNBA has reached a fork in the road: Either we continue with gentle commentating and remain in this space of gendered expectations of mediocrity from women athletes, or we push everyone to see the WNBA as the home of physical, skillful basketball. If the WNBA decides we are too vulnerable to be critiqued, they are undercutting the experience of true enthusiasts. Those broadcasting the WNBA have to hire the best to bring out and represent the true essence of what the WNBA is and push it to be entertaining.

I don't say this to incentivize bullying of players. Critique is not the same as denigrating or shit talking. Critique is productive, honest, and solutions-oriented. It's never personal. Strong critique requires reporters, analysts, and personalities to hold significant knowledge, expertise, experience, and game-analysis insights in order to contextualize real-time plays and outcomes. That is the crux of sports to begin with. Players, teams, and stats are lined up against one another to decide who the best performing individuals and teams are. Trusted critics are the key holders and queen makers of the game because they set the bar for what is deemed average, excellent, and exceptional. It is not feminism for those translators of the game to have lower expectations of women or to treat us as less capable of rising to the bar.

As of the early 2020s the WNBA has begun to roll out more pre-game and postgame shows, which are able to tell the story and get people excited about whom and what they're about to see. But the reporting is still not as robust as it needs to be, and it's still clunky with mid-game interviews with coaches who are clearly distracted. Further, many of the broadcasters have clear biases and don't truly tell the players' stories. I want the same conversations surrounding the game winner that Sabrina Ionescu hit in game three to be as loud and boisterous as when Luka Dončić knocked down the three over Rudy Gobert. However, I also want the white gloves to come off when Breanna Stewart missed two free throws to win game one to be the same storyline as when we were wondering if LeBron James could be clutch. It's time production is innovative and maybe the game is produced and shot in a different way to showcase the women's game in a grander way. Let's not just copy and paste production. To bring that level of depth and excitement, commentators need to be students of women's basketball, and unfortunately many of them are not. We need to expect more of the so-called experts coming to the table and shaping basketball for viewers. After all, commentators are just as much a part of the viewer experience as the players.

White-glove treatment of WNBA players is what trickles down into the myths that women hoopers are less than. We deserve rigorous critique and to have broadcast programming that reflects the passion and talent that steps out on the court each season. The people who are able to tell those stories are going to be the ones who catapult women's basketball to a space that people from all backgrounds enjoy year after year. That's what women athletes deserve. The resources to do their jobs well and the platform to have their work be properly seen, valued, and respected. Oh, and the referees . . . find better ones (ha ha!).

Know Your Audience

The 2024 WNBA season amplified a number of issues the league and its players have always faced. However, it was now subject to debate from a wider audience and a fan base new to the league. The WNBA is made up in majority of the minority in this country—the players and what they look like and the communities they represent aren't always celebrated historically in our country. Why would we believe the WNBA would be any different? With growth comes responsibility, and the league as a whole did not prepare, stand for, or support their players in navigating the racism, sexism, and homophobia that came with new fans and new viewers. The WNBA was not proactive in protecting players with security. Yes, security guards were reactionary, but taking a stance against "fans" spewing racist and homophobic vitriol at players needed to come from the top. The responsibility can't only fall to individual players to rein in and set standards for fan behavior. The WNBA should be at the forefront of leading the discussion and not shying away from something so important in not only what impacts the players, but what is right. By failing to get out in front of this developing toxicity online and in arenas everywhere, the WNBA was forced to play catch-up publicly and in the process lost the faith of a great deal of players. Time and time again the league turned a deaf ear to the growing need to lead the discussion and not be reactive to it. It was quickly evident that there was even more division among fans and a huge need for players to be protected and advocated for. The league needed to do better.

Ultimately, the explosive 2024 season was a by-product of shifts taking place nationwide. Vehement racism had been on the rise in the years and months leading up to 2024, largely driven by Donald Trump and his Make America Great Again movement. Basketball isn't immune to sociopolitical shifts, but we have a responsibility as a league by and for women—built primarily by Black and LGBTQ+ women—to account for and proactively maintain a safe space for players, coaches, and other fans. Certain things should not and cannot be tolerated, particularly when it comes to in-arena behavior. This is not a case of ideological differences; this is about workplace safety and creating an environment where players can do their jobs without fear of physical or emotional abuse.

Black women and LGBTQ+ players have powered the league for nearly thirty years with little recognition or celebration, few leadership pipelines, and silence around the issues that matter most to us. For so long, even the LGBTQ+ fans weren't marketed to. We have been a league that up until recently ran away from who it was and failed to lean into authenticity and the true identities of a lot of its players.

Desperate times call for more of a need for a sense of direction, strategy, and leadership at the top. But the WNBA has been unsteady with leadership shifts over the last two decades. Once Val Ackerman stepped aside as the WNBA commissioner in 2005, after having been in the role since the league's inception, there wasn't much stability. Donna Orender took over from 2005–2011, then Laurel Richie took over until passing the baton to Lisa Borders in 2015. In 2018, there was a gap year where Mark Tatum, then–deputy commissioner of the NBA, filled in until Cathy Engelbert took the job in 2019. The

WNBA as a whole lacked direction and brand clarity during some of its most challenging times.

Players need to feel heard, protected, supported, and uplifted. When league executives know their players and foster meaningful relationships with them, it builds trust. With that knowledge comes awareness of what players need to thrive and continue growing the league. When players feel sidelined, invisible, and taken for granted, it breeds resentment and misunderstanding.

Particularly when it comes to activism, WNBA players have historically always spoken up and advocated around issues of racial and gender justice, as Black women do, and often without any support or institutional amplification. Ignoring that advocacy was one thing, but with time, executives began actively punishing players for using their platforms. In 2016, players on three WNBA teams wore black T-shirts with messages speaking out against gun violence and police brutality. The WNBA issued fines to the teams as well as individual players, hiding behind a uniform policy as the justification. These fines were double the amount of the average WNBA technical foul fine and came only months after NBA protests against gun violence were widely celebrated. The punishment was obviously disproportionate, and players knew the message hidden between the lines: Stay in line and do only as you're told.

Why didn't gun violence or public safety also matter to WNBA executives if it directly impacted the very communities that their players came from? How were they so out of touch with the movements that galvanized not only the players but the fans? The move sparked backlash as leaders in both the sports and political worlds pushed back against league executives. But it shouldn't have taken that. Pat Summitt said it best: "Leaders listen first." When we know what motivates the people around us, what keeps them up at night, what wakes them up in the morning . . . we can work better together. Unfortunately, right now, executives are moving one way in the name of progress but leaving behind the very backbone of the league.

How can we proclaim to grow the game when we turn our backs on the generations, contributions, and expertise that came before us? How can we purport to be visionaries without engaging our imaginations and holding ourselves accountable? We have to tell better stories about our legends, veterans, and active players. All of them. What we celebrate will grow. What we neglect will wither away.

If Not Us, Then Who?

When Kobe Bryant put on his orange WNBA sweatshirt, it was both an invitation and an affirmation. An invitation to enjoy hoopers, regardless of their gender. If someone as cool and committed to great basketball like Kobe could fall in love with our game, no one was "above" watching women's basketball. It was an affirmation that we were just as entertaining and deserving of the love that a legend like Kobe meted out. Kobe has always been synonymous with excellence and doing the challenging thing regardless of what others thought of him. Each time he sat courtside at an NBA game repping women, he lifted us higher.

Kobe's investment wasn't out of charity. On the contrary, Kobe knew overlooking the WNBA was a disservice to lovers of basketball. He poured his attention, time, capital, and visibility into making girls and women more seen and heard. He did it without expectation of anything in return, like a true ally does. Kobe was one of one in that regard, and paved the way for the mainstream support we are seeing today. It took foresight to dream up this league and to grow the game to where it is today. It will take creativity and commitment to grow the WNBA to the heights it deserves. There is no greater time for women's sports and women's basketball than now. This is our 1996 moment revisited. What will we do with it?

We should be the premier league for women basketball players globally. Little girls and boys should be glued to their screens and in the stands watching their future. I believe we're uniquely positioned for the job and we can embrace that opportunity to be the vanguard for great sports and even greater equity. It takes thinking beyond cookie-cutter approaches and experimenting with new ideas like developing more of an international presence and relationships with those countries where basketball is going to continue to grow like China, Japan, Belgium, France, and India. To be the destination for impeccable basketball and not miss out on the full range of talent out there, we need players from around the world to come to the United States to play and not exclusively the other way around.

This moment is also bigger than any one sport. I want to see a race to the top with athletic associations competing to be the premier space for women athletes with the WNBA leading the way. Women's soccer and the US Women's National Soccer Team have already been revolutionizing the way women play and are compensated for their labor. The USWNT's 2022 Collective Bargaining Agreement (CBA) transformed pay equity in the sport and revealed creative pathways to making the numbers make sense for hardworking and *winning* women athletes. The US Soccer Federation, in tandem with the men's and women's national teams, agreed to equalize prize winnings and pool some of their broadcast, ticket, and sponsorship revenue between the two teams. The CBA also created parity around match venues, fields, hotel accommodations, charter flights, and staffing. In one sweep, these teams proved will and innovation are what we need most to shift the landscape of women's athletics. Billie Jean King, in 1970 recognized the unequal prize money women received in women's tennis. It was known as "Dollar Rebellion" because players signed contracts of one dollar to part ways with a system that didn't value them as female athletes. Look where women's tennis is today. Wimbledon pays equal prize money to women and men. Change and progress have always fallen on the backs of players who demand for leagues to be better.

Looking around at successful models elsewhere empowers us all to move forward more boldly and to say that we can do better. I want to advocate for those coming up next so that they can enter a league that has their longevity, health, and wholeness top of mind. The WNBA should improve every year and continue shattering glass ceilings without allowing the shards of glass to cut players on the way down. The WNBA can be an association that facilitates good basketball, champions women, and makes dreams come true. That's the league I fell in love with and the one I will continue to challenge to be better! Once again, the entire world is watching women's sports, just like in 1996. The WNBA has an opportunity to be proactive in ownership, player experience and development, and with its fans and viewers. In twenty years, how will we define this moment?

PART FOUR

The Dash

FIFTEEN

My Life, My Choices

You've never arrived.
You are always working toward something.

—PAT SUMMITT

I watched a TV show with my wife called *Dark Matter*. An has always been the one more interested in the sci-fi shows, while I prefer true crime documentaries, so when she suggested it, I initially rolled my eyes. But the moment I watched the trailer, I was hooked! The show follows a physicist named Jason Dessen, who lives happily with his wife and son. One day Jason is kidnapped and thrust into a parallel universe. He realizes later that it was in fact another "him" who kidnapped himself. Soon he learns that every decision he makes births a brand-new version of himself, as well as an alternate universe. Big decisions and small decisions all impact the world he lives in and all the people in it. You all really should watch this show yourselves, but my point in summarizing it is that we are all on a journey and are active participants in it. The very choices and directions we make impact who we are and who we surround ourselves with.

Growing up, I approached every decision like a fork in the road. One way was right and the other was wrong. I would imagine all the wrong turns I made and which "Candace" didn't exist as a result. Trusting the chosen path was always difficult when I was an active participant. I excelled when things happened to me because I could always adapt, but actively choosing my next move sent my mind racing with scenarios that left my head spinning and my heart and head at odds. The what-ifs used to keep me up at night. The gift of having a life of choices sometimes left me questioning whether it was a luxury or a curse.

For someone so passionate and stubborn, I can be surprisingly avoidant of decision-making. In some ways, I blame the first decision I ever had to make on my own. As the baby girl of the family, I've had to claw out my own identity for myself, so the first real chance I got to assert myself was in choosing where to attend college. This was a big decision, determining where I'd spend my basketball career, and it terrified me to have so much power in my hands and to realize that it would affect so many others. Alternate realities loomed, and this decision could determine whom I married, my best friends, where I would return to for the rest of my life, and what team I would spend my entire life wearing proudly across my chest. This decision would shape my entire existence.

A tad melodramatic looking back on it, but that's how anxious I was at the time. I couldn't think about the present because I was consumed by all the consequences stacking on top of one another. It became incredibly hard for me to narrow down what was important if each decision connected to thousands of things. I felt a tremendous amount of pressure, and my mind was constantly turning with the different scenarios. An opportunity of a lifetime, to literally pick wherever I wanted to go to school, turned into something I dreaded.

During the recruitment period, I narrowed down my choices to five different universities. As the number one recruit in the country, I struggled even trimming schools I knew I would never go to from the list. But I could actually see myself enjoying any of the five campuses. When I closed my eyes, I could visualize myself strolling through an expansive campus green wearing different shades of orange, blue, or red. I imagined myself in the different dorm rooms

I'd visited and gymnasiums I'd toured. Sitting in the classrooms of the school of communications or business. Attending football games.

My trajectory would definitely look different at each place, but nothing immediately stuck out to me as a bad fit. I knew no matter what I'd be following my basketball dreams on an elite Division I team and in a community that really loved women's basketball. Coaching and the culture of the team would play a big part in what came next, so I knew I wanted a program that would prepare me to become professional. That part was nonnegotiable. But that wasn't all I wanted out of my college experience. I may have been a teenager at the time, but I was thinking about the long haul. I wanted a university with a great business or communications major, a vibrant community of diverse people, and a college-town experience that would offer a lot of activities and sporting events to attend, and though I didn't want to stay too close to home, I wanted to stay close enough to have family attend my most important moments. Which school could give me that?

With the months dwindling down and the time to commit inching closer and closer, I was more torn than I'd been when I first began the process. I could feel my parents skewing their questions and highlights toward Tennessee. They'd say things like, "You said you want to play for a school with a solid football team, right?" and it was clear where they hoped I'd commit. They both spoke with Coach Summitt quite often; they admired her aura and personality. I get it, and they weren't wrong. But the more they were drawn to her and pulled me along with them the more I resisted. Meanwhile, the other four coaches were doing everything they could to sway me to their side. Many would call me up and share a piece of information I just "had" to know about another coach. The recruitment process was getting dirtier and dirtier, and the trash talk was only getting in my head. There was entirely too much noise, and I simply couldn't concentrate on what my heart and mind were trying to tell me.

Things boiled over after I went on an official visit to the University of Maryland. My brother Marcus accompanied me on the trip, and

I chose to leave my parents behind. This was my first act of complete defiance of my parents' wishes. They were so against me attending the university that they refused to join me, which infuriated me. It wasn't just the decision of where to play; it was all the added pressure of what came with it. They had shared what they thought but promised that this was ultimately my decision, and yet, they were trying to manipulate me out of my own choice. When I returned from the trip, I got into a huge argument with them where they threatened not to come to my games if I went through with committing there. Up until that point in my life, I could count on one hand how many games my parents had missed in my entire life. I was hurt and stressed out so much because the joy of choosing felt snatched from me. This wasn't how I'd imagined the beginning of the rest of my life playing out.

After a heated week of discussions, I was essentially on nonspeaking terms with both my parents. One day, my dad came home with roses. One for me. One for my mom. This was his olive branch or white flag. "Let's remember we're all on the same team here," he said, and I was grateful for the reminder. There were so many points where I worried about how invested everyone was in the calls I was making. And as a parent now, I understand why my parents were so fearful that I'd do something I regretted. Sometimes it's a juggling act to balance your wants and desires for your child versus trusting that you raised them to understand theirs. But more than anything, I needed to feel as though my parents trusted and believed in me. That no matter which decision I made, we would figure it out together, and I would always have their support.

We cried, apologized to one another, and hugged away all the tension that had been blocking what should have been an exciting moment. College would mark the beginning of the rest of my life and I wanted to make the decision that would leave me happiest at the end of the day. But because I was letting so much unimportant stuff come into my mind—like what other people thought and expected of me as well as the negative recruiting from the coaches—I began to doubt myself. I respected each coach and team immensely, so the thought of telling four people no didn't feel good to me. For weeks, I'd been sacrificing my own happiness to make other people comfortable. In reality, saying no to one team didn't mean their program was wrong overall, just not right for me. With a clear mind and heart, I could finally admit to myself that my parents knew me well and Tennessee really was the best for me from coaching style to academic support and beyond. When I canceled out the noise, it was like flipping a coin and knowing where you wanted it to land while it was in the air. Tennessee checked almost every box. But Coach Summitt had the unique ability to teach me to be a great player, while also modeling how to be a great human. She walked in morals and navigated with great discipline. The only thing I didn't love about Tennessee was that they already had championships, and I wanted to establish a winning team and be synonymous with a collegiate dynasty. In the end, I settled for reestablishing a winning record at Tennessee since they hadn't won a title in nearly six years.

On Tuesday November 11, I entered the ESPNZone in downtown Chicago with a bob cut, Enyce shirt, and sparkling teeth freshly braces free. That day, I became the first woman to announce my college decision on ESPNEWS as people around the country tuned in to see where I'd land. My dad handed me a Tennessee number-three jersey on camera, and it was official. The weight of the decision was off my shoulders, and I could focus on my future. Orange would be my color, and Tennessee would be school, for life. We listened to "Rocky Top" on the way home, and all I could do was think about was what I wanted to accomplish and the championships I wanted to win wearing that Tennessee-orange jersey with the number three across my chest.

The key to decision-making, I realized, was finding that inner stillness. In decision-making we normally know which way we are leaning. Usually you self-talk your way out of something. If that's the case, you have your choice. That quiet space where I could hear myself think and not have my own voice drowned out by others'. It allowed me to focus on the nonnegotiables and not let the sub-choices pile up. I'm truly the only one who knows what I want.

What had made decision-making so difficult for me was how much I both deferred to and defied the advice from people around me. The emotions of decision-making drained me as I worried about hurting or disappointing others, or the perception of my final decisions. I valued the opinions of the people around me immensely, but also I resented being told what to do. With time, I learned to anticipate those reactions and not ask for feedback until I had checked in with myself and slept on it twice. By the time most people know I'm on the verge of something new, I've nearly made up my mind and am simply gut checking. Doing so has allowed me to trade self-doubt for self-assurance, knowing that no one knows what's best for me but me.

Go Where You Are Watered

I'll be blunt: A lot of people have played in my face across my career. I get it; expectations are a privilege. No one has higher expectations than I have for myself. I've never expected things to be handed to me, but I wasn't prepared for how often it seemed my humility and grace were downplayed, my name was disrespected, and my greatness always came with an asterisk. I do my best not to compare myself or my journey to others. But at some point, it became glaringly obvious that I wasn't playing the same figurative game as some of my peers. I rarely speak on the disrespect, and I've often been asked how I restrain myself or keep from succumbing to that anger. I've always treated negativity as fuel and refused to give people more space in my life than they deserved. I keep it moving, but I never, ever forget. At some point, standing on business is standing on truth.

I've never liked Geno Auriemma, the head coach at the University of Connecticut, and I'm pretty sure he's never liked me. In some ways,

I inherited the tension and conflict between him and Pat Summitt. Coach Pat was my person, and Geno coached a rival team, so I never assumed that our competitive relationship was anything but good basketball. I'd dunked at UConn in 2007, to Geno's disdain, and we had snatched two championships from him in the three years I was a Lady Vol. But when 2012 rolled around and it was time to gear up for the Olympics in London, I suited up and kept it professional under the leadership of my temporary Coach Geno.

We won gold, even though our working relationship hadn't been easy. In particular, the politics and power plays were difficult to get used to. The smart remarks, jabs and comments were something I could look past, but the silent treatment at times was deafening. I understand the political nature of the game; there's no denying the advantage certain players have just by previously having him as a coach. I get that, but USA basketball was as political as it got because our women's team was DOMINANT. We could field three teams and probably medal gold, silver and bronze! So picking the team and playing time was left open to desire and not necessity. Geno did what he wanted and answered to no one, a stark shift from Pat Summitt's policy of hearing everyone out. Geno yanked me out of the starting lineup after the first game for "not bringing the right energy" and would order me to take off my headphones, which most other coaches at this level had evolved away from college-like rules— including men's USA Coach K (who is notorious for running a disciplined Duke program). I don't have a problem with rules that make sense, but we were grown women playing basketball for our country, not children in a classroom to be micromanaged. He would insist that I shouldn't dribble the basketball or bring the ball up the floor. That was like telling Steph Curry not to shoot. That was what my game was all about, and has always been. Asking me to not do something that made me who I was as a player was confusing.

Those little moments of pettiness confounded me. Quickly, I realized that I wasn't being held nor judged by the same standards as my teammates. *Why would a coach opt for a power play on this stage?* I often was frustrated, I would look to the men's team and see grown men treated with respect and when it came to us, we were treated like we were still in college. Don't like me off the court, fine, but in between the lines we should be able to work together. I took major steps back where needed in order to play my role under Geno's leadership. I was proud of myself, despite the mind games, I was ready when my number was called. In the crucial gold medal game, our team got off to a rough start. He reluctantly pointed to the end of the bench and I went in. Bringing energy, running the floor, defending, scoring, and doing whatever the team needed me to do. Leaving the 2012 Olympics with both a gold medal and the honor of being deemed the Most Outstanding Player despite the circumstances, gave me a deeper belief in myself. I was excited to go for gold again four years later.

To my dismay, Geno Auriemma was named to a second stint as Team USA coach for the 2016 Olympic cycle. Usually, coaches only serve one Olympic cycle. Shortly after the announcement, the Director of Basketball, Carol Callan, organized a call between myself and Coach Auriemma to "get on the same page." We talked, squashed our beef, chuckled and agreed to move forward from a place of understanding and tried to reset. In 2015, it was time for our fall training camp tour for Team USA. I had a lot on my plate professionally and personally. My knee had begun to act up again, and I was forced to undergo another cleanup surgery the year prior, causing me to miss the world championships. Despite all of that, I was excited for a third shot at Olympic gold in Rio de Janeiro. When a European tour was being put together to play a few games in Barcelona, Rome, Naples, and Prague, I was asked to be a part of the camp. The timing wasn't ideal and would mean more time away from my baby girl right after a grueling playoff period. *This is the process*, I told myself. *This is what it takes. Big sacrifices build up to big wins.*

With only a few weeks of rest, I headed to Europe where we dominated, and I proved I was very much one of the best players in the world. In fact, my knee finally felt normal, so much so that a couple of my USA basketball teammates, including Breanna Stewart, and I put on an impromptu dunk contest. All types: lean ins, two hands, and from distance. It was so much fun competing with and against the best players in the world. In our match against Spain's national team, my triple-double helped Team USA absolutely eviscerate our competition. At one point during one of the games as I made my way to the bench, Geno grabbed me and told me that "I am one of the top three players in the world, my mindset should be to prove to everyone in the gym I am number one every time I step on the floor."

Coming out of Europe, I was excited about what we could do the coming year as well as my growth in the international game. I knew Team USA had some challenging decisions to make, as there were so many worthy players, but I never felt like I was in jeopardy of not making the team. My main reason for even considering competing in another Olympics was so that my then seven-year-old daughter could actually remember it. So when Team USA again asked for more of my scarce offseason time, I acquiesced.

Again, the winter of 2015, I traveled with three other players on a press tour drumming up anticipation for the coming games. Though no rosters would be set in stone for some months, I was already being touted as one of the faces of Team USA's 2016 women's basketball team. I even appeared on the Rio 2016 Olympic commercial. I played the part expected of me, and I went out of my way to be available whenever needed. I FaceTimed my daughter in between junkets and made promises for all the fun we'd have when Mommy was back. "It's only for a little while," I'd tell her. "Just a few more sleeps." This was something I always had dreamed of as a kid, way back in 1996 on that couch all those years ago. Donning USA across my chest and representing my country.

When national team director, Carol Callan, called to let me know
I would not be on the Olympic team the following spring, my initial
reaction looked a lot like most of America's. As Carol chattered on
about how important I was to the organization but that they'd gone
in a different direction that year, I sat silently with the phone wedged
between my ear and shoulder. All I could think about was if Pat was
well, none of this would have happened. I was more speechless than
I'd ever been at any other point of my life until I heard the words,
"We have so much respect for you and your career, we would like to
give you the opportunity to withdraw your name and opt out of the
2016 Olympics on your own." Immediately, I came back to reality.
HELL NO! You announce this and face the backlash that is to come.
Why would you offer this proposition if what you were doing was
right? I quickly and kindly dismissed her and ended the conversation.

When I hung up the phone, my disbelief turned into rage. For
a fleeting moment, I had let Carol plant the seed in my mind that
there might be a rational reason behind my exclusion from the team.
Did they not think I was healthy? That couldn't be. I'd put on a damn
good show in Europe for Team USA and led the Sparks' playoff
showing only months before. Were they upset that I didn't go to the
World Championships? I'd had injuries, but I'd healed and recovered
from those surgeries and had the stats to show it.

When the news was announced publicly, players, fans, and analysts alike were all baffled by the move. The speculation as to what
was really going on began almost immediately. It was hard not to
read into the theories swirling around, considering none of the official statements made any sense. The overwhelming takeaway was that
Geno simply didn't like me. Considering the committee had stacked
Team USA with UConn alums, the biases felt obvious. Quickly I
understood this was a business and they were playing politics and
games. In years past, "certain" players were passed on and excluded
from Team USA and not even given a chance, Deanna Nolan, Becky

Hammon, Courtney Vandersloot, and Nneka Ogwumike. Now, I could add my name to the list. Throughout the years there is understanding that there are different rules for different players and quickly I realized there were certain players that were in fact untouchable. Support, standards, and judgement looked different depending on who you are, even to this day.

There was no logical reason for leaving me off the team, but that's not even what angered me most. What makes my blood boil to this day is thinking of all the time I'll never get back. The fact that no matter what I did, I was not going to make that team. Instead of them just saying that, they wasted my time and theirs. A lot of people wanted to see me snap. It would have been my right, to be honest. I wouldn't stoop to anyone else's level and let them "prove" that I wasn't a good fit. In retrospect, I would have rather been cut from the team than waste time going to Rio and been miserable as a result of the mind games that were surely to be played. I expressed my disappointment with the decision, wished the players well, and made my non-negotiable: I would never have my time and energy wasted like that again in an environment that I knew wasn't for me because I'd never play for Team USA ever again. We went on to win the 2016 WNBA Championship with not a single player from the Olympic team roster.

Sometimes the hardest decisions to make are the ones where we decline or turn down an opportunity. There can be mixed emotions of regret, uncertainty, and fear. My clarity has come from recognizing that what is for me, will *feel* like it. That doesn't mean the road will be easy and paved with rose petals, but there's a gut instinct when you are out of place and in a room where you aren't valued. Knowing when to say no and how to value myself regardless of what others did, became essential to maintaining my peace throughout my career.

One Percent, Each Day

Once you stop doubting yourself, the next hurdle in decision-making is actually executing. My competitive streak doesn't let me half-ass much of anything, but I do know a thing or two about being unfocused and scattered. Sometimes, an inner voice still mulling over a recent decision would keep me from giving my all to the space I committed to. But you can't have one foot in the door and the other outside of the frame. If a decision doesn't work out, we can always pivot but not without giving full and earnest effort first.

My parents raised my brothers and me to embrace hard work as essential to the journey. A lot of those qualities carry over in different parts of life because it's hard to turn off wanting to be good or striving for excellence. But the sacrifices that come with hard work make the journey a bit uncomfortable at times. Working toward your goals means making sure that the time you've allotted to achieving your goals matches up with what you wish to accomplish. To summarize my childhood life lessons, tell me how you spend your time, and I'll tell you how serious you are about your goals. The real winners are the ones who fall in love with that process recognizing that you don't luck up and hit a game-winning shot without setting aside comfort and working toward that.

Success is a muscle that gets stretched and built up over time. That's the message I internalized from my parents. With age, I adapted some of these lessons into a succinct framing that helped me move intentionally throughout my basketball career. Then one of my coaches in Los Angeles broke down our season using a similar method that I have now adapted now for my everyday life. Coach Brian Agler showed us on a whiteboard one practice what our telescopic goal was: to win the championship. After that, he broke down how we would accomplish it every day through our microscopic goals. Telescopic goals are the long-term visions we have for ourselves. Telescopic goals also tend to be the big, exciting goals that we dream of and salivate over, like winning a championship, owning and operating a successful business, being promoted at work, launching a new creative venture, owning your dream home, building generational wealth, or building and cultivating a positive relationship. To get to those telescopic plans requires day-to-day diligence. That's where microscopic goals come in. In setting more short-term goals that can be attacked and achieved more quickly, we essentially lay out breadcrumbs for ourselves that lead to the destinations we've imagined.

The timing of letting go of something you love is critical as you balance your heart and head and remain grounded in your core values. I prefer to start with what I want to achieve and work backwards from there. Whether it's in picking a partner, buying a house, timing career movements, or letting go of something that is no longer serving you, procrastination is a natural response. Adding time to think any major decision over is important, but there is such a thing as overthinking. I've done everything under the sun to help with making tough, life-changing decisions. Flipped a coin, made a pros-and-cons list, prayed, daydreamed about outcomes, and so on. We mull over the big choices, but our focus should really be on the everyday habits that we develop and choose. Those are the decisions that can make or break who you are. Doing what you say you will. Committing to the process. Working out. Being disciplined. Putting in the work. All those intangibles matter far more than the big choices we make, because they scaffold up and compound over time. When I started committing to who I was and what I woke up to be every morning, it was easier to ensure that my decision-making aligned with my morals.

SIXTEEN

Love Is a Verb

Nobody cares how much you know until
they know how much you care.
—THEODORE ROOSEVELT

I am a quintessential Aries. If you look up an Aries in the dictionary, it should have a photo of me directly underneath because every personality trait ascribed to the fire sign describes me to a T. I'm passionate, energetic, lively, ambitious, confident, and self-motivated. I am also slightly stubborn, impulsive, impatient, and a tad bit confrontational. I wear my emotions on my sleeve, I always have a plan, and I don't fit into anyone's box.

Being a mother and a professional basketball player tested me to no end because I was constantly being forced into preconceived notions of what a successful player and an attentive mother looked like. The same was never expected of my male peers, who could play hard and dedicate themselves to their sport without anyone wondering where their children were or who was caring for them. I, on the other hand, was never really allowed to separate who I was on the court and who I was to my children. Especially after carrying Lailaa, there was no choice but to be fully involved with breastfeeding, nap schedules, and everything in between. I wouldn't have wanted it any other way, but I hated the double standards that came with having a high-stakes professional career and needing to be so hands-on.

"Where's Lailaa?"

In 2009, I was a new mom with a lot on my plate. First and foremost, my body just underwent a lot of changes, and my mind was still catching up to the pace and physicality. Things weren't as easy as they once were just a season ago during my rookie year, and nothing about 2008 was a cakewalk. Adjustment was the name of the game. I tried to give myself grace as my body adjusted to the changes I had endured during pregnancy and childbirth. Mentally, I had a lot to juggle in balancing the newness of motherhood and working my way back into the physicality and pace of basketball shape.

I was also managing the logistical nightmare of being a breastfeeding mom to a newborn while actively playing professional basketball just weeks after giving birth. That meant that in addition to hours of workouts, practices, and games each day, I was also coordinating a feeding, nap, and childcare schedule so that both Lailaa and my team got the best of me at any given moment. At times, I was sleep-deprived and delirious, but I was in my happy place playing basketball and being a first time mom. Sometimes I had to remind myself I was doing a damn good job. There wasn't much time left over for me but motherhood required some sacrifice and I was proud to be so present with my daughter without trading in my sneakers. Women can do both.

On one particular day, I was traveling with the Sparks for an away game, which meant that Lailaa was traveling with us, too. The morning of the game, I woke up earlier than normal to get both her and myself ready for the day ahead. After she was fed and I'd pumped enough milk for my time away, I headed out to the bus to meet the team for practice. I remember being exhausted every moment of every day, and this day was no different. I pumped in the locker room before our shootaround and was already planning out the next week to make sure Lailaa's childcare could be covered.

We were going through a warmup when one of the reporters present asked me, "Where's Lailaa?" My blood grew hot, and my

skin became flush as I cocked my head to the side at the ridiculous-
ness of the question. This was my legendary teammate Lisa Leslie's
last year in the WNBA, and we were headed into a huge game that
had implications for our seeding in the playoffs. A lot was on the line
for us, and I had locked into what we were on the court to do. This
reporter wasn't asking about defensive coverage or what my mindset
would be that night playing in a big game. All he could think about
was where Lailaa was?

NBA fathers were never asked about the whereabouts of their
children or about who was caring for them in their father's absence.
The expectation is that another parent or loved one or caretaker is
on the job. Why would that same assumption not be made for me?
In fact, I'm sure most NBA dads don't travel with their children and
continue operating as the primary parent in season. My child was a
few miles away getting rest before the game, not that it was anyone's
business. Could others say the same?

What really irked me about the question, though, was the insinu-
ation that if Lailaa were not with me that I would be seen as a negligent mom. When I'd first announced my pregnancy, everyone was
anxious to see me return postbirth. Now that I was back, I realized
people were hypercritical of how I parented and what support I used
to be at the top of my game. I was lucky to have a mother who often
traveled with me and her granddaughter. But if that weren't the case
and I did need to make different choices, that decision would definitely come with judgment.

In the end, I brushed the question off with a smile and bit my
tongue—as I had done so many times in my life. I always wore being
a mom front and center on my chest. But, as I got deeper into the
game, I realized there was very little separation that was made by
others. We work, but we are still supposed to be physically present in
our kids' lives at all times.

My commitment to my child and to the sport I loved were constantly being called into question. It infuriated me but also poked at

a deep insecurity of mine: that Lailaa wouldn't have the childhood I'd had and that she'd resent me for it. Or worse, that Lailaa would be raised by other people and hardly know me. I didn't want someone else spending more time with my kid than me, or knowing that she sneezes three times in a row each time. That she loves to be put to sleep on the right side and not the left or that she scrunches her nose and arches her back when she gets tired. I was super sensitive about knowing every detail. Every move I made from the moment I found out I was pregnant was done with Lailaa—and these fears—in mind. It was all a major shift from the Candace Parker just a few years before who had centered her life around basketball.

On Christmas Eve, years before that interview, Shelden and I piled into the car to find out the sex of the baby growing inside me. Shelden was hoping for a boy but thought we were having a girl. I was the complete opposite. In the end, we both would have been happy with a healthy child, no matter the sex, but I was secretly holding out hope for my baby girl. Since I was little, growing up around two older brothers, I'd always wanted a little sister or more feminine energy around. I never did get that little sister, but a daughter would be even better.

As I lay on my back with the ultrasound technician moving the wand over my belly, I stared at the screen in anticipation. Finally the attendant wrote out what she'd seen: "GIRL." Shelden immediately laughed and joked that I always get what I want, and that's exactly how I felt. Everything I'd ever wanted was on its way to me. My job was to protect that little girl and be the mother I'd always dreamed of.

That's the thing, though. I had the kind of stay-at-home mother who was there for everything and everyone. Sometimes I forgot my homework and my mom would warn, "This is the last time I am going to bring it." (But she never did turn me down.) Other times, Mom would pop up at my school with a surprise hot lunch or anytime we needed a parent volunteer. Even if I had one line in a play, my mom was front row. Whenever I needed her, she was there to save the day. That's what motherhood looked like to me, and I knew my career would keep me from that level of omnipresence.

I wrote letters to Lailaa almost every day of my pregnancy and then during most major milestones of our lives. I wanted to keep a journal that she could look back at and see a record of her life and the love she was surrounded by from the very beginning. I also wanted to speak to her from a place of being a young mom, before I turned into an uncool, rigid mom who doesn't remember what it's like to be going through life. That space for reflection helped me to realize that my motherhood journey would definitely look different than the one I'd grown up admiring. But different didn't need to mean worse. Instead of living a life in fear of what I'd get wrong, I wanted to be proactive about showing Lailaa just how much she was the center of my world. I may not be physically present all the time, but the intention I brought into the time we did have and how I stayed in touch while away would make all the difference.

I wrote letters about lessons Lailaa taught me. Like the time she lost a game and threw a *huge* tantrum. When I scolded her and said we don't cry or act that way when we lose, Lailaa threw me back at me: "But that's how you acted when you lost a game." Mind you, that "game" she is referring to was a huge playoff game against the Minnesota Lynx that slipped from our grip in the very last second. I started a rebuttal, *But that was a different loss.* Before I spoke, I realized that, in her eyes, the example she remembers had given her permission to do the same! Lesson learned. Kids will check you on your bullshit and remind you to be who you say you are. I wrote a letter about this for Lai to read with hindsight. Letter writing became a way to stay connected no matter the distance, and to be the kind of mother who is emotionally attuned to what's changing for my daughter, and for me.

From my letters to her, I wanted Lailaa to know that I labored for thirty hours straight and when she finally came all I felt was gratitude and adoration. She was worth the wait, worth the pain, and worth everything to come. I wrote to her during some of the toughest moments in my life when I was struggling with motherhood, divorce, tough losses, and pivotal life changes. I wrote to Lailaa from a perspective that felt unique to that time in my life. I would never ever get to have an open dialogue with her at that youthful and inexperienced stage. Hopefully when she reads the letters later, she'll relate to me clumsily moving through life. Even better, maybe it will help us have deep discussions when she comes of age. As parents, we think we are doing right by never showing our kids emotions or weakness. In actuality, we are doing our children a disservice if we aren't modeling how to navigate their feelings and how to deal with them.

Ultimately, I wanted Lailaa to hear how motherhood had changed me in infinite ways. That I looked out at strangers now and thought, *That's someone's Lailaa.* How Lailaa opened up my heart to a level of love and care I didn't know possible. And that I would do anything and everything to make my actions match these words.

Live Your Life Your Way

To be the mother I'd always dreamed of, while also being the athlete I knew I was, required a lot of sacrifice. Initially, I wore that sacrifice like a badge of honor. This is what being a working mom required, I thought. Sleepless nights, endless scheduling and rescheduling, and bending over backward. I had no free time; everything I had—and sometimes didn't have—went toward motherhood and basketball. Over time, I realized that it was a disservice to both Lailaa and me to deplete myself. My fatigue left me irritable and erratic most of the time. I'd forget to feed myself until it affected my milk supply, or I'd skip out on napping to get an extra workout in but find myself yawning through the day. I was dropping balls both literally and figuratively. In trying to be everywhere and do everything, I wasn't giving anyone my best, and that had to change.

I had to reject martyrdom, first and foremost. Women are socialized to care for everyone around us, putting ourselves at the bottom of our to-do lists. But when I was struggling to stay afloat, unable to keep up, who would step in and make everything better the way I'd done for them? There's only one me, and I had to stop overcommitting and underdelivering. It took me quite a bit of time to realize that I deserved to enjoy motherhood, not simply go through the motions. I had to be more disciplined with my time, for *me*.

When I accepted that both Lailaa and I deserved more and that I had to be the one to make different decisions, one of my first orders of business was to shed my shame of enlisting more help. When I first became pregnant, many people hinted that childcare and a nanny might help me balance my many responsibilities. I was immediately resistant, and even judgmental, about that advice. Why would I off-load the care of my child to a stranger? Seeing others do so initially seemed almost lazy to me and not the sort of thing I'd do as a parent.

I was so afraid of the stigma around moms who used nannies. Growing up, I remember my mom turning her nose up at people with extra childcare. I reasoned from a young age that either you lived modestly and your parents were around with no nannies, or you lived in a big house with many luxuries but your parents were gone all the time and you were raised by nannies. It was an either-or. I wanted in so many ways to disprove this theory. I didn't want to fall into the category of not being a part of my daughter's life, choosing wealth and material luxuries over quality time and after-school pickup. With time I realized that we each do life differently and have different things on our plates, so I could never judge or blame anyone for securing support in whatever way they need. Being a zombie with your tank completely empty is not a way to succeed at work or at home.

Creating more time is about figuring out what is worth sacrificing. I don't care what anyone says, you can buy time by prioritizing
what you want to do over what you have to do. Some things are
worth the sacrifice (financial or otherwise) if it means less time being
stretched thin and more time enjoying my family. Those trade-offs
may be ideal for one and not worth the added stress for someone else.
Instead of surrendering to envy over whose grass is greener, I had to
trust that my shade of green is the perfect one for me.

Missing anything of Lailaa's used to plague me with guilt and
keep me awake at night worrying about how she would feel looking out into the audience and not seeing her mom front and center.
Would she resent me? Would she think that I was choosing basketball over her? From a very young age, I would do my best to remain
as present as I could even when I had to be away. I would send my
entire village to support her. If I couldn't be there, her grandmother,
aunts, uncles, and a host of family friends would. For the first class
award that she earned in elementary school, our people showed up
and celebrated, cheered, and even held me up on FaceTime when she
went up to take pictures with the principal. To see Lailaa's toothless
grin at all the love and support that our family has for her made me
realize that motherhood is just about doing the best that you can.

I am grateful for my mom for being such an integral part of my
daughter's life. My mom allowed me a sense of calm when I had to
be away. I knew that Lailaa would be loved and have all of her needs
met! Traveling the world with my mom and daughter was an adventure. Watching Lailaa try her first solids in Turkey, crawl in Spain,
and take her first steps at a hotel in Phoenix was special because I
was achieving my wildest dreams with two of my favorite people by
my side. I never felt alone. At times, I did feel overwhelmed. There
weren't enough hours in the day to balance being a completely present mom, weights, two practices, treatment, and solid sleep to recover.
I ended most days exhausted and even more so if I tried to squeeze in
a bit of "me" time. I felt guilty for my daughter being overseas cooped

up in a small apartment. I struggled at times parenting alongside my mom. I worried about being in a foreign country when Lailaa got sick or her fever spiked. I had very little time to prioritize myself. I bent over backward to be attached to Lailaa at the hip whenever I wasn't suited up for practice or a game. I couldn't physically continue down this path. I was not a machine even though, for a while, I was pretending to be. The first time I left Lailaa behind on a road trip was when she was 3 years old. I cried the entire way to the airport and hugged her goodbye as I choked back even more tears. The two days away stretched on like weeks and weeks as my body ached to be back with my little girl. And yet, I hadn't slept so well in years. After what felt like the best rest of my life, I was able to wake up early and lift weights without worrying about a morning breakfast or waking my Mom. I then stayed later after practice to get up extra shots. I even snuck in an entire pregame nap with no interruptions. When the game actually came, I felt more energized and ready to go than I'd been in a while. I remembered for a moment what I used to do regularly.

When I returned home, I missed Lailaa like crazy and couldn't wait to jump back into our flow. At the same time, that trip was like ripping off the Band-Aid of a realization I'd needed to come face to face with long before. I wanted to be great at basketball and greatness takes time, extra time. Though I felt guilty about being away from Lai, I was ultimately skipping necessary steps in workouts to be with her. Motherhood had to include my needs as well. Being tired, irritable, and having low energy was impacting who I was on and off the court. I needed to find more balance to be any good to either of us. It's okay for Lailaa to be away from me.

Ultimately, my biggest breakthrough came when I stopped thinking I was the only one who could do anything for Lailaa. It was wearing me thin trying to do the job of an entire village. I held a lot of guilt over the reality that I needed support to do what my mom had done alone, but I had to remember that my mom and I were leading different lives at different times so of course motherhood would look different as well. Who was I trying to prove something to and why did it have to involve so much struggle? When I was growing up, my mom wasn't splitting her time between three little ones and a rigorous schedule of playing professional sports. Sometimes, work would have to take precedence for me, and if I was proactive about the support I had in those moments, it would make things a lot easier for everyone involved. It's okay for Lailaa to be away from me especially when she's in the care of people who are trusted and equipped. My being away is what made our beautiful life and afforded me the ability to lean on others. Time to take advantage of what all that hard work made possible.

I did everything in my power to be like Pat: to be where my feet were and make everyone feel as though I was 100 percent full and ready to give all I could that day. Balancing help and finally ridding myself of mom guilt allowed me to be even better on the court and at home. I wasn't completely depleted when I returned home from a long day at the gym; I was excited and energetic to see my kids. This balance led me to play some of my best basketball of my career. After receiving the 2013 MVP trophy, I realized I had figured out the perfect balance. That night I returned home and read our favorite book to my baby girl, *Giraffes Can't Dance!* I'll never forget as I kissed her good-night, Lailaa in her cute little voice saying, "Good job, Mommy!" I wasn't quite sure what she was talking about, the MVP or mommy-ing! I didn't ask. I was proud of both.

Presence, Not Presents

For the first two and a half decades of my life, my competitive side pushed me to hustle hard with little time for playing or resting. If I wasn't practicing, working out, or studying, I was likely rehabilitating, getting surgery, or otherwise preparing to be on a court. In college, I can count on two hands how many times I actually went out. I wasn't about the nightlife because I had a goal and I would rather rest and recover and spend an evening in, watching bad scary movies with my college roommate, than be out wasting time and drinking. My boyfriend and I, in college, would go to the Stokely Athletic Center and shoot at all hours of the night and sometimes on the way home stop and grab a bite at IHOP. We would always run into college mates just finishing partying and I loved feeling like I got better while they were chilling.

Welcoming balance into my life had required me to almost rewire myself. Did I want to be the best on the court and give my family the last of me? There are many greats who've done this and have the accolades and honors to show for it. But I didn't want my professional legacy to outshine who I was to the people I love. I want a life full of Saturday farmers markets and Sunday brunches, school drop-offs and carpool lines, nerding out over documentaries, having time to read a new book, being at my kids' activities, hiking with my dogs, and taking random trips to the beach eating lobster rolls while soaking our toes in the cold Pacific Ocean. This isn't what people tell you to aspire to. Of course in addition to beautiful travels and yummy food, I also want to send my children to the best schools and ensure they have a world full of options, as all parents do. Beyond that, however, most of the things I want out of life aren't as flashy as a closet full of things, never-ending red carpets, and constantly taking on more. But I didn't want to be a boss if that meant not being a mom and wife. Nobody tells you how important balance is. I shifted to envying the people who excelled at it.

When you're doing something different, you have to teach people how to treat you and your priorities accordingly. My manager, agent, coaches, teammates, and other colleagues all had to understand who and what came first for me, so I put calendar holds for personal commitments and stuck to them with the same rigor as business calls. Whether that was school pickups, volleyball games, or chaperoned field trips, I did everything in my power to be there for those moments. Some conflicts are unavoidable but, with pre-established priorities, being consistent isn't as difficult as we think. My work-life balance also pushed me to be more efficient when I *was* on the clock because if I could work smarter and finish my to-do list earlier, it would mean even more time with my loved ones. I'd never give less than what I've committed to no matter what—it's not who I am. But I would absolutely get strategic to build a strenuous schedule around my family. Ensuring the people around me got what my priorities were made work-life balance easier.

I didn't pick up that trick entirely on my own. I've always believed that the smartest people surround themselves with the ideas and perspectives of even smarter people. Being inspired by how other people, including nonathletes, organize their lives and careers has allowed me to piecemeal a life that works for me. No one person will have identical values to me, but by borrowing little things that work for me from a wide range of people, I can build a tapestry of life lessons, advice, and tidbits that keep me aligned with what I want for myself. That's how I learned to keep some of my time nonnegotiable.

Netflix cofounder Marc Randolph tweeted one day about his definition of success. "The thing I'm most proud of in my life is not the companies I started," he began. "It's the fact that I was able to start them while staying married to the same woman." He did this by prioritizing weekly date nights, no matter what. "Rain or shine, I left at exactly 5 pm and spent the evening with my best friend . . . Those Tuesday nights kept me sane. And they put the rest of my work in perspective." At first, I'm sure Randolph had to really wrestle with people about that boundary. With time, they began to realize that if they needed something from him it had to either get to him before 5:00 p.m. or wait until Wednesday morning.

Oftentimes, our boundaries with work help teach people what line they can and can't cross with you. The misconception is that if you don't only work you are lazy and if you don't respond at all hours of the night you aren't ambitious. Boundaries are put in place to help keep us balanced, physically and mentally. It doesn't change work ethic or the ability to get things done. The same work and requirements and standards can all be in place, but the details and rules of how it is accomplished may be different. Quality over quantity. Tear down the false premise that just working long and hard is enough or even desired; be efficient and smart. In order for me to have success on the court, home has to be taken care of. In order for me to have peace of mind in the studio or boardroom, I have to know my priorities, but also live them. Avoid the one-size-fits-all approach of all or nothing. Missing work doesn't mean you don't care. In fact, establishing priorities, expectations, and goals and working backward to make the time to accomplish them actually leads to more effective work. Boundaries are another form of discipline to help you excel long term, and no is a complete sentence. Maybe in essence the reason Marc Randolph was able to succeed in business was as a result of his success in his marriage.

During times where work pulled me away, I made my presence known in other ways: Frequent FaceTimes scheduled around our various time zones. I went through great lengths to keep our shared calendars up-to-date with our various responsibilities including work, school, and playdates, to know when everyone was available. Another practice we established were family sleep calendars. I was somewhat inspired by a CEO I heard speak at a conference. The woman said before work trips she made little trinkets and crafts with her kids and traded the things they'd made. Every time they video chatted while away, the CEO showed the trinket she'd traveled with, and it was a reminder that they were always with one another even from afar. I loved the simplicity of making something together and using it as a reminder even when away. Lailaa and I began creating sleep calendars when I had to travel without her, which were colorful markers of how many nights or sleeps I'd be away. Each night we talked, we crossed off a number, counting down until there was only one sleep left. It allowed Lailaa to understand our time away while also spending quality time talking during our craft time.

Through Pat Summitt, I learned to show people how much they mean to you through daily actions. Pat did that for me in ways I'll never be able to put into words. She did it for all her players, coaching staff, and Lady Vols team. Pat went out of her way to be there for people at their absolute lowest. And when Pat achieved wins that she'd worked her ass off for, she refused to hog the moments for herself and shared that spotlight with the people around her. Pat was always we in the wins and me in the losses. Coach wanted everyone to look internally at what they could do to be better for the team, so she had no problem falling on the sword to the media.

I also learned from Pat's regrets that you can be a visionary without sacrificing everything. That's when we make decisions to choose love over legacy and presence over presents. Early on, I knew that I wanted to give Lailaa the world without spoiling her.

What we had built as adults was much different than what either Anya or I had as kids. In many ways, it's what our parents had worked so hard to make possible for us. But we struggled to operate from these new positions we were in. My parents said no to material things not because they didn't want us to have them but because we couldn't afford them at the time. If I was telling our kids no because "we shouldn't," at times it was difficult to discern what was appropriate.

Our answer was to spend money on presence, not just presents. In essence, creating more time, making things easier, moments, sprinkles on top of experiences supersede things—designer clothes, expensive cars, jewelry, etc. We do the best to ensure our actions as a family indeed align with our values and our intentions.

My kids may not remember every memory or moment but I hope they will carry on the "habits" and traditions like mother/daughter trips, Sunday game days, Friday morning breakfasts before school, holiday cookie decorating, and our absolute love for Halloween and family costumes. I heard someone once say that your biggest flex as a parent is your kids not needing you as adults, but wanting you around. It's nearly impossible not to worry as a parent. My friends and I joke and ask ourselves what our children will say in therapy about us fifteen years from now. I am far from perfect but I hope my children remember the quality time. It doesn't matter whether we were eating a five-star meal or our favorite HiHo cheeseburger, whether we were dipping our toes in the house pool or decorating a Christmas tree far, far away in Xinjiang, China. What mattered was the moment.

Traditions and quality time eased my mind that no matter how often we moved from place to place, there would always be something stringing our life together. No matter where we were, we did those same traditions with a spin. Now fast-forward to Lailaa splitting holidays between her dad and me, it doesn't matter if we actually have her on Thanksgiving or Christmas, we celebrate the same way. No matter if it's a Friday instead of a Thursday or the twenty-eighth instead of the twenty-fifth it's the act and the moments that count not the technicalities. When I changed my focus to that it eased things for her and me. What you focus on changes perspective a great deal in difficult times and especially when you are just doing the best you can as a parent.

As parents we oftentimes wonder if our kids are "getting" what we are trying so hard to instill. Airr turned three recently and I was scheduled to fly out of town to be in the studio for my TNT Tuesday show. The previous weekend we celebrated and threw him a birthday party and had a great time. As Monday concluded and I packed to leave early Tuesday morning, I felt the guilt of missing his real birthday creeping in. I boarded my flight the next morning and upon landing, I received pictures from my daughter of the birthday breakfast she got up early to make for Airr! I got emotional because she did for her little brother what I did for her when she was little. A special birthday breakfast plate filled with all of her favorite things was something she always looked forward to! Quality time and special traditions are the currency that feeds our relationships. Whether for you those relationships are with children, parents, extended family, friends, neighbors, or colleagues, find your people and lean into your time with them. Pat used to always tell me, chase people and passion in your life and you will never fail.

I was exhausted from years and years of planes, trains, and automobiles. Six months of WNBA and the other six months spent overseas. Every vacation was rushed, we were constantly dealing with time zone changes, I had to miss big events like the Super Bowl and holidays, my off days were few and far between, and an offseason didn't exist for me. By 2017, Lailaa and I had been on the road for seven years, the vast majority of her little life.

I had decided enough was enough. We were done overseas. I would figure out another way to spend my offseason. That summer in 2017, the WNBA season was already underway, and I actually missed two games for the Los Angeles Sparks while playing abroad in Istanbul, Turkey. Exhaustion was an understatement. Between jet lag, body soreness, injuries, and end-of-season woes, it was hard to jump right back into the beginning of a new season. Between tougher practices, travel, games, and learning new teammates, switching gears was tough. And that's just the basketball part. Lailaa missing school, extracurricular activities, and friends was also a challenge. The steady constant she had in all of this was *me*.

One June summer day, we sat in an airport exhausted in God knows what city, headed to a WNBA game. Just one month earlier, I had donned a Fenerbahçe jersey competing for a Euroleague championship, and now I was in my tenth season in the WNBA. The phone rang. I picked up and listened as my agent told me about the opportunity I simply couldn't refuse. One more season in China the following year. Just one, he promised. In exchange, the team was willing to pay me the kind of money that could make certain aspects of our lives set. Endorsements made life in the WNBA worthwhile, but this type of money I couldn't pass up. Could I really turn down a couple months of work that could change our future lifestyle?

I wavered. I had promised my daughter we were done flying over oceans to dribble an orange ball and being far away from our home. But *this* opportunity made me doubt my ability to keep my word. I knew the answer was yes. I couldn't turn it down. Before I even hung up the call, I felt deflated. This isn't the typical response to securing such a major deal like this, of course. But I'd promised my baby girl, and I hated to walk that back. I turned to Lailaa and gently broke the news to her. She turned away fast, but I could still see the tears forming in her eyes. With her back facing me, moving up and down as she cried, my heart broke into a million pieces. Lailaa had endured so many places, adjustments, changes, and environments and always with so much grace. This was her breaking point. After a few moments, in a mature nature far exceeding her eight young years, she turned back around and simply said, "Okay." She gave me her trust . . . again.

As parents, we are constantly making decisions that impact our little hearts outside our chests. Our kids rely on us to balance wants and needs, now and later, what's a small sacrifice versus which costs are too great. We are measuring and weighing things, like in math, but the units of life aren't convertible. How can you compare money and comfort? Whether it's moving cities or continents, our literal and figurative moves as adults impact the little humans we are responsible for. The fear as a parent is you won't be there for your kids emotionally but, also, the fear of not being able to financially support their needs, as well. In the midst of finalizing a divorce and becoming the primary breadwinner, I knew I could use the financial security.

Again, I was flooded with the reality that this wasn't the childhood I'd had. Did the money mean anything if it left my child so gutted? The answer, I came to realize, wasn't so black-and-white. Sometimes, there is a right or wrong thing to do. We are needed by the people we love, and that has to come first. Other times, we have to face the reality that the career span of the average professional athlete is much shorter than others. I couldn't be casual about my high-earning years if I was going to ensure a certain life for my family. Sometimes, we have to hustle hard and make the sacrifice. But it wasn't just my sacrifice. As parents, at times, we feel a need to protect our children from discomfort or hurt. But as they get older and develop their own values, they'll surprise you in their ability to navigate obstacles and carry burdens with wisdom far beyond their years.

My father has always been a superhero in my eyes. Capable of anything. Invincible to all harm coming his way. He's a bionic man who bounces back from any and everything thrown at him, so when he became sick just as I was beginning to play for the Sky, it crushed me. Though I was starting anew with a fresh franchise, I knew immediately that I needed to prioritize my father in whatever ways he needed me. Thankfully, people around me understood that with no hesitation. A number of my friends and colleagues could relate as they had to care for their own parents during physical and health challenges. In an instant, the dynamic of who takes care of who is flipped on its head.

More test results and opinions revealed the full story: Dad needed chemotherapy followed by a stem cell transplant. This was the first time that I knew my dad needed me. As children we are used to our parents showing up for games, cleaning our wounds, and taking care of us when we are sick or have surgery. No one warns you that as you get older, so do your parents. The dynamic of your relationship changes and at times I was appalled at my dad not wanting to accept my help or my desire to be there for him as he had for me! Pride got in the way of his willingness to allow his child to care for him. As parents we feel that we are put on this earth to do the caring, not the other way around. After I refused to be pushed away, my dad finally let down his guard and allowed me to be there for him. I flew in after studio shows and drove to his house early on off days during the season to accompany him to chemo. I was grateful that he wanted me around in such a vulnerable and scary time. All the doctor visits, taking care of him post-op, and phone calls strengthened our bond.

As fond as I was of my dad before, I'm even more so now. I saw so much of myself in him throughout his journey back to good health. I learned I was great at showing up for the ones I loved. It was second nature. But I was bad at receiving support and love because like my dad, I never want to be a burden or an inconvenience. When you love someone with all of your heart, you don't mind sacrificing and prioritizing them. Life is tough enough, I had to learn to stop pushing people away in moments I needed support the most. No matter how old we get, parents can still be life's best teachers!

SEVENTEEN

Rule of Threes

You are the sum total of everything you've ever seen, heard,
eaten, smelled, been told, forgot—it's all there.

—MAYA ANGELOU

The rule of threes is universal. There's a natural symmetry in things that come in threes, and we see it all around us in pop culture: the three little pigs, the Three Musketeers, three square meals a day . . . I could go on and on. Experts have studied why ideas or things that come in threes are so memorable to us, and there's no one answer. But items that come in threes—and messages conveyed in threes—are more memorable than any other number. When I chose to wear three on my back, in 2004, I had no idea how much the number would follow me.

The rule of threes took on new meaning after winning my third WNBA championship in 2023 and having my third child the following year. Across my three WNBA wins with three different teams, I learned so much about myself and how my perspective on life shifted over time. Winning, losing, and battling it out for something you love changed me and my approach forever. Similarly, my motherhood journeys varied immensely when it came to Lailaa, Airr, and Hartt. They've each taught me so much about parenting, leadership, grace, time, and love.

Lai entered my world when I was fresh out of college, newly married for the first time, thrust onto a new stage, and still figuring out this thing called life and balance. Before her, I was a young woman wrapped in a world that had me at the center. Lailaa immediately entered my universe and became the Sun that I rotated around. I tried to do it all, but Lai sensed that I was a well-intentioned amateur. In true first-born-daughter fashion, she was patient, well-mannered, and had an easygoing nature. Whether traversing continents, learning new languages, or being the only kid in the room, Lailaa handled everything in stride. Through and with her, I learned what it meant to put someone else's needs before my own.

When Lailaa was around six years old, one of my coaches challenged me to treat my teammates with the same tenderness, love, care, and patience that I treated my daughter. I didn't initially lean all the way into that mode of thought, still believing the only way to get to what you want is through toughness. Somewhere along the way, I'd lost sight of the Tennessee way of leaning into your teammates, leading by example, and hustling hard *together*. Undesired results will do that; they'll convince you that you have no one but yourself to fall back on. Trust is the hardest thing to establish and develop when you are navigating uncharted territory. My daughter helped me understand life better off the court, which eventually translated to team rapport and how I approached the women I played alongside.

There's nothing like the newness of your "first" anything. The thrill. The angst. The uncertainty. There's so much you don't know the first time you do anything . . . I didn't even know just how much I didn't know! But, through my daughter, I learned that leading with vulnerability, respect, love, care, and developing and demonstrating trust even in uncertainty is who I wanted to be. She helped me learn that. Motherhood is the most challenging role I've held, and because I was a mother, I also learned in time to be a better, more dependable teammate. I 100 percent attribute that mindset shift to how and why we came away with the 2016 WNBA championship—or at least my role in that win.

But, when navigating firsts, you question yourself, your purpose, and your setbacks. *Am I doing the right thing at the right time and will it lead me to my desired outcome?* There were moments when I wondered if I was meant to win a championship in the WNBA. I doubted myself as a first-time mom. Lailaa taught me not to fear the uncharted path, but to adapt and lean in even more to the qualities that make those around me better. I relinquished control and bought into the process. Lailaa shifted my perspective on what it takes to win and be successful. Before motherhood, I measured winning by points, the scoreboard, and record. After her, I measured it by how successful I was at making the people around me better. My daughter helped reestablish a blueprint that had been laid for me by my parents and Coach Summitt. One that I'd lost sight of somewhere along the way. I learned through motherhood that though I can do everything, I'm not at my best when I attempt to do it all alone. In basketball and in life, I needed my teammates to be great for the days when I wasn't at my best.

Lailaa also helped me realize how to enjoy the journey. After all I'd fought to accomplish, the accolades weren't what I was truly in pursuit of. I wanted what was on the other side of the accomplishment: fulfillment, pride, family, camaraderie, and the realization that my mind and body had carried me to a new height. And the best part is that once you've done something before, a calmness washes over you. It doesn't make the next attempt "easy" per se, but you can walk in with the awareness that you've climbed that mountain before. Every battle or hurdle thrown your way is simply part of the process.

So Nice, Do It Twice

I never imagined donning another WNBA jersey other than the Los Angeles Sparks. When the media day came and I looked down at the Chicago Sky logo across my chest, I realized that sometimes the best things for you are the ones that happen when you least expect them. You can plan, map out, and envision all you want, but you'll still end up somewhere and in something you never expected. Most times, it's somewhere you should be.

Joining the Chicago Sky after thirteen years in the WNBA was an opportunity to be a part of a city, team, style of play, and environment that felt full circle. *Home.* I went home, back to where I first learned to play the game of basketball, in front of people who watched my career from the start, and alongside teammates who reminded me of why I picked up the ball in the first place. For the first time, I didn't worry about perception or opinions, and instead made the best decision for me and my family. With Anya as my wife, our journey helped me realize that magical things are possible when you block out the noise and fear of others' perception. Heading to Chicago was a shot at more happiness and greater purpose.

I was brought to the team as an experienced veteran who had seen what it takes to win a championship in the WNBA. Leadership, experience, and belief is what I immediately felt I could bring to the Sky. There wasn't a better fit for me in the league than them, at the time. They played with pace, loved to move the ball, had athletes who could space the floor and knock down shooters. In some ways I feel as though they were my missing piece and I was theirs.

It sounds elementary—because most things we learn early in life are most important — but sharing really is caring. I learned on the path to my first WNBA championship win that no matter how talented your teams are or how badly you think you want it, if everyone on the team isn't focused on the same goal and synchronized in that effort and on the same page—from the coaches to the players to the assisting staff—it was a futile effort. By locking in with one another, communicating intentionally, and battling until the end, we could achieve most anything.

Our team in Chicago was hungry enough to push any and all ego to the side. Our season record wasn't great as we struggled to get our footing. Along the way, my new teammates wholeheartedly welcomed my insights, and I, in turn, vowed to learn from the new environment and fresh energy of the younger players around me. Syncing our efforts in that way made for the perfect storm, and, together, we made it to the playoffs as the sixth seed, fought our way through the finals, and battled the Phoenix Mercury. This was my third time in the finals. I won one in 2016 and lost one in 2017. During both crucial close-out game fours, I had failed to will my team to victory. That was on my mind from the time I entered the arena. What would it take to get over the hump and close out a series? Dressed in a white collared shirt, leather biker jacket, and leather pants, I tucked a Chicago Bulls Michael Jordan red jersey in my backpack for good luck. Growing up, the image of MJ jumping on the scorer's table and pumping his fist with confetti falling was cemented in my mind. Experience taught me fate didn't make my responsibility for doing my part any less, I still had to grab the pen and finish writing the story.

In game three, we blew Phoenix out by thirty-six points! Somehow, I felt my entire journey had prepared me for this exact moment. I felt the team, and the organization as a whole, relax. Before individual warm-ups, someone messaged our team's group chat asking for names for the postgame championship celebration. I immediately reminded everyone that we had not won anything yet! I was furious at how casual everyone acted, expecting Diana Taurasi, Brittney Griner, and Skylar Diggins-Smith to just roll over and wave the white flag. I knew better than that!

Phoenix came out in game four with a vengeance. We got down by as many as fourteen points late in the third quarter. I could sense the momentum shifting. Big moments aren't always at the end of games. Sometimes games are won in pivotal, energy-changing plays. I knew this was what Chicago brought me there to do: to lead, step up, and be the voice of reason. We needed a steady ship and big plays! Failure had taught me that my losses came as a result of being scared of the moment instead of searching for it. I knew it was time to step up and be the hunter, not the hunted. Our team huddled after a time-out, and I spoke confidence into the group, reminding everyone that we don't have to hit home runs to win. "Let's just keep swinging and chip away with singles." I backed up my words with my play and made big buckets to keep us within striking distance as we entered the fourth quarter. Allie Quigley and I had timely baskets that kept the game from getting out of hand.

With 1:57 left, the Mercury were up 69–72. Sloot, our point guard, drove off of a Stefanie Dolson screen and I stayed spaced opposite the action. In that moment, my mind shut off. The possibilities, outcomes, and all other distractions disappeared. My hands were ready when the ball arrived, and, as I had done thousands of times, the ball settled on my fingertips before my shot. I let it go and held my follow-through. Splash! The crowd erupted and the game was tied. That moment and that feeling is probably one of the greatest I've ever experienced in my career. All the ups, downs, struggles, and heartbreak prepared me for that moment.

Though five years separated me from the last time I'd brought home that trophy, everything about winning in 2021 felt different. When the clock ran out, I raced to An and my parents who'd been sitting courtside together. This was An's and my first time celebrating a WNBA championship together. Winning in LA was a personal fight to prove our team was capable of making it all the way, but winning in Chicago was about pure love for the game. Chicago and Naperville are where I first picked up a basketball. To win there in front of family, friends, former coaches and teammates, was one of the most full-circle moments in my career. That playoff season was the perfect way to cap off a year that was up and down. Moving teams, moving our life from LA to Chicago, grinding through injuries, and growing our family.

Even before the WNBA season even began, Anya and I knew that we'd soon be welcoming a little Parker into the world. From the beginning, we were extremely up front with our family and friends about the fact that we wanted to have children together and what that journey would look like. By leveling with the people around us and meeting everyone's natural curiosity with a learning opportunity, we got ahead of the questions and created space for people to be cautiously optimistic with us.

We knew our journey was going to look different from what some of the people around us were used to—I mean, we were still learning the range of options available to us. I'd been a mother before, but kind of like winning a championship, I hadn't done it this way and with this team. With Anya carrying our child, there was so much I had to learn about supporting someone else through pregnancy and childbirth. But no matter what, this was still *our* child. I'd played an integral role in choosing our sperm donor and we talked nonstop about every single decision and how it made us feel, settling on a path to motherhood that suited us perfectly. Anya and I took our partnership very seriously, and that deep communication was the perfect foundation.

When the spring of 2021 rolled around, we were deep into our baby-making process having tried rounds of both intrauterine insemination (IUI) and in vitro fertilization (IVF). I was traveling on the road for work and was settling in at the Minneapolis Airport when Anya FaceTimed me. "Guess what," she asked before blurting out the answer: "We're pregnant!" I tried to temper my reaction so I wouldn't look completely insane in the midst of the terminal, but I couldn't help squealing in glee. When Anya zoomed out and I saw more of her background, I realized she was at my dad's house with my best friend Justine, who was the person who purchased the pregnancy tests for me when I found out little Lai was growing inside of me. Having her there with Anya when she found out about little Airr was incredibly full circle for me. When Anya and I first admitted our feelings for one another, I always wondered what we'd be trading off to make space for our love. But there in that moment, I knew we hadn't let go of anything important.

My heart swelled as Anya's belly grew throughout the WNBA season. At an ultrasound appointment during the second trimester, we first saw his little head and arms moving around. Just as the ob-gyn confirmed that Airr was measuring big, a SportsCenter alert appeared on my phone. I joked that it was divine timing and foreshadowing that Airr would be a hooper one day! Already I felt proud of and excited for my unborn son. When we won the championship in mid-October, the public may not have known what Anya meant to me, but they saw us embrace as the confetti fell on the court.

Almost two months after the championship, on Anya's and my two-year wedding anniversary, we shared for the first time publicly that we were married and expecting a baby together. When Airr finally arrived in February 2022, all I felt was love. Love, love, love. When the doctors laid his body on Anya's chest, she immediately began sobbing, and I looked on at them both feeling the emotions surge through my body. At last, our baby boy was here with us. I wish that moment could have lasted a lifetime, but eventually our golden hour of skin-to-skin time was up as a range of medical professionals buzzed around caring for Airr. The protective mama bear in me immediately showed its face, refusing to allow our baby out of my sight while also advocating for Anya. Both of my babies needed to be okay, and it was my job to protect them.

When I became a mom for the first time, I couched my insecurities behind an armor of overconfidence. By putting on a good face, I thought I might be able to fake it till I made it. There was a lot of trial and error along the way, so that by the time Airr came around with his stubborn personality, I learned to embrace the unknown.

That mentality served me with parenting my second child *and* securing another WNBA championship ring. I leaned on experience and what I had learned from my past struggles. There's a calmness that comes with a journey that you have embarked on before. The second time is different, but you understand the importance of moments that much more!

The Third Time's the Charm

When I joined the Las Vegas Aces, I was finally secure in who I was as a player and a person. I'd weathered countless storms—injuries, grief, triumph, failure, disappointment, and joy. At some point, I looked myself in the mirror and said three words I needed to hear and believe: "You deserve it." Why was I obsessed with choosing a difficult or heartbreaking path? I felt like that old parable about a drowning man believing God would save him but turning away all life-saving support. Did I subconsciously think it's what was required to "earn" success?

I reminded myself that I had nothing else to prove to anyone except myself. I wanted a third championship, yes, but really at this stage in my career I didn't want to just play, I wanted to win. In my last year of playing professional basketball, I deserved the joys of a nice locker and state-of-the-art facility at the very least. No more battling for scraps. No more starting from the bottom. I'd been there and done that. Time to shine, baby.

Though I was a veteran, joining the Aces was slightly different from moving to the Chicago Sky. For one, I entered with a lot of humility around what my body could and couldn't withstand. By that season, I'd been playing in the WNBA for fifteen years and had been navigating serious injuries, surgeries, and rehabilitative journeys for more than twenty years. I can't lie and say I dealt with my feelings perfectly. For quite some time, I had to process the unfairness of working so hard at the expense of my body all to turn around and be seen as someone using shortcuts. But I never ever could allow myself to be the angry, bitter vet. I love the game of basketball too much, and I had so much respect and admiration for the incredible talent on the Las Vegas Aces. Getting to play with friends and players like Chelsea Gray and A'ja Wilson gave me confidence in the state of women's basketball.

Naturally, I saw a lot of myself in A'ja. Not just the skill but also the burden. Heavy is the crown, they say, but very few offer to lighten the load. I had been around vets that uplifted and empowered me and those who added weight to the load. A'ja was special, and I knew my responsibility was to be for her what I needed someone to be for me. I was at the end and she was in her prime. A tough pill to swallow, but an opportunity for me to demonstrate maturity and grace throughout the process. Was I perfect? Hell no! No one prepares you for the feelings you have when Father Time catches up to you. But I knew who I wanted to be, and every day I worked toward that goal of leading, making others around me better, and remaining humble.

I would be lying if I told you that this Las Vegas championship didn't feel different. Instead of being soaked in a sweaty jersey with champagne and confetti, I was in street clothes barely off of crutches from my season-ending navicular fracture surgery. There's nothing like playing and making plays to lead your team to victory. From the sideline, I did my best to shout out advice to A'ja and offer ideas to the coaching staff, but I never imagined being on the bench watching the game play out. Ultimately, it was through this journey that I learned who I was far exceeded and surpassed the game of basketball. Time with my family while I recovered from surgery gave me the opportunity to see my daughter's first varsity volleyball game, take Airr to school, and be still for once. Our third child grew in Anya's belly, and there was a calmness throughout the pregnancy. There was no rush or urgency, but instead slow mornings and traditions that began because for the first time in my entire career I had time. I realized during this process that I was far more than an orange ball, and that my teammates at home, my wife, and my children would 100 percent fill the void I would have from retiring from the game of basketball.

Time teaches us not to self-sabotage or shortchange ourselves. With my first two children, I similarly assumed a martyr-like position of wanting to protect my babies—and partner—that I didn't stop to enjoy the pregnancy period, which was as important as preparing for our baby's entrance. Similar to my basketball career, I rushed through motherhood assuming more days lie ahead. With Lailaa, I was a young rookie with my career ahead of me, and with Airr I was protecting my and Anya's privacy. As a result, I hadn't experienced the bliss of openly sharing a baby bump or planning for a growing family without first calculating the career risks. By the time Hartt rolled around, I was indignant about having earned the right to be loud and proud of our beautiful family. No more omission.

When Hartt entered our lives, even when he was in the womb, I truly slowed down and relished the moments, both big and small. I held on tighter to the Sunday morning cuddles where all five of us piled into our bed with all three dogs to laugh and snuggle. I shared about him publicly, no longer feeling the fear of what came from others' judgment. When he was finally earthside, I reveled in smelling his baby scent. I was no longer counting down to what was next; instead I was savoring each moment as if it might be the last. Hartt made me realize how grown-up my first baby had gotten. Lailaa was in high school, and it seemed like just yesterday I was nursing her in the wee hours of the morning.

Each of my children has pulled a different version of parenting out of me and taught me what it means to lead. I've had to push my own idea of what is best to the side and listen in for what will work best for them. I learned to love the game differently and to do so while keeping family central. Slowing down didn't need to mean stopping. Even if I wasn't on the court, I found paths to keep basketball part of my life as a broadcaster, producer, Adidas executive, and investor.

Motherhood taught me that there are countless ways to show love and be present. The same goes for championships. Each title had a different journey and required me to display a variety of skills to come out on top. There is no cookie-cutter method that could work on each of my children in the same way that there's no one formula for succeeding in basketball. If there were, we'd all raise perfect children and the playoffs would be a lot less interesting. There's no outsmarting life. We have to go by feel and constantly evolve in response to the setbacks and opportunities we face. On the other side of that evolution and experimentation is the key to really winning.

PART FIVE

Opportunity

EIGHTEEN

I Did It My Way

I faced it all and I stood tall.

—FRANK SINATRA

Familiar music blared from the speakers, the lights went black, and a laser light show filled the court with the red, fierce Chicago Bulls logo. The crowd erupted and then a legendary voice, that of Ray Clay, overpowered the roars, "And nowwwwwww, your starting lineup for YOUR Chicago Bulls!" I was eight years old and to this day I still remember how magical that moment was. "From Norrrrtttthhh Carolina . . . at guard . . . 6'6" . . . Michael Jordan!" That game would change my perspective on basketball; I learned through that experience that it was so much more than just a game, it was entertainment!

When games weren't on local WGN, we would tune in from home early to watch the NBC pregame show and I would sing along to the NBA on NBC theme song by John Tesh, "Roundball Rock." I loved watching the pregame shows and hearing the analysis of the matchup. I would flip the channel to postgame highlights and discussions on ESPN SportsCenter and I fell in love with Stewart Scott and his hip-hop references while covering some of sport's greatest moments. "Cooler than the other side of the pillow," "Boo-YAH!" "Straight Butter!" I noticed immediately that my experience watching the same game was different depending on who was covering it from a newscaster and analyst perspective. Robin Roberts represented for the ladies, and was one of the first newscasters I saw on television who looked like me. Men dominated sports, both on the floor and off, so seeing a woman on the desk was important to me as a young Black girl. It made a career in sports seem possible. I watched and loved sports just as much as others, so why were most of the opportunities in sports automatically delegated to men? Women deserve to help tell the stories as well. I was a fan of the game of basketball and all that contributed to making the viewer's experience exciting! On the weekends I would eat my breakfast and watch Ahmad Rashad and Willow Bay host *Inside Stuff*. My favorite episode was when Shaquille O'Neal tried to dunk fiercely and shattered the backboard, falling flat on his back! The coverage of the game pulled me in even more. Basketball was more than just in between the lines. Broadcasts help viewers get to know their idols and take the game more in depth.

As I grew in the game as a player, I became a student of the game as well. Soaking in as much basketball as I could. I fell in love with the way analyst Hubie Brown explained the game and broke down the X's and O's during live play. *Inside the NBA* was a show my family and I loved to watch. Ernie Johnson Jr. ran point position as the host and he ran the offense on the desk with Shaq, Charles Barkley, and Kenny Smith. The show was about basketball, but it was pure must-watch entertainment. Craig Sager manned the sideline with his unique fashion of loud suits. For the first time, people tuned in to watch the pregame show and postgame show, at times more so than the actual game. That desk had a chemistry, a way of blending together personalities and making it seem like they were at home in their living room discussing the game of basketball.

When the opportunity came in late 2015, I couldn't wait to jump into broadcast work. There was no ego in it for me; I was grateful and excited to be part of the game in a new way. I always believed playing basketball was the best job in the world and a close second was being paid to *talk* basketball. I talk basketball all day everyday anyways. My family literally can't get me to *stop* talking about basketball. I'm the person who watches the game, then watches the highlights and analysis of the game postgame on a loop. Then the next morning I get up and watch all the shows that analyze said game. I'm a basketball junkie and I know most of the time, my wife and daughter especially just want me to change the damn channel! Now someone was willing to pay me to discuss the game that I love? Sign me up!

I started out covering SEC college games like Alabama, Ole Miss, and Georgia. This was during the WNBA offseason, and I was flying out to cities across the Southeast. It was brutal in the beginning: landing at airports, renting a car, and driving an hour and a half to go call games that maybe one hundred people were watching. It didn't matter to me if there were only two people listening in; I prepared, researched, and poured my energy into it.

I pride myself on being super knowledgeable and prepared for everything I go into. I studied the teams I'd be covering, the injury reports and stats on each player, and the history between the coaches. Part of it was my competitive nature and need to be the best, but the other aspect was wanting to do justice to the game I love and to players that I have great respect and empathy for. I know how it feels to wonder if the broadcasters are paying as much attention to the game as we are. When you're playing basketball, the game moves fast, and we're doing everything to keep up. While on the court, we have to be both in our bodies and able to see the game aerially to get where we need to be and make plays happen. When you do all of that and find out later that the broadcasters barely knew players' names and relied on their general basketball knowledge, it's discouraging. The game is more entertaining with intimate awareness of what's on the line, what these moments mean for the players on the court, and how they're pivoting and showcasing true skill.

That's the aspect of broadcasting that can't be taught. There's a craft to thriving on the fly, but a core part of it is a sincere love of basketball. Either you have that or you don't, but it's hard to instill in someone. That love pushed me to do the work and be excited about being a rookie again. It was nice to be doing something out of my comfort zone and where I could experiment more without people's preconceived expectations of me. They'd seen me play, but now they'd get to really grasp my basketball IQ and passion.

The Rookie and the Vet:
Putting in Ten Thousand Hours

Though I was committed to a slow-and-steady grind in broadcast, my ambitious side made itself known. I set my sights early on toward doing live and in-studio coverage across both men's and women's basketball. It would take time and serious work, but that was my telescopic goal. Malcolm Gladwell's 10,000-hour rule really carried me during this time. In his book *Outliers*, Gladwell writes, "Ten thousand hours is the magic number of greatness," and that consistent practice is what fuels success, more than serendipity or lucking up.

Professional athletes are used to doing the work to get to where we need to go within our sports—to climb, to set and break records, to win. But outside our respective sports that most of us have been playing for decades, we sometimes forget about how much time and repetition is involved in mastering anything. While broadcasting didn't strain my body in the same way physically, it took humility to realize that I didn't know everything . . . yet. With time and practice, this new frontier could be a thrilling one, but I wouldn't get there through wishful thinking and name recognition alone. And I didn't want to. I wouldn't want anyone thinking I've had any part of my career handed to me. Dealing with tough feedback at my big age was a harsh blow to take. I wanted to be coachable. In order to get better, leaning into what you need to improve on is key.

During my first WNBA offseason, in 2009, I was pregnant and unable to play in Russia until the following year. In the meantime, as I nested and prepared for my baby girl to arrive, I asked my agent to help me explore other ventures. I was fresh out of college and proving that I could and would live up to all the hype surrounding me, so why would broadcasting be any different? I'd grown up watching the NBA and TNT until the WNBA was formed and that, too, consumed my life. Racing home and watching the greats discuss other greats was the highlight of my week. I couldn't wait to emulate that and bring my own personality to the table.

My agent came back with the chance to call a few NCAA women's basketball games, and I leaped at the chance. I traveled to East Lansing for the Michigan State Spartans' game against Ohio State, where I was the color analyst for ESPN2. That day was incredible, and I loved getting to witness the behind-the-scenes action of an arena in a whole new light. Entering Breslin Center, I quickly settled in next to my cohost and reviewed my notes. I felt a jittery and anxious energy, but as soon as tip-off came, I got in my zone. The day was a bit of a blur, but I walked away feeling pretty good about how I did.

That game gave me my first understanding of how different on-the-ground coverage can be from in-studio shows. I didn't know what was expected of me and was doing things on the fly. No one told me how to prepare, so I just gathered notes, researched stats, and showed up. The challenge of in-game broadcasting is you are reacting on the fly. The goal is to bring the viewer in to what it is like in that arena. Insights and replays happen fast, and as a result you have to be quick and ready to tell a story that you don't have a lot of time to think through. Despite my nervousness and need to learn how to even communicate with production in the truck, where the cough button was, etc., I was proud of how I did and was excited to keep going. I felt confident I would get the chance to call the upcoming NCAA tournament.

ESPN called me the night of the game to debrief, and my jaw dropped when they said that would be my last game of the year. They detailed a number of mistakes in my reporting and how I sounded, but all I heard was "You aren't good, and you can't call for us anymore." I felt empty and dejected after hanging up the phone with my then-boss at ESPN. My entire life, I've prided myself on having a high basketball IQ and here I was being told I couldn't call games. I was devastated. It had been a long time since I'd been bad at something, and it hurt even more that I didn't register my performance as inadequate. I'm normally my harshest critic and have never been one to lie to myself. Clearly my radar was off, and I didn't fully grasp what good broadcasting looked like.

I took that feedback hard and threw myself into other work to distract myself from those analyst dreams. It was years later before I even thought about doing television again. My anger and defensiveness kept me away from the work that would eventually bring me back to broadcasting stronger than ever. When I did get over my initial embarrassment, I finally was able to admit that I could do and be better. Mediocrity is not something I have ever accepted. I had a lot of work to do, and they'd cared enough about me and my performance to give it to me straight. What I did with that feedback was on me.

When I'd nursed my wounds enough to try again, I was ready to start logging my hours toward the analyst career I knew was possible for me. *Can't* isn't in my vocabulary. There wasn't a question that I knew enough about basketball to do well at calling games. If my delivery, cadence, and response time needed work, then I would put in the time. Just as I watched film as a player, I studied the analysts I admired and wanted to emulate. There was no better production to study and start with than learning from one of the greatest sports shows ever made: Inside the NBA on TNT. I learned that no one takes themselves too seriously and that curiosity is valued above all. Authenticity is important, but the key to being an outstanding broadcaster is to listen! When you listen and then formulate your thoughts, the chemistry jumps off the television. It's crazy how Pat's lessons keep showing up, no matter what I do! Listening to your producer, host, fellow analysts and the game itself. You can never try and pre-tell the story, the game itself will help you tell it. The mentality at Turner was that when we each make one another look good, we all succeed. The people there had accomplished so much, won all the awards, and been inducted into their respective hall of fame associations yet were on a constant quest toward humility and respect. I wanted to be like *that*. I wanted to learn to listen and not be afraid of criticism or messing up. I wanted to be a part of adding value, knowledge, and especially entertainment to those who watched.

Being new at something again isn't easy, but I've always asked a lot of questions and humbled myself enough to recognize things don't have to come easily to me for me to find success eventually. I asked tons of questions for months and months, never letting pride get in the way of my probing. Any new space I entered, I wanted to know what success looked like, what the unwritten rules were, and how people have been able to find longevity in the space. I wanted the recipe, and I wasn't ashamed to admit it.

Michael Strahan was one of the first people I looked to for mentorship. Michael had an incredible fifteen-year career as a defensive end with the New York Giants. After absolutely dominating on the field, setting records for single-season quarterback sacks, and retiring with a Super Bowl win under his belt, Michael flawlessly transitioned to media where he became a household name again. Hosting football-pregame shows gave way to even more opportunities, and now, Michael is an Emmy Award–winning and beloved cohost for one of America's top morning shows. I wanted to know how he did it all and made it seem so easy. The man says good morning to millions of people each morning and reads off a teleprompter as if it was second nature. People have fun with him, learn from him, and remain glued to their screens hanging on to his every word.

Thankfully, Michael was incredibly kind and giving of his time, though I know he had so little of it. He told me how, in the beginning, while he was still playing for the Giants, he'd get up early on Monday mornings after late Sunday night finishes to do NFL radio. While everyone else was celebrating or going home to their families, Michael was clocking in. It could be grueling at times, he'd say, but he'd rather do the hard things early. Doing that always made life easier later. We had countless conversations like that where he encouraged me to keep my head down, roll up my sleeves, and stay in it for the long haul. I thought broadcasting would be immediate and easy, but the sacrifices Michael made traveling and grinding during his playing career made him great and opened up opportunities. It might have looked easy, but there were no shortcuts.

The beautiful thing about opening myself up to being a student was finding so many teachers and support systems all around me. Robin Roberts is another luminary I turned to for guidance and support at various stages of my journey in television. Robin set records as a multi-sport athlete in high school and a standout basketball player for her collegiate team. After graduating before the days of the WNBA, Robin jumped almost immediately into sports journalism and anchoring various shows across both radio and television. Less than a decade after beginning her reporting career, Robin began working with ESPN and became the first woman to co-host NFL Primetime. As an adult, being mentored by a Black woman who looked like me made me feel seen and valued at a critical juncture in my life where insecurities can leave crater-sized holes in our paths. Her ability to not only thrive in the world of sports anchoring but then transform and land at *Good Morning America* also taught me about the importance of evolution. Society will tell you that you've hit your ceiling and it's on us to hear our own voices louder than anyone else's.

Across my career up until this stage, I didn't always benefit from working with people who were receptive to inquisitive minds or mentorship in general. Thankfully the people I met in broadcasting wanted to share what they've learned. When they saw that I was receptive, people easily opened up with tips, tricks, and lessons. Many of them shared advice I'd heard often along my basketball journey: You have to put the time into learning the game. In the broadcasting world, that meant always being prepared and professional but also recognizing that having a voice comes with great responsibility. As the spokesperson of whatever game you're covering on a given day, the audience is depending on you to translate what is happening in front of them and what they may not see that is shaping the performances on the court. The fans you're speaking to want fun and nuanced coverage that leaves them more empowered and excited about the next game where they can apply what they saw and learned. But each person in the audience is incredibly different. You're speaking to a grandmother, a basketball head, a novice, a teenager, a superfan, and a former player all at once. You haven't done your job if you can't speak to each and every one of them. How you deliver a message that leaves them each with something they didn't know they needed is what separates a decent analyst from a great one.

I never wanted to be one of the guys. I wanted to be one of the players. People lean in and listen intently like the gospel to Stephen A. Smith, which they should. He's knowledgeable, entertaining, and great at what he does. When they watch me, no matter how knowledgeable or how on point my analysis or comments may be, I am discounted because I never played in the NBA. I always am blown away because neither did Stephen A. Smith. Men don't have to constantly fight through the challenges women in sports do. But it's okay, I'm game. I played basketball at the highest level I could have achieved and won as well. It's interesting because the disrespect doesn't come from the hall of fame and all-stars and champions; it comes from random fans who haven't earned even a middle school participation trophy. I had to eventually not let it impact me on a level that changed what I was doing, but I kept the understanding that I owed it to future women to continue to say the necessary things and be present even more on those shows. Exposure and visibility matter. Seeing something over and over, it's not going away; more people become accustomed to accepting and listening. Realize the good. Diversity is important, including diversity of thought.

Broadcasting challenged me in ways that I hadn't been in a while. I found myself reverting to familiar methods of immersion. I cut out most distractions and buckled in for watching film, studying other commentators, and doing the hard stuff early. I'm very hands-on when I'm focused: asking tons of questions, watching others in their prime, and tweaking according to my needs. It's how I've approached private equity and managing the business behind my many interests. I wanted to get the blueprint directly from the experts and do my part to earn a spot next to them. Then I listened to President Obama give an interview one day where he said, "don't let anyone make you think you don't belong. Once you sit at these tables with folks with fancy titles, and you go 'oh they ain't all that!'" President Obama pushed back against the idea that people are more special, smart, or savvy than you because they had the name or the connections to get the opportunity; that illusion is more a product of their confidence and what environments they've been exposed to. Our job as individuals is not to be intimidated but, on the contrary, to be someone who accepts the task of being a lifelong student and letting that speak for you.

There's nothing better than being told you can't do something and proving them wrong. As Kobe said, it's always better the hard way.

Preparation Meets Opportunity

For a few years I'd been calling college games and doing broadcasting work here and there, but I was ready to break out and take up more space. I'd learned from some of the best to ever do it and didn't want to miss the chance to splash onto the scene and prove that women hoopers are hoopers first and foremost. We understand basketball just as much as our male peers and have insights to bring to the table. But a lot of entertainment and television production is a waiting game for your big break.

Tara August has been the former Senior Vice President of Talent Relations and Special Projects for nearly two decades at Warner Bros. Discovery Sports, formerly known as Turner Sports. Under Tara's leadership, TNT has ushered in, established, and cemented top shows with everyone from Shaquille O'Neal to Charles Barkley and beyond. In 2017, Tara called with an opportunity that would have pushed my broadcasting career to the next level. The only problem was that it conflicted with the contract offer I'd just received to play in China during the WNBA offseason. The money being offered by the team was astronomically high, almost double what I'd ever been paid by a team to play basketball. I couldn't say no to the offer, so I told Tara that this season wouldn't work for me. I trusted that what was meant for me would come back around.

Tara was disappointed with me. As a woman in sports, she understood that opportunities for women don't come along every day. Tara operated among the many decision-makers in sports and, unfortunately, just like there aren't many Black women in sports in front of the camera, there were even fewer in her position. She's been creating great sports television longer than most, and I believe she saw my trajectory ahead of me and wanted me to jump at this moment. Saying no then could mean turning down my one shot. "I can't promise that this opportunity will be around for you next year," she warned earnestly, wanting me to be sure before I officially turned them down. I completely understood the position she was in. All I could do was hope I was making the right decision for my family and me at the time. If broadcasting was truly for me, I had to trust the alignment and be patient and ready enough for my moment and that I'd have more than one chance.

After returning from China, I received another call, this time about covering the NCAA men's regular season. The opportunity was in-studio analysis, which was a lot more glamorous than my SEC days of traveling across the South and Midwest, driving myself to games and reporting from the sideline. As they detailed the timing and logistics of the role, my mind began to spin with fear. I normally wait until the NCAA tournament to truly keep up with men's basketball teams. *How am I going to broadcast this?* I asked myself. I didn't feel as ready as I wanted to be, and the fear of blowing it immobilized me.

I thought of Lailaa and wondered what I'd tell her if a golden opportunity was before her. Without a question, I'd encourage her to take it! No one ever thinks they are ready or prepared fully for growth and more. But you have to trust what got you to that point and sometimes you have to trust your own potential. My entire life, I had always taken risks and bet on myself. Pat didn't recruit the two-time WNBA MVP and complete finished product version of me, she recruited the hungry, curious state champion who loved basketball and wanted to climb bigger heights. Broadcasting was the same. Fear of failure could not be the reason for not accepting. As the saying goes, when you stay ready, you don't have to get ready. The universe grants us chances to prove ourselves. Saying no before was because the timing didn't work out. Saying no now would be fear of failure. I'd rather try and fail than never try at all.

Saying yes to that trial run with Turner Sports snowballed into more chances to get in front of new audiences and larger platforms. In 2018, I became the only woman analyst during that season's men's NCAA March Madness, and I continued to cover the men's tournament in-studio for the next seven years straight. The next offseason I turned down a lucrative offer to return to Russia and play alongside Breanna Stewart and, instead, bet on myself to stay stateside and do commentating. TNT began to test me out for NBA coverage. It started small with me filling in for analysts who were out sick and joining shows as a guest for one-off broadcast episodes. Back in 2016, I did a guest appearance on *Area 21* with Kevin Garnett and Gary Payton. We got into a friendly and passionate debate about traveling that ended up going viral on social media afterward. KG was one of my favorite players growing up, and to be on TNT having friendly debates with him about basketball was something fifteen-year-old Candace would have never believed! I loved talking about sports, and I believe my passion and genuine joy for the game shined through to the many viewers.

I was calling a Lakers-Celtics game one day, alongside legend Reggie Miller and the best play-by-play voice, Kevin Harlan, and I'll never forget the feeling I had. My job was literally to sit courtside at a Lakers game, sit next to legends I grew up watching and listening to, and break down the game of basketball. All those years ago, I tuned in to learn from others about the game, and now I was able to do some of the teaching. Jason Tatum was on fire at the time and on a mission to prove himself against Lebron James and the Lakers. Two rival franchises with a combined twenty-seven titles between the two. I knew what it was like to be young and ready to take over on a big stage against someone you were trying to be and be better than. The desire to prove yourself and show the world that you belonged in the same conversation as one of the GOATs. On the other hand, I knew what it was like to be Lebron and not yet ready to hand over the keys to an upcoming future great. The arena was packed full of fans and celebrities alike and the energy in the audience was electric! Everyone was on the edge of their seats when Tatum went right at the matchup with Lebron and scored a tough mid-post jumper to solidify the game and a Boston Celtics win. Reggie and I stood up in the closing moments; each working while remaining true fans of the game. Did Tatum just take the league over? I hyped up the moment, but made sure to bring perspective. He had a lot of work to do before he could be mentioned in the same breath with Lebron James, but that day was a start.

Another game I think back fondly on was when the Golden State Warriors were playing Phoenix and I was calling the game alongside Kevin Harland and Reggie Miller once again. Steph Curry stepped up to the free throw line and Kevin reminded viewers that Steph was on one of his longest free-throw streaks. Sure enough, right when Kevin said those words, the ball circled the rim and bounced out of the basket. I immediately knew he'd jinxed Steph and Steph did too. Before shooting his second free throw, Steph pointed at Kevin with a knowing look and we all burst into laughter. Reggie and I egged Steph on even more pointing and tattling that Kevin did indeed do what Steph thought, the doomed "announcers jinx."

These are the moments basketball fans live for and I'm getting paid to be front and center for it all. Best of all, I get to do it with people I love and care about. At TNT Sports, respect is shared from the top talent and senior executives all the way to the producers, runners, make-up artists, and assistants. We sincerely enjoy one another because we trust one another enough to stick to the vision. In an environment like this, the bad apples truly weed themselves out because maintaining that team culture is a group project that no one slacks on. That's the team chemistry that fans feel on the other side of their screens and the camaraderie that makes good basketball accessible to millions more than can squeeze into the stands.

Being in the commentator's seat has given me an entirely new vantage point and voice within basketball. It has expanded my dash and renewed my purpose. It's also taken my dreams to new heights to envision broadcasting, producing, and other levels of equity in this game I love. In 2023, I became the first woman to call an NBA All-Star Game. As I said during the pregame show when asked about how the moment felt, "I hope that I inspire people that look like me out there, but I also hope I inspire the business and the leaders that are putting people in these positions. . . . It's just opportunity that's separating us." I'm not the first woman to be qualified for the job, just the first woman to be extended the chance. By taking up space unapologetically, I hope to be the first in a wave of expansion that says: Women athletes have something to say, and we're listening.

The responsibility that comes with knowing you're part of a legacy bigger than you is major. No matter how many games I call or laughs I share on air, nothing will make me forget the giddy and nerve-racking feeling I had when I was just getting started. Sweat beaded all over my body as I tried to act natural with the countdown to live television playing in my ear piece. 3, 2, 1. Time slowed and my heart beat out of my chest before I jumped right in. After the cameras were off, I retraced my steps and analyzed everything I'd said and done. Those nerves were part of being the new kid on the block and, with time, I became a lot more sure of myself. What I'm proudest of is that I had the courage to get back up and do it in spite of the fear. Despite my discomfort or self-doubt, I said yes to unsure things. Some of those decisions propelled me forward and opened more doors while others taught me lessons that I carry over and apply to this day. What I never regretted was saying yes, taking the leap, asking the questions, leaning on veterans, having the courage to be imperfect, and loving what I do.

Preparation meets opportunity. My life is proof of that on all levels. When you put in the work, the universe rewards you. It can be frustrating to wonder if it's all in vain, but trust me, it's not. Now that I'm a regular cohost of *NBA* on TNT Tuesdays and regularly covering March Madness with TNT and CBS, those ESPN days of being told I was trash feel so far away. I used to stay late after practice as a player and get extra shots up, that's what those SEC days were. Extra reps. What once felt foreign is now a normal day in the office, and I'm so grateful for every setback that gave me time to hone my skills and continue to get better.

Broadcasting and working with TNT Sports opened my mind to a whole new way of connecting with lovers of basketball. Storytelling is a huge part of athletics generally, but seeing the behind-the-scenes of how commentary, television, and films make it to audiences excited me. I started my own production company, Baby Hair Productions, to steer the stories I wanted to see and that I think will empower the next generation of women in basketball. Our first documentary, "Title IX: 37 Words that Changed America," was a love letter to the landmark bill that changed sports in America forever. My mother didn't have the opportunity to play sports in high school or college but, in the span of one generation, I've been able to live out my wildest dreams on the court and beyond. And to imagine the landscape ahead for my daughter is that much easier as a result of pioneers who opened doors so more little girls could continue to dream! Celebrating that fight and reiterating the importance of continued progress was the honor of a lifetime, and I wouldn't have been able to do it without my co-producers, Scout Productions and Turner Sports. I hope to continue to tell stories, especially of women in sports. Sports changes lives. It changed mine, and I hope to continue through storytelling to inspire the next generation to be unapologetic in pursuing their dreams!

Broadcasting has cushioned the blow of retirement and eased my transition to the sideline. This new career has allowed me to continue to remain a part of the game of basketball, long after my time on-court. It has also opened my mind to all the ways I can reinvent myself and leverage the platform that basketball has gifted me. I've walked the runways of Paris Fashion Week, interviewed the first Black President of the United States, become President of Adidas Women's Basketball, written a book, and generally achieved more dreams than I dared to imagine for myself. I'm grateful for the process and the journey that is behind me and I am excited for the possibilities that lie ahead. It's the second-best job in the world, and after years of living my dream, it's full circle to be starting out with another.

NINETEEN

What More Can I Say?

Pressure is a privilege.

—BILLIE JEAN KING

In 1986, when I was born, my grandpa continued a tradition he'd first started with my older brothers. He gifted me a one-dollar bill and wrote,

> to Candace Parker from Grandpa Bill
> "Emergency Fund"
> God Bless
> 10-5-1986

Though it wasn't a ton of money or the start of a trust fund, I still have that dollar bill as a reminder of family and legacy. A legacy is what you leave behind—tangible or intangible—for people to remember you by. Legacy can be wealth and assets, or it can be core values and blueprints to follow. A legacy is more than what you say but also what you do and how you do it. It's what people think of before you've even opened your mouth, and it outlives you. Your legacy, core values, and intentions should jump out and precede you or define you when it's all said and done. The game of basketball doesn't last forever. By the time you hit your late thirties, you are considered a dinosaur. What the experience of retiring serves as is a mini-death, in a way. A game you have dedicated your life to, all of a sudden, is gone. People mourn your playing career and reflect on your contributions to the game. The end is something we never plan for, but is inevitable. How will you live the rest of your life?

I love my people hard, and I've never wanted my wife and kids to get the world's sloppy seconds out of me. I bring the same energy and enthusiasm to play sessions, tummy time, school drop-off, and family vacations as I do to my on-the-court time because they are my most tangible fingerprint left on the world. Of course I also want my children to be proud of my trophies or the two-time MVP, all-star, and championship rings I worked for. I want all of that to serve as family heirlooms that get passed down as reminders of who I was in the process.

Tyler Summitt (Pat's son) so graciously sent me Pat's watch, her first-ever Final Four appearance and national championship tickets, and other priceless items. I keep them near and they serve as constant reminders of all the work she put in and all the doors she opened for others within women's sports. I spray Angel perfume before big meetings or big games to serve as a tangible reminder to be like Pat. She wore Angel all the time and everyone who knew her is reminded of her when they smell it. When fans come up to me and ask me what it was like to play for Pat and what I learned and how cool it must have been to play for a coach like her, what I remember most about her, I'm sure they are taken aback when my response is jalapeño corn. That represents the countless home-cooked meals she prepared for the team and myself and how many dinners we spent sitting around the table talking at Pat's pool house. I think of the love and care and purpose she gave each of us. Yes, the banners are an added layer and winning championships with her truly was remarkable, but Pat's legacy in my eyes will live in the moments, who she was in those moments, and who she inspires me to be now. I hope my children see my trophies representing battling back after setbacks and obstacles. The accolades and achievements are celebrated but they're more so reminders of the work it took and the balance of keeping priorities in alignment with the daily grind. I hope they remember the impromptu beach trips, the car rides, and the care. I hope they remember that life is about humility. Constantly trying to evolve and grow and learn. I hope those family heirlooms inspire curiosity and evoke a desire to learn.

What I leave to and for my family is also my legacy, and basketball is a big part of that. From the moment I touched a basketball, it electrified me. I was born into a country that didn't yet have a home for professional women basketball players. The moment one appeared, I knew my mission in life would be to grow women's basketball to a place where people of all genders could enjoy and partake in the sport. I wanted to have a daughter one day who could choose from a menu of options and not be limited by what people assumed she was capable of. I wanted the name Candace Parker to become synonymous with doing anything and everything at the highest level. Being multifaceted and multihyphenated in who I was and what I represent. Depth and versatility in whatever lane I choose, but refusing to stay in the lane the world dares to try and place me in. It's beautiful and surreal to watch your mission evolve into a legacy and to see what my passion could fuel in others. That women could be superheroes and are worthy of being looked up to and modeled after. Women are thought leaders and innovators, trailblazers, movers, shakers. We deserve not just a seat at the table; we deserve to be at the head. I'm grateful for my upbringing and mostly my parents for instilling in me the confidence to push boundaries and sit at tables that the world itself never imagined for me. How could I not when I admired women who proved so much was possible through our defiance? Women like Mia Hamm, Billie Jean King, Cheryl Miller, Dominique Dawes, Robin Roberts, First Lady Michelle Obama, and countless others.

My love for basketball superseded winning alone. It was bringing a team of people together, working relentlessly, and proving to one another what you can do that made me feel alive. The pursuit of the win is where lifelong relationships were formed and how I saw a way to merge my love for people and my passion for this sport. I've played with Americans of all races, sexualities, and socioeconomic backgrounds, as well as Australians, Russians, Chinese people, Turkish people, and people of dozens of other nationalities. What united us was this orange basketball and two hoops. Playing together bridged divides and gave us something to connect over. Working together so intimately helps you see one another's greatest fears and grandest hopes. Once you've seen someone cry out of frustration and out of joy, it's hard not to care about them in that same way.

Depending on others through injuries, motherhood, and losses taught me to be someone others could depend on when their journeys proved challenging. Everybody loves telling these comeback stories of beating the odds after having been down and out. I've been down and out, and it is anything but glamorous to be at the bottom of the hill climbing your way up. Once you've overcome and been victorious, everyone applauds you, but the work to get there is often done alone. What about those people who haven't reached that point of telling their stories and being celebrated for them? I remember being on the sideline my entire college freshman year and wishing somebody—anybody!—would look over at me doing physical therapy while they sprinted. I wanted just one person to see me and my effort. To say, "Yo, great rep," or, "Great leg raises, Candace."

That year I didn't have a jump shot for people to clap at. I couldn't dunk or outrun anyone. I was in a season of baby steps that I hoped would get me back on the court and being able to play the way I knew I could. I always promised myself that if I ever got out of being on the sideline, I would never leave people behind, ever. That's what it feels like when you're putting in the work that's not amounting to any visible triumphs. I've been in that position more times than I can count. Whether it's recovering from surgery, pushing through a dry spell, returning from maternity leave, or starting over on a new team, no one wants to feel like they're standing still as the world passes them by. *When you get out of this*, I'd tell myself, *open up more doors and listen to people the way you wanted people to hear you.*

I started out organically reaching out to any hooper who got injured. Whether we were close beforehand or not, I do and say what I would have appreciated when I was in those same shoes. Sometimes that means being an ear to vent to, and other times people need a light at the end of the tunnel. I try to instill confidence in the people around me because we're part of the same family, industry, and ecosystem. What hurts one player has the potential to harm each of us. No matter how much talent a team possessed, low morale or unexpected circumstances could always undo that. This is a league full of real people who have feelings and real life happening outside of games and tournaments. If we don't have space to honor our humanity, we are nothing.

I work to lead in ways that aren't always flashy or popular. Loud acts garner the most attention but that doesn't always mean it left the greatest impact. I give what I craved and appreciated most: a simple acknowledgment on a down day, a phone call to check in, an encouragement shouted to the sideline, a hug without words. I want to instill confidence in the new mom who doesn't think she can find balance or the injured athlete who thinks they can't return to who they once were. Being that ear to listen and that understanding voice when someone is feeling unheard makes all the difference when the walls close in and your circumstance leaves you lonely. Trust me, I know. I've been in that position more times than I want to count and I'm eternally grateful to those who didn't forget about me, and showed it with their actions. I only know who I want to be because people either were those role models for me or inspired me to look at my life from a different perspective. I am living proof that if you invest in women, it becomes a ripple effect and everyone around them wins. I want to repay and pay it forward for the people who are told they can't or shouldn't keep pushing for more. I want to be an example that when the ball stops bouncing doesn't mean it is the end. Retired athletes are still valuable and your story is still being written.

Pat Summitt taught me invaluable lessons about pouring into the people around you. I was tough when my teammates needed to be pushed, but I'd also catch people one on one. I wanted to know how their mom was doing, to get updates on whatever happened with their little ones, to see pictures of their pets, and to know what consumed them during the offseason. It came from an earnest place of giving what I knew I wanted to receive. Having balance in our lives is additive, not a burden, and the stakes of our game don't always let us trust that. Though the world sometimes wants me to think the opposite, I know I'm a better player because of Anya, Lailaa, Goose, and Hartt. The more we bring our full selves to work, the better leaders can anticipate what keeps players happy.

Taking the time to learn about the people around me would become a major part of my legacy. The year before I retired, *The New York Times* reported on my relationship with Kahleah Copper, writing, "Parker tends to the league by seemingly preparing it to be in fertile condition when she eventually leaves it." The next year when I did retire from the WNBA, so many players took the time to give me my flowers and honor my contributions to basketball beyond athleticism. At a surprise party in Arizona, not far from the arena where I played my first-ever WNBA game, everyone from Kahleah Copper and Aliyah Boston to Chelsea Gray, Nneka Ogwumike, and Sue Bird brought me to tears with their reflections. I couldn't help thinking of my first year in the WNBA, learning under Lisa Leslie's tutelage. Making life easier for those coming behind us is the job of any trailblazer. I benefited from the guidance of women like her, and now I had the chance to do the same.

Be the Change You Wish to See

I was attending an invitation-only talk at the Obama Foundation where Barack Obama was giving a speech. He opened the floor to questions and I immediately raised my hand. How many times do you get the chance to ask the first Black president of the United States a question? I was curious about how leadership shaped his parenting approach and vice versa. "You and First Lady Obama are both great parents," I began, "and you seem to have raised Sasha and Malia to be level-headed in a world of craziness. What values do you hope to instill in them and other young people?" I asked. His answer surprised me. "It's not always about you," President Obama replied. "The more you can realize that and get outside of yourself and help people because you're supposed to and not because of what it can do for you, the better."

It reminded me of an article that was written right after the WNBA was launched, lamenting the lost generation of women athletes that never had the opportunity to play beyond high school. "We got next" was a rallying call for some women to run toward, but this article was the first time I began to imagine what it was like to watch society get better in ways that you wouldn't be able to benefit from. It felt unbelievably unfair that for so long talented women stopped playing in their teen years or traveled abroad to continue following their passions. Why did it take the Olympics recognizing the greatness within our borders for us to look closer to home? Why is it that someone has to first do it to believe that it can be done?

Across my career I've oscillated between feeling sorry for myself and being excited to leave the world better than I received it. The former emotions stemmed from knowing that life could be easier and that playing sports didn't need to be such a constant battle. When women could finally play, everyone wanted to talk about everything but basketball. What we wore, how we looked, whether we were too aggressive or catty, if we could handle the physical nature of good defense or had the physical advantages to play great offense and make the shots that men could. The second-guessing was an incessant distraction keeping us from being our full selves: gutsy, calculated, dynamic, animated, and fun. But if we were too busy proving ourselves instead of being, we'd never get the chance to show it.

There was no full-length career mold or archetype I was able to follow as I climbed my way through the world of American women's basketball. The pioneers I looked up to were also my teammates and competitors. They offered me ample advice and guidance, but many of them were face-to-face with sexism and racism themselves. These mentors were also fumbling through life trying to establish enterprises and carve out lanes for women athletes to be respected as business women. The person who came closest for me was Magic Johnson, who pivoted masterfully from athlete to mogul and executive. He changed the game for what NBA players could imagine for themselves post-retirement in the business world, and I want to do the same for women athletes. To prove how limitless our potential is. There were other people I admired in many ways, but our paths were too distinct to model my own after. Thankfully, I've never wanted to. Being different is a badge of honor that I wear, knowing I have the agency to create a life tailor-made for me. But just because I've found my way doesn't mean it should be this hard for those coming behind me.

In this next chapter of my life, I'm constructing a table wide enough for all of us to eat. Even beyond Adidas, I sit on boards and invest in companies and brands that align with my values and vision for the world. I've always wanted to be a team owner and, in 2025, I officially submitted a bid to establish a WNBA team in Pat Summitt's honor alongside leaders and fellow athletes who I value immensely. After sixteen years as an athlete ambassador of Adidas, I transitioned into the role of President of Women's Basketball. I have worn Adidas since I was fifteen years old with acne and braces. They sent me a pair of exclusive Tracy McGrady shoes, and I have been in three stripes ever since. This lengthy partnership filled with growth, progress, growing pains, love, support, and empowerment has contributed to my career immensely. Now, I get to help do the same for those young girls out there who are next. Women deserve to have signature shoes, be on the cover of video games, star in commercials, and walk the runways in Paris—but also have a seat at the table in the boardroom. I am living proof that finding the right partner to provide support and opportunity can lead to magical outcomes. My aim in this expanded role is to further the growth of the game by investing in girls and women like we deserve. Keeping people and passion at the forefront, I want to help not just the superstars and potential professional players, but embody the reality that sports has the ability to change lives. We want to do that as a brand for as many young girls and women as we can.

Jay-Z always inspired me to do more than just your hustle. I was blown away by his lyrics, but more so his clothing line, investments, building his own record label, and carving out equity with the Ace of Spades Champagne. He was the first rapper to put on a suit and play the game so an entire era of hip-hop could benefit. Perception matters when talking about opportunity. I am among many other female athletes who understand the value of having a seat at the table. I hope to continue to curate rooms of influence that are centered around ownership, equity, compensation, and building pipelines for women athletes to keep taking up space. Even beyond Adidas, I sit on boards and invest in companies and brands that align with my values and vision for the world. Whether it's Avenue Capital Sports Fund and learning from my mentor Marc Lasry, getting a chance to possibly create with one of my favorite directors in Gina Prince-Bythewood, or being a strategic advisor for Fifth Down Capital, I love learning about and being exposed to all parts of the business. I learn from these spaces, but I believe they learn as well. They learn the importance of including, investing in, and empowering female athletes. Hopefully, my work makes it that much easier for women to play, analyze, develop strategy, and continue defying expectations. Women athletes are valuable, and the next few decades will prove that. Just watch.

Live On

Kobe Bryant has always held an incredibly special place in my heart. First, he was the ferocious player whose energy and passion I loved. Then, once I met and got to know him, I saw Kobe as a family man who left it all on the court. He was humble enough to be on time to pick up his wife and children but confident enough to shoot every shot knowing that he'd put in the work long before his hand released the ball. I was mesmerized by Kobe's work ethic and took any chance I had to learn new footwork techniques and learn what set him apart from the rest of the pack. Kobe made time for me and so many other WNBA players because he loved it. He only did things he loved. Witnessing him with his girls, coaching Gigi, writing children's books, and amplifying women's basketball was a master class. Kobe did everything with excellence, and I never understood where he found the time in the day. But however he managed to do it, I knew I could, too.

Kobe was a larger-than-life person whom I selfishly and foolishly believed I'd have all the time in the world to learn from. His passing rocked the world of basketball to our core both because he was a legend of the game we all loved but also because Kobe Bryant's legacy and mission never wavered. No one needed to speak for him for us to understand what carrying on his light would entail. Holding our loved ones close, embracing a Mamba Mentality, learning and growing from past mistakes, and making the world brighter for those coming behind us is what Kobe lived and breathed. I wanted that same level of clarity in my life so that my actions spoke before me long before and after my mouth opened.

Pat Summitt's death hit me in similar ways. Losing community pillars and groundbreaking champions makes us feel uncertain for a reason. Their impact was felt, so surely their absence will be, too. But grief is an unexpected teacher; our sadness makes us resent grief, but grief activates something in us that whispers, "Live the way they would have wanted." For Kobe and Gigi, I continue to grow women's basketball while carving out time for my family—and his—any chance I get. For Pat, I teach her Definite Dozen principles to my children as if it is the start of a new Lady Vols season. Just like she would have.

Though Goose and Hartt have never met Pat or Kobe, they carry those lessons with them. When Goose makes a basket, he throws up his hands and shouts: "*Kobe!*" He doesn't need to have met him to know and feel his impact. Legacies never die so long as the living persist. I am a tapestry of all the people who trusted pieces of their legacies with me, physical or otherwise.

Now I'm charting out my own legacy in even more explicit ways so there is no confusion whom or what Candace Parker stands for. When the story of my life is told and when my future great-grandchildren are asked about me, I want them to have something as special as my grandpa Bill's emergency-fund deposit to remember me by. I was born into a world that didn't know women could be so great, and my children were born into a world where women being great is the norm. I want people to think back fondly on the fact that players like me planted seeds and watered soil in gardens we knew we may never get to tend. But from my vantage point I can tell that the flowers smell sweet and that they're only growing more beautiful and stronger with time. That figurative garden is my legacy, and I'm not finished watering yet.

My love for basketball began on Naperville courts with my parents and brothers. The weekend didn't truly begin until everyone piled into the car for a family day at Spring-Field Park. When I was playing for the Sky, I woke everyone up early so we could journey back to those same basketball courts where it all began. Hartt wasn't born yet but the rest of us—Anya, Lailaa, and Airr—all streamed into the car to bounce an orange ball on the same court where I first beat my dad one-on-one. The emotions hit me like a brick house because the court that my family played, laughed, competed, loved, and made memories on now donned a new name: Candace Parker Court.

A few years back in 2009, the court was renamed after me in an amazing dedication and unveiling where I was also gifted a key to the city that raised me. Everyone from the community showed up including the mayor, my friends and family, teammates, classmates, old babysitters, principals, and teachers. Everyone was there to honor my work, my family, and the impact we've left on Naperville. The basketball court at Spring-Field Park represented so much more than just a game. It represented the seed that was planted decades before. The genuine love for basketball and how it could bring people together and make us all strive for more. Where my love of basketball was inspired, developed, and molded. Where I watched my brothers play and sat on the sideline waiting my turn, where I realized I was tired of sitting on the sideline and I was ready to make my mark.

Taking my family back there was like Daniel-san from *The Karate Kid* becoming the teacher. The young Jedi knight becoming Yoda. As my kids stepped on the court and my wife grabbed a ball, I blinked hard to hide the emotion that I felt. During this journey, the days have been long and the years have been short. The time has flown by, but at the same time I'm right where I need to be. Here with my happy, my reason, my present, and the future. I am because of those moments all those years back on the court. And my kids get the Mommy they have because of the investments people made in my life. My parents told me I could and worked like hell to give me as many opportunities as they can; as a result, I do so for my kids. This court doesn't represent a game; in the court I see the faces of my brothers, my mother, and my father. Taking my kids back to where it all started made me realize I owe everything I am to my start, but I will give everything I am to them, my future.

ACKNOWLEDGMENTS

Thank you to every single reader who made space on their shelves for me. It's scary to consolidate your career and life's lessons into a book for people to engage with. I hope you feel seen, challenged, inspired, and supported in following your dreams and actualizing them with the CAN-DO mentality.

Thank you to my entire team at WME: Zack Miller, Andrea Blatt, Ginger Chan, Sabrina Taitz, Jake Wolken, Morgan Montgomery, Josh Levy, Lee White, Josh Pyatt, and Kelly Sherman. Zack, you have been family for a long time—longer than I've known I wanted to write a book. I'm so grateful to get to work with you through so many pivotal life moments. Thank you for introducing me to Andrea, who made sure this book found a home!

Thank you to Team Candace: Gary Scharf and the entire NKSFB team, Lindsay Gregg and Adidas, Turner Sports, Tara August, Mikki Farrar, Eric Thomas, Nicole Pullman and Goldman Sachs, Marc Lasry and Avenue Capital, Andrew Spellman and Fifth Down Capital, Mike's Hot Honey, and the many people who help me succeed.

To my editor, Sarah Ried, thank you for being so patient during this process and ensuring I could tell my story my way. I knew I couldn't embark on such an important new chapter without vulnerability, and you made space for the story I had inside me. Thank you to the entire team at Zando who made this book possible including Molly Stern,

Andrew Rein, Ashley Alberico, Sam Mitchell, Nathalie Ramirez, Sarah Goldstein, and so many others.

Thank you Brea Baker for working with me so closely on this book and helping me make sense of everything I wanted to get out on the page. This has been a labor of love, and I appreciate you listening to understand and being patient with my process. We made something beautiful, honest, and real.

My family is my North Star in every sense of the word. I owe so much gratitude to each and every one of them: my wife, my children, my parents, my siblings, and everyone who had a hand in making me who I am today. Thank you!

Thank you to all my teammates, coaches, organizations, and amazing people I got to meet throughout my years of playing basketball. And, not to be forgotten, even my opponents and competitors are crucial parts of my story. All of the challenging moments shaped and made me better; each and every one of you has been essential to my journey in the game we all love. From the bottom of my heart: Thank you.

And, lastly, to basketball: You were my first love and are still allowing me to achieve my wildest dreams.

ABOUT THE AUTHOR

CANDACE PARKER has already solidified herself as one of the most influential athletes of this generation. After being selected as the No. 1 overall pick in the 2008 WNBA Draft by the Los Angeles Sparks, following a champion career at Tennessee, Parker went on to become the first player to earn WNBA MVP and Rookie of the Year honors in the same season, win three WNBA championship titles, and take home two Olympic gold medals. Off the court, first and foremost, she is a wife and mother of three children and three dogs. Since retiring, she serves as a public speaker, activist, entrepreneur, and studio broadcaster for men's and women's basketball.